The Org Mode 8 Reference Manual

A catalogue record for this book is available from the Hong Kong Public Libraries.

Published by Samurai Media Limited.

Email: info@samuraimedia.org

ISBN 978-988-13277-0-3

This manual is for Org version 8.2.

Table of Contents

13 Publishing

14 Working with source code

1 Introduction

1.1 Summary

Org is a mode for keeping notes, maintaining TODO lists, and project planning with a fast and effective plain-text system. It also is an authoring system with unique support for literate programming and reproducible research.

Org is implemented on top of Outline mode, which makes it possible to keep the content of large files well structured. Visibility cycling and structure editing help to work with the tree. Tables are easily created with a built-in table editor. Plain text URL-like links connect to websites, emails, Usenet messages, BBDB entries, and any files related to the projects.

Org develops organizational tasks around notes files that contain lists or information about projects as plain text. Project planning and task management makes use of metadata which is part of an outline node. Based on this data, specific entries can be extracted in queries and create dynamic *agenda views* that also integrate the Emacs calendar and diary. Org can be used to implement many different project planning schemes, such as David Allen's GTD system.

Org files can serve as a single source authoring system with export to many different formats such as HTML, LaTeX, Open Document, and Markdown. New export backends can be derived from existing ones, or defined from scratch.

Org files can include source code blocks, which makes Org uniquely suited for authoring technical documents with code examples. Org source code blocks are fully functional; they can be evaluated in place and their results can be captured in the file. This makes it possible to create a single file reproducible research compendium.

Org keeps simple things simple. When first fired up, it should feel like a straightforward, easy to use outliner. Complexity is not imposed, but a large amount of functionality is available when needed. Org is a toolbox. Many users usilize only a (very personal) fraction of Org's capabilities, and know that there is more whenever they need it.

All of this is achieved with strictly plain text files, the most portable and future-proof file format. Org runs in Emacs. Emacs is one of the most widely ported programs, so that Org mode is available on every major platform.

There is a website for Org which provides links to the newest version of Org, as well as additional information, frequently asked questions (FAQ), links to tutorials, etc. This page is located at http://orgmode.org.

1.2 Installation

Org is part of recent distributions of GNU Emacs, so you normally don't need to install it. If, for one reason or another, you want to install Org on top of this pre-packaged version, there are three ways to do it:

- By using Emacs package system.
- By downloading Org as an archive.
- By using Org's git repository.

We **strongly recommend** to stick to a single installation method.

Using Emacs packaging system

Recent Emacs distributions include a packaging system which lets you install Elisp libraries. You can install Org with *M-x package-install RET org*.

Important: you need to do this in a session where no `.org` file has been visited, i.e. where no Org built-in function have been loaded. Otherwise autoload Org functions will mess up the installation.

Then, to make sure your Org configuration is taken into account, initialize the package system with `(package-initialize)` in your `.emacs` before setting any Org option. If you want to use Org's package repository, check out the Org ELPA page.

Downloading Org as an archive

You can download Org latest release from Org's website. In this case, make sure you set the load-path correctly in your `.emacs`:

(add-to-list 'load-path "~/path/to/orgdir/lisp")

The downloaded archive contains contributed libraries that are not included in Emacs. If you want to use them, add the `contrib` directory to your load-path:

(add-to-list 'load-path "~/path/to/orgdir/contrib/lisp" t)

Optionally, you can compile the files and/or install them in your system. Run `make help` to list compilation and installation options.

Using Org's git repository

You can clone Org's repository and install Org like this:

```
$ cd ~/src/
$ git clone git://orgmode.org/org-mode.git
$ make autoloads
```

Note that in this case, `make autoloads` is mandatory: it defines Org's version in `org-version.el` and Org's autoloads in `org-loaddefs.el`.

Remember to add the correct load-path as described in the method above.

You can also compile with `make`, generate the documentation with `make doc`, create a local configuration with `make config` and install Org with `make install`. Please run `make help` to get the list of compilation/installation options.

For more detailed explanations on Org's build system, please check the Org Build System page on Worg.

1.3 Activation

Since Emacs 22.2, files with the `.org` extension use Org mode by default. If you are using an earlier version of Emacs, add this line to your `.emacs` file:

(add-to-list 'auto-mode-alist '("\\.org\\'" . org-mode))

Org mode buffers need font-lock to be turned on: this is the default in Emacs[1].

There are compatibility issues between Org mode and some other Elisp packages, please take the time to check the list (see Section 15.10.2 [Conflicts], page 222).

The four Org commands `org-store-link`, `org-capture`, `org-agenda`, and `org-iswitchb` should be accessible through global keys (i.e., anywhere in Emacs, not just in Org buffers). Here are suggested bindings for these keys, please modify the keys to your own liking.

(global-set-key "\C-cl" 'org-store-link)
(global-set-key "\C-ca" 'org-agenda)
(global-set-key "\C-cc" 'org-capture)
(global-set-key "\C-cb" 'org-iswitchb)

To turn on Org mode in a file that does not have the extension `.org`, make the first line of a file look like this:

        MY PROJECTS   -*- mode: org; -*-

which will select Org mode for this buffer no matter what the file's name is. See also the variable `org-insert-mode-line-in-empty-file`.

Many commands in Org work on the region if the region is *active*. To make use of this, you need to have `transient-mark-mode` (`zmacs-regions` in XEmacs) turned on. In Emacs 23 this is the default, in Emacs 22 you need to do this yourself with

(transient-mark-mode 1)

If you do not like `transient-mark-mode`, you can create an active region by using the mouse to select a region, or pressing *C-SPC* twice before moving the cursor.

1.4 Feedback

If you find problems with Org, or if you have questions, remarks, or ideas about it, please mail to the Org mailing list emacs-orgmode@gnu.org. You can subscribe to the list on this web page. If you are not a member of the mailing list, your mail will be passed to the list after a moderator has approved it[2].

For bug reports, please first try to reproduce the bug with the latest version of Org available—if you are running an outdated version, it is quite possible that the bug has been fixed already. If the bug persists, prepare a report and provide as much information as possible, including the version information of Emacs (*M-x emacs-version RET*) and Org (*M-x org-version RET*), as well as the Org related setup in `.emacs`. The easiest way to do this is to use the command

---

[1] If you don't use font-lock globally, turn it on in Org buffer with (add-hook 'org-mode-hook 'turn-on-font-lock)

[2] Please consider subscribing to the mailing list, in order to minimize the work the mailing list moderators have to do.

```
M-x org-submit-bug-report RET
```

which will put all this information into an Emacs mail buffer so that you only need to add your description. If you are not sending the Email from within Emacs, please copy and paste the content into your Email program.

Sometimes you might face a problem due to an error in your Emacs or Org mode setup. Before reporting a bug, it is very helpful to start Emacs with minimal customizations and reproduce the problem. Doing so often helps you determine if the problem is with your customization or with Org mode itself. You can start a typical minimal session with a command like the example below.

```
$ emacs -Q -l /path/to/minimal-org.el
```

However if you are using Org mode as distributed with Emacs, a minimal setup is not necessary. In that case it is sufficient to start Emacs as `emacs -Q`. The `minimal-org.el` setup file can have contents as shown below.

;;; Minimal setup to load latest 'org-mode'

;; activate debugging
(setq debug-on-error t
      debug-on-signal nil
      debug-on-quit nil)

;; add latest org-mode to load path
(add-to-list 'load-path (expand-file-name "/path/to/org-mode/lisp"))
(add-to-list 'load-path (expand-file-name "/path/to/org-mode/contrib/lisp" t))

If an error occurs, a backtrace can be very useful (see below on how to create one). Often a small example file helps, along with clear information about:

1. What exactly did you do?
2. What did you expect to happen?
3. What happened instead?

Thank you for helping to improve this program.

How to create a useful backtrace

If working with Org produces an error with a message you don't understand, you may have hit a bug. The best way to report this is by providing, in addition to what was mentioned above, a *backtrace*. This is information from the built-in debugger about where and how the error occurred. Here is how to produce a useful backtrace:

1. Reload uncompiled versions of all Org mode Lisp files. The backtrace contains much more information if it is produced with uncompiled code. To do this, use

   ```
   C-u M-x org-reload RET
   ```

   or select `Org -> Refresh/Reload -> Reload Org uncompiled` from the menu.

2. Go to the `Options` menu and select `Enter Debugger on Error` (XEmacs has this option in the `Troubleshooting` sub-menu).

3. Do whatever you have to do to hit the error. Don't forget to document the steps you take.

4. When you hit the error, a `*Backtrace*` buffer will appear on the screen. Save this buffer to a file (for example using `C-x C-w`) and attach it to your bug report.

1.5 Typesetting conventions used in this manual

TODO keywords, tags, properties, etc.

Org mainly uses three types of keywords: TODO keywords, tags and property names. In this manual we use the following conventions:

`TODO`
`WAITING`   TODO keywords are written with all capitals, even if they are user-defined.

`boss`
`ARCHIVE`   User-defined tags are written in lowercase; built-in tags with special meaning are written with all capitals.

`Release`
`PRIORITY`   User-defined properties are capitalized; built-in properties with special meaning are written with all capitals.

Moreover, Org uses *option keywords* (like `#+TITLE` to set the title) and *environment keywords* (like `#+BEGIN_HTML` to start a `HTML` environment). They are written in uppercase in the manual to enhance its readability, but you can use lowercase in your Org files[3].

Keybindings and commands

The manual suggests a few global keybindings, in particular `C-c a` for `org-agenda` and `C-c c` for `org-capture`. These are only suggestions, but the rest of the manual assumes that these keybindings are in place in order to list commands by key access.

Also, the manual lists both the keys and the corresponding commands for accessing a functionality. Org mode often uses the same key for different functions, depending on context. The command that is bound to such keys has a generic name, like `org-metaright`. In the manual we will, wherever possible, give the function that is internally called by the generic command. For example, in the chapter on document structure, `M-right` will be listed to call `org-do-demote`, while in the chapter on tables, it will be listed to call `org-table-move-column-right`. If you prefer, you can compile the manual without the command names by unsetting the flag `cmdnames` in `org.texi`.

---

[3] Easy templates insert lowercase keywords and Babel dynamically inserts `#+results`.

2 Document structure

Org is based on Outline mode and provides flexible commands to edit the structure of the document.

2.1 Outlines

Org is implemented on top of Outline mode. Outlines allow a document to be organized in a hierarchical structure, which (at least for me) is the best representation of notes and thoughts. An overview of this structure is achieved by folding (hiding) large parts of the document to show only the general document structure and the parts currently being worked on. Org greatly simplifies the use of outlines by compressing the entire show/hide functionality into a single command, `org-cycle`, which is bound to the `TAB` key.

2.2 Headlines

Headlines define the structure of an outline tree. The headlines in Org start with one or more stars, on the left margin[12]. For example:

```
* Top level headline
** Second level
*** 3rd level
    some text
*** 3rd level
    more text


* Another top level headline
```

Some people find the many stars too noisy and would prefer an outline that has whitespace followed by a single star as headline starters. Section 15.8 [Clean view], page 219, describes a setup to realize this.

An empty line after the end of a subtree is considered part of it and will be hidden when the subtree is folded. However, if you leave at least two empty lines, one empty line will remain visible after folding the subtree, in order to structure the collapsed view. See the variable `org-cycle-separator-lines` to modify this behavior.

2.3 Visibility cycling

2.3.1 Global and local cycling

Outlines make it possible to hide parts of the text in the buffer. Org uses just two commands, bound to `TAB` and `S-TAB` to change the visibility in the buffer.

TAB   org-cycle
          Subtree cycling: Rotate current subtree among the states

---

[1] See the variables `org-special-ctrl-a/e`, `org-special-ctrl-k`, and `org-ctrl-k-protect-subtree` to configure special behavior of `C-a`, `C-e`, and `C-k` in headlines.

[2] Clocking only works with headings indented less then 30 stars.

```
,-> FOLDED -> CHILDREN -> SUBTREE --.
'-----------------------------------'
```

The cursor must be on a headline for this to work[3]. When the cursor is at the beginning of the buffer and the first line is not a headline, then `TAB` actually runs global cycling (see below)[4]. Also when called with a prefix argument (*C-u TAB*), global cycling is invoked.

S-TAB   org-global-cycle
C-u `TAB`   *Global cycling*: Rotate the entire buffer among the states

```
,-> OVERVIEW -> CONTENTS -> SHOW ALL --.
'--------------------------------------'
```

When *S-TAB* is called with a numeric prefix argument N, the CONTENTS view up to headlines of level N will be shown. Note that inside tables, *S-TAB* jumps to the previous field.

C-u C-u TAB   org-set-startup-visibility
Switch back to the startup visibility of the buffer (see Section 2.3.2 [Initial visibility], page 8).

C-u C-u C-u TAB   show-all
Show all, including drawers.

C-c C-r   org-reveal
Reveal context around point, showing the current entry, the following heading and the hierarchy above. Useful for working near a location that has been exposed by a sparse tree command (see Section 2.6 [Sparse trees], page 11) or an agenda command (see Section 10.5 [Agenda commands], page 111). With a prefix argument show, on each level, all sibling headings. With a double prefix argument, also show the entire subtree of the parent.

C-c C-k   show-branches
Expose all the headings of the subtree, CONTENT view for just one subtree.

C-c TAB   show-children
Expose all direct children of the subtree. With a numeric prefix argument N, expose all children down to level N.

C-c C-x b   org-tree-to-indirect-buffer
Show the current subtree in an indirect buffer[5]. With a numeric prefix argument N, go up to level N and then take that tree. If N is negative then go up that many levels. With a *C-u* prefix, do not remove the previously used indirect buffer.

C-c C-x v   org-copy-visible
Copy the *visible* text in the region into the kill ring.

---

[3] see, however, the option `org-cycle-emulate-tab`.

[4] see the option `org-cycle-global-at-bob`.

[5] The indirect buffer (see Section "Indirect Buffers" in *GNU Emacs Manual*) will contain the entire buffer, but will be narrowed to the current tree. Editing the indirect buffer will also change the original buffer, but without affecting visibility in that buffer.

2.3.2 Initial visibility

When Emacs first visits an Org file, the global state is set to OVERVIEW, i.e., only the top level headlines are visible[6]. This can be configured through the variable `org-startup-folded`, or on a per-file basis by adding one of the following lines anywhere in the buffer:

```
#+STARTUP: overview
#+STARTUP: content
#+STARTUP: showall
#+STARTUP: showeverything
```

The startup visibility options are ignored when the file is open for the first time during the agenda generation: if you want the agenda to honor the startup visibility, set `org-agenda-inhibit-startup` to `nil`.

Furthermore, any entries with a 'VISIBILITY' property (see Chapter 7 [Properties and columns], page 62) will get their visibility adapted accordingly. Allowed values for this property are `folded`, `children`, `content`, and `all`.

`C-u C-u TAB`   org-set-startup-visibility
    Switch back to the startup visibility of the buffer, i.e., whatever is requested by startup options and 'VISIBILITY' properties in individual entries.

2.3.3 Catching invisible edits

Sometimes you may inadvertently edit an invisible part of the buffer and be confused on what has been edited and how to undo the mistake. Setting `org-catch-invisible-edits` to non-`nil` will help prevent this. See the docstring of this option on how Org should catch invisible edits and process them.

2.4 Motion

The following commands jump to other headlines in the buffer.

`C-c C-n`   outline-next-visible-heading
    Next heading.

`C-c C-p`   outline-previous-visible-heading
    Previous heading.

`C-c C-f`   org-forward-same-level
    Next heading same level.

`C-c C-b`   org-backward-same-level
    Previous heading same level.

`C-c C-u`   outline-up-heading
    Backward to higher level heading.

`C-c C-j`   org-goto
    Jump to a different place without changing the current outline visibility. Shows the document structure in a temporary buffer, where you can use the following keys to find your destination:

---

[6] When `org-agenda-inhibit-startup` is non-`nil`, Org will not honor the default visibility state when first opening a file for the agenda (see Section A.9 [Speeding up your agendas], page 236).

`TAB`	Cycle visibility.
`down / up`	Next/previous visible headline.
`RET`	Select this location.
`/`	Do a Sparse-tree search

The following keys work if you turn off `org-goto-auto-isearch`

`n / p`	Next/previous visible headline.
`f / b`	Next/previous headline same level.
`u`	One level up.
`0-9`	Digit argument.
`q`	Quit

See also the option `org-goto-interface`.

2.5 Structure editing

M-RET   `org-insert-heading`

Insert a new heading/item with the same level as the one at point.

If the cursor is in a plain list item, a new item is created (see Section 2.7 [Plain lists], page 12). To prevent this behavior in lists, call the command with one prefix argument. When this command is used in the middle of a line, the line is split and the rest of the line becomes the new item or headline. If you do not want the line to be split, customize `org-M-RET-may-split-line`.

If the command is used at the *beginning* of a line, and if there is a heading or an item at point, the new heading/item is created *before* the current line. If the command is used at the *end* of a folded subtree (i.e., behind the ellipses at the end of a headline), then a headline will be inserted after the end of the subtree.

Calling this command with `C-u C-u` will unconditionally respect the headline's content and create a new item at the end of the parent subtree.

If point is at the beginning of a normal line, turn this line into a heading.

C-RET   `org-insert-heading-respect-content`

Just like *M-RET*, except when adding a new heading below the current heading, the new heading is placed after the body instead of before it. This command works from anywhere in the entry.

M-S-RET   `org-insert-todo-heading`

Insert new TODO entry with same level as current heading. See also the variable `org-treat-insert-todo-heading-as-state-change`.

C-S-RET   `org-insert-todo-heading-respect-content`

Insert new TODO entry with same level as current heading. Like *C-RET*, the new headline will be inserted after the current subtree.

`TAB`   `org-cycle`

In a new entry with no text yet, the first `TAB` demotes the entry to become a child of the previous one. The next `TAB` makes it a parent, and so on, all the way to top level. Yet another `TAB`, and you are back to the initial level.

M-left   `org-do-promote`

Promote current heading by one level.

`M-right`   `org-do-demote`
　　　Demote current heading by one level.

`M-S-left`   `org-promote-subtree`
　　　Promote the current subtree by one level.

`M-S-right`   `org-demote-subtree`
　　　Demote the current subtree by one level.

`M-S-up`   `org-move-subtree-up`
　　　Move subtree up (swap with previous subtree of same level).

`M-S-down`   `org-move-subtree-down`
　　　Move subtree down (swap with next subtree of same level).

`M-h`   `org-mark-element`
　　　Mark the element at point. Hitting repeatedly will mark subsequent elements
　　　of the one just marked. E.g., hitting `M-h` on a paragraph will mark it, hitting
　　　`M-h` immediately again will mark the next one.

`C-c @`   `org-mark-subtree`
　　　Mark the subtree at point. Hitting repeatedly will mark subsequent subtrees
　　　of the same level than the marked subtree.

`C-c C-x C-w`   `org-cut-subtree`
　　　Kill subtree, i.e., remove it from buffer but save in kill ring. With a numeric
　　　prefix argument N, kill N sequential subtrees.

`C-c C-x M-w`   `org-copy-subtree`
　　　Copy subtree to kill ring. With a numeric prefix argument N, copy the N
　　　sequential subtrees.

`C-c C-x C-y`   `org-paste-subtree`
　　　Yank subtree from kill ring. This does modify the level of the subtree to make
　　　sure the tree fits in nicely at the yank position. The yank level can also be
　　　specified with a numeric prefix argument, or by yanking after a headline marker
　　　like '`****`'.

`C-y`   `org-yank`
　　　Depending   on   the   options   `org-yank-adjusted-subtrees`   and
　　　`org-yank-folded-subtrees`, Org's internal `yank` command will paste
　　　subtrees folded and in a clever way, using the same command as `C-c C-x C-y`.
　　　With the default settings, no level adjustment will take place, but the yanked
　　　tree will be folded unless doing so would swallow text previously visible. Any
　　　prefix argument to this command will force a normal `yank` to be executed,
　　　with the prefix passed along. A good way to force a normal yank is `C-u C-y`.
　　　If you use `yank-pop` after a yank, it will yank previous kill items plainly,
　　　without adjustment and folding.

`C-c C-x c`   `org-clone-subtree-with-time-shift`
　　　Clone a subtree by making a number of sibling copies of it. You will be prompted
　　　for the number of copies to make, and you can also specify if any timestamps
　　　in the entry should be shifted. This can be useful, for example, to create a

number of tasks related to a series of lectures to prepare. For more details, see the docstring of the command `org-clone-subtree-with-time-shift`.

`C-c C-w`   `org-refile`

Refile entry or region to a different location. See Section 9.5 [Refile and copy], page 94.

`C-c ^`   `org-sort`

Sort same-level entries. When there is an active region, all entries in the region will be sorted. Otherwise the children of the current headline are sorted. The command prompts for the sorting method, which can be alphabetically, numerically, by time (first timestamp with active preferred, creation time, scheduled time, deadline time), by priority, by TODO keyword (in the sequence the keywords have been defined in the setup) or by the value of a property. Reverse sorting is possible as well. You can also supply your own function to extract the sorting key. With a `C-u` prefix, sorting will be case-sensitive.

`C-x n s`   `org-narrow-to-subtree`

Narrow buffer to current subtree.

`C-x n b`   `org-narrow-to-block`

Narrow buffer to current block.

`C-x n w`   `widen`

Widen buffer to remove narrowing.

`C-c *`   `org-toggle-heading`

Turn a normal line or plain list item into a headline (so that it becomes a subheading at its location). Also turn a headline into a normal line by removing the stars. If there is an active region, turn all lines in the region into headlines. If the first line in the region was an item, turn only the item lines into headlines. Finally, if the first line is a headline, remove the stars from all headlines in the region.

When there is an active region (Transient Mark mode), promotion and demotion work on all headlines in the region. To select a region of headlines, it is best to place both point and mark at the beginning of a line, mark at the beginning of the first headline, and point at the line just after the last headline to change. Note that when the cursor is inside a table (see Chapter 3 [Tables], page 19), the Meta-Cursor keys have different functionality.

2.6 Sparse trees

An important feature of Org mode is the ability to construct *sparse trees* for selected information in an outline tree, so that the entire document is folded as much as possible, but the selected information is made visible along with the headline structure above it[7]. Just try it out and you will see immediately how it works.

Org mode contains several commands for creating such trees, all these commands can be accessed through a dispatcher:

---

[7] See also the variables `org-show-hierarchy-above`, `org-show-following-heading`, `org-show-siblings`, and `org-show-entry-below` for detailed control on how much context is shown around each match.

`C-c /`   `org-sparse-tree`

     This prompts for an extra key to select a sparse-tree creating command.

`C-c / r`   `org-occur`

     Prompts for a regexp and shows a sparse tree with all matches. If the match is in a headline, the headline is made visible. If the match is in the body of an entry, headline and body are made visible. In order to provide minimal context, also the full hierarchy of headlines above the match is shown, as well as the headline following the match. Each match is also highlighted; the highlights disappear when the buffer is changed by an editing command[8], or by pressing `C-c C-c`. When called with a `C-u` prefix argument, previous highlights are kept, so several calls to this command can be stacked.

`M-g n` or `M-g M-n`   `next-error`

     Jump to the next sparse tree match in this buffer.

`M-g p` or `M-g M-p`   `previous-error`

     Jump to the previous sparse tree match in this buffer.

For frequently used sparse trees of specific search strings, you can use the option **`org-agenda-custom-commands`** to define fast keyboard access to specific sparse trees. These commands will then be accessible through the agenda dispatcher (see Section 10.2 [Agenda dispatcher], page 99). For example:

(setq org-agenda-custom-commands
    '(("f" occur-tree "FIXME")))

will define the key `C-c a f` as a shortcut for creating a sparse tree matching the string 'FIXME'.

The other sparse tree commands select headings based on TODO keywords, tags, or properties and will be discussed later in this manual.

To print a sparse tree, you can use the Emacs command **`ps-print-buffer-with-faces`** which does not print invisible parts of the document[9]. Or you can use `C-c C-e C-v` to export only the visible part of the document and print the resulting file.

2.7 Plain lists

Within an entry of the outline tree, hand-formatted lists can provide additional structure. They also provide a way to create lists of checkboxes (see Section 5.6 [Checkboxes], page 55). Org supports editing such lists, and every exporter (see Chapter 12 [Exporting], page 137) can parse and format them.

Org knows ordered lists, unordered lists, and description lists.

- *Unordered* list items start with '-', '+', or '*'[10] as bullets.

---

[8] This depends on the option `org-remove-highlights-with-change`

[9] This does not work under XEmacs, because XEmacs uses selective display for outlining, not text properties.

[10] When using '*' as a bullet, lines must be indented or they will be seen as top-level headlines. Also, when you are hiding leading stars to get a clean outline view, plain list items starting with a star may be hard to distinguish from true headlines. In short: even though '*' is supported, it may be better to not use it for plain list items.

- *Ordered* list items start with a numeral followed by either a period or a right paren-thesis[11], such as '1.' or '1)'[12]. If you want a list to start with a different value (e.g., 20), start the text of the item with `[@20]`[13]. Those constructs can be used in any item of the list in order to enforce a particular numbering.
- *Description* list items are unordered list items, and contain the separator ' :: ' to distinguish the description *term* from the description.

Items belonging to the same list must have the same indentation on the first line. In particular, if an ordered list reaches number '10.', then the 2–digit numbers must be written left-aligned with the other numbers in the list. An item ends before the next line that is less or equally indented than its bullet/number.

A list ends whenever every item has ended, which means before any line less or equally indented than items at top level. It also ends before two blank lines[14]. In that case, all items are closed. Here is an example:

```
** Lord of the Rings
   My favorite scenes are (in this order)
   1. The attack of the Rohirrim
   2. Eowyn's fight with the witch king
      + this was already my favorite scene in the book
      + I really like Miranda Otto.
   3. Peter Jackson being shot by Legolas
      - on DVD only
      He makes a really funny face when it happens.
   But in the end, no individual scenes matter but the film as a whole.
   Important actors in this film are:
   - Elijah Wood :: He plays Frodo
   - Sean Austin :: He plays Sam, Frodo's friend.  I still remember
     him very well from his role as Mikey Walsh in The Goonies.
```

Org supports these lists by tuning filling and wrapping commands to deal with them correctly[15], and by exporting them properly (see Chapter 12 [Exporting], page 137). Since indentation is what governs the structure of these lists, many structural constructs like `#+BEGIN_...` blocks can be indented to signal that they belong to a particular item.

If you find that using a different bullet for a sub-list (than that used for the current list-level) improves readability, customize the variable `org-list-demote-modify-bullet`. To get a greater difference of indentation between items and their sub-items, customize `org-list-indent-offset`.

The following commands act on items when the cursor is in the first line of an item (the line with the bullet or number). Some of them imply the application of automatic rules to

---

[11] You can filter out any of them by configuring `org-plain-list-ordered-item-terminator`.

[12] You can also get 'a.', 'A.', 'a)' and 'A)' by configuring `org-list-allow-alphabetical`. To minimize confusion with normal text, those are limited to one character only. Beyond that limit, bullets will automatically fallback to numbers.

[13] If there's a checkbox in the item, the cookie must be put *before* the checkbox. If you have activated alphabetical lists, you can also use counters like `[@b]`.

[14] See also `org-list-empty-line-terminates-plain-lists`.

[15] Org only changes the filling settings for Emacs. For XEmacs, you should use Kyle E. Jones' `filladapt.el`. To turn this on, put into `.emacs`: `(require 'filladapt)`

keep list structure intact. If some of these actions get in your way, configure `org-list-automatic-rules` to disable them individually.

TAB   org-cycle

> Items can be folded just like headline levels. Normally this works only if the cursor is on a plain list item. For more details, see the variable `org-cycle-include-plain-lists`. If this variable is set to `integrate`, plain list items will be treated like low-level headlines. The level of an item is then given by the indentation of the bullet/number. Items are always subordinate to real headlines, however; the hierarchies remain completely separated. In a new item with no text yet, the first TAB demotes the item to become a child of the previous one. Subsequent TABs move the item to meaningful levels in the list and eventually get it back to its initial position.

M-RET   org-insert-heading

> Insert new item at current level. With a prefix argument, force a new heading (see Section 2.5 [Structure editing], page 9). If this command is used in the middle of an item, that item is *split* in two, and the second part becomes the new item[16]. If this command is executed *before item's body*, the new item is created *before* the current one.

M-S-RET   Insert a new item with a checkbox (see Section 5.6 [Checkboxes], page 55).

S-up
S-down   Jump to the previous/next item in the current list[17], but only if `org-support-shift-select` is off. If not, you can still use paragraph jumping commands like *C-up* and *C-down* to quite similar effect.

M-up
M-down   Move the item including subitems up/down[18] (swap with previous/next item of same indentation). If the list is ordered, renumbering is automatic.

M-left
M-right   Decrease/increase the indentation of an item, leaving children alone.

M-S-left
M-S-right

> Decrease/increase the indentation of the item, including subitems. Initially, the item tree is selected based on current indentation. When these commands are executed several times in direct succession, the initially selected region is used, even if the new indentation would imply a different hierarchy. To use the new hierarchy, break the command chain with a cursor motion or so.

> As a special case, using this command on the very first item of a list will move the whole list. This behavior can be disabled by configuring `org-list-automatic-rules`. The global indentation of a list has no influence on the text *after* the list.

---

[16] If you do not want the item to be split, customize the variable `org-M-RET-may-split-line`.

[17] If you want to cycle around items that way, you may customize `org-list-use-circular-motion`.

[18] See `org-list-use-circular-motion` for a cyclic behavior.

`C-c C-c`   If there is a checkbox (see Section 5.6 [Checkboxes], page 55) in the item line, toggle the state of the checkbox. In any case, verify bullets and indentation consistency in the whole list.

`C-c -`   Cycle the entire list level through the different itemize/enumerate bullets ('-', '+', '*', '1.', '1)') or a subset of them, depending on `org-plain-list-ordered-item-terminator`, the type of list, and its indentation. With a numeric prefix argument N, select the Nth bullet from this list. If there is an active region when calling this, selected text will be changed into an item. With a prefix argument, all lines will be converted to list items. If the first line already was a list item, any item marker will be removed from the list. Finally, even without an active region, a normal line will be converted into a list item.

`C-c *`   Turn a plain list item into a headline (so that it becomes a subheading at its location). See Section 2.5 [Structure editing], page 9, for a detailed explanation.

`C-c C-*`   Turn the whole plain list into a subtree of the current heading. Checkboxes (see Section 5.6 [Checkboxes], page 55) will become TODO (resp. DONE) keywords when unchecked (resp. checked).

`S-left/right`
This command also cycles bullet styles when the cursor in on the bullet or anywhere in an item line, details depending on `org-support-shift-select`.

`C-c ^`   Sort the plain list. You will be prompted for the sorting method: numerically, alphabetically, by time, by checked status for check lists, or by a custom function.

2.8 Drawers

Sometimes you want to keep information associated with an entry, but you normally don't want to see it. For this, Org mode has *drawers*. They can contain anything but a headline and another drawer. Drawers look like this:

```
** This is a headline
   Still outside the drawer
   :DRAWERNAME:
   This is inside the drawer.
   :END:
   After the drawer.
```

You can interactively insert drawers at point by calling **org-insert-drawer**, which is bound to `C-c C-x d`. With an active region, this command will put the region inside the drawer. With a prefix argument, this command calls **org-insert-property-drawer** and add a property drawer right below the current headline. Completion over drawer keywords is also possible using `M-TAB`.

Visibility cycling (see Section 2.3 [Visibility cycling], page 6) on the headline will hide and show the entry, but keep the drawer collapsed to a single line. In order to look inside the drawer, you need to move the cursor to the drawer line and press `TAB` there. Org mode uses the **PROPERTIES** drawer for storing properties (see Chapter 7 [Properties and columns], page 62), and you can also arrange for state change notes (see Section 5.3.2 [Tracking TODO state changes], page 51) and clock times (see Section 8.4 [Clocking work time], page 78) to be stored in a drawer LOGBOOK. If you want to store a quick note in the LOGBOOK drawer, in a similar way to state changes, use

`C-c C-z`   Add a time-stamped note to the LOGBOOK drawer.

You can select the name of the drawers which should be exported with `org-export-with-drawers`. In that case, drawer contents will appear in export output. Property drawers are not affected by this variable: configure `org-export-with-properties` instead.

2.9 Blocks

Org mode uses begin...end blocks for various purposes from including source code examples (see Section 11.3 [Literal examples], page 130) to capturing time logging information (see Section 8.4 [Clocking work time], page 78). These blocks can be folded and unfolded by pressing TAB in the begin line. You can also get all blocks folded at startup by configuring the option `org-hide-block-startup` or on a per-file basis by using

```
#+STARTUP: hideblocks
#+STARTUP: nohideblocks
```

2.10 Footnotes

Org mode supports the creation of footnotes. In contrast to the `footnote.el` package, Org mode's footnotes are designed for work on a larger document, not only for one-off documents like emails.

A footnote is started by a footnote marker in square brackets in column 0, no indentation allowed. It ends at the next footnote definition, headline, or after two consecutive empty lines. The footnote reference is simply the marker in square brackets, inside text. For example:

```
The Org homepage[fn:1] now looks a lot better than it used to.
...
[fn:1] The link is: http://orgmode.org
```

Org mode extends the number-based syntax to *named* footnotes and optional inline definition. Using plain numbers as markers (as `footnote.el` does) is supported for backward compatibility, but not encouraged because of possible conflicts with LaTeX snippets (see Section 11.7 [Embedded LaTeX], page 133). Here are the valid references:

[1]   A plain numeric footnote marker. Compatible with `footnote.el`, but not recommended because something like '[1]' could easily be part of a code snippet.

[fn:name]
             A named footnote reference, where **name** is a unique label word, or, for simplicity of automatic creation, a number.

[fn:: This is the inline definition of this footnote]
             A LaTeX-like anonymous footnote where the definition is given directly at the reference point.

`[fn:name: a definition]`
>   An inline definition of a footnote, which also specifies a name for the note. Since Org allows multiple references to the same note, you can then use `[fn:name]` to create additional references.

Footnote labels can be created automatically, or you can create names yourself. This is handled by the variable `org-footnote-auto-label` and its corresponding `#+STARTUP` keywords. See the docstring of that variable for details.

The following command handles footnotes:

`C-c C-x f`   The footnote action command.

>   When the cursor is on a footnote reference, jump to the definition. When it is at a definition, jump to the (first) reference.

>   Otherwise, create a new footnote. Depending on the option `org-footnote-define-inline`[19], the definition will be placed right into the text as part of the reference, or separately into the location determined by the option `org-footnote-section`.

>   When this command is called with a prefix argument, a menu of additional options is offered:

>>   s   Sort the footnote definitions by reference sequence. During editing, Org makes no effort to sort footnote definitions into a particular sequence. If you want them sorted, use this command, which will also move entries according to `org-footnote-section`. Automatic sorting after each insertion/deletion can be configured using the option `org-footnote-auto-adjust`.

>>   r   Renumber the simple `fn:N` footnotes. Automatic renumbering after each insertion/deletion can be configured using the option `org-footnote-auto-adjust`.

>>   S   Short for first `r`, then `s` action.

>>   n   Normalize the footnotes by collecting all definitions (including inline definitions) into a special section, and then numbering them in sequence. The references will then also be numbers. This is meant to be the final step before finishing a document (e.g., sending off an email).

>>   d   Delete the footnote at point, and all definitions of and references to it.

>   Depending on the variable `org-footnote-auto-adjust`[20], renumbering and sorting footnotes can be automatic after each insertion or deletion.

`C-c C-c`   If the cursor is on a footnote reference, jump to the definition. If it is a the definition, jump back to the reference. When called at a footnote location with a prefix argument, offer the same menu as `C-c C-x f`.

`C-c C-o` or `mouse-1/2`
>   Footnote labels are also links to the corresponding definition/reference, and you can use the usual commands to follow these links.

---

[19] The corresponding in-buffer setting is: `#+STARTUP: fninline` or `#+STARTUP: nofninline`
[20] the corresponding in-buffer options are `fnadjust` and `nofnadjust`.

2.11 The Orgstruct minor mode

If you like the intuitive way the Org mode structure editing and list formatting works, you might want to use these commands in other modes like Text mode or Mail mode as well. The minor mode **orgstruct-mode** makes this possible. Toggle the mode with *M-x orgstruct-mode RET*, or turn it on by default, for example in Message mode, with one of:

(add-hook 'message-mode-hook 'turn-on-orgstruct)

(add-hook 'message-mode-hook 'turn-on-orgstruct++)

When this mode is active and the cursor is on a line that looks to Org like a headline or the first line of a list item, most structure editing commands will work, even if the same keys normally have different functionality in the major mode you are using. If the cursor is not in one of those special lines, Orgstruct mode lurks silently in the shadows.

When you use **orgstruct++-mode**, Org will also export indentation and autofill settings into that mode, and detect item context after the first line of an item.

You can also use Org structure editing to fold and unfold headlines in *any* file, provided you defined **orgstruct-heading-prefix-regexp**: the regular expression must match the local prefix to use before Org's headlines. For example, if you set this variable to ";; " in Emacs Lisp files, you will be able to fold and unfold headlines in Emacs Lisp commented lines. Some commands like **org-demote** are disabled when the prefix is set, but folding/unfolding will work correctly.

2.12 Org syntax

A reference document providing a formal description of Org's syntax is available as a draft on Worg, written and maintained by Nicolas Goaziou. It defines Org's core internal concepts such as **headlines**, **sections**, **affiliated keywords**, **(greater) elements** and **objects**. Each part of an Org file falls into one of the categories above.

To explore the abstract structure of an Org buffer, run this in a buffer:

M-: (org-element-parse-buffer) RET

It will output a list containing the buffer's content represented as an abstract structure. The export engine relies on the information stored in this list. Most interactive commands (e.g., for structure editing) also rely on the syntactic meaning of the surrounding context.

3 Tables

Org comes with a fast and intuitive table editor. Spreadsheet-like calculations are supported using the Emacs `calc` package (see *Gnu Emacs Calculator Manual*).

3.1 The built-in table editor

Org makes it easy to format tables in plain ASCII. Any line with '|' as the first non-whitespace character is considered part of a table. '|' is also the column separator[1]. A table might look like this:

```
| Name  | Phone | Age |
|-------+-------+-----|
| Peter |  1234 |  17 |
| Anna  |  4321 |  25 |
```

A table is re-aligned automatically each time you press **TAB** or **RET** or *C-c C-c* inside the table. **TAB** also moves to the next field (**RET** to the next row) and creates new table rows at the end of the table or before horizontal lines. The indentation of the table is set by the first line. Any line starting with '|-' is considered as a horizontal separator line and will be expanded on the next re-align to span the whole table width. So, to create the above table, you would only type

```
|Name|Phone|Age|
|-
```

and then press **TAB** to align the table and start filling in fields. Even faster would be to type |Name|Phone|Age followed by *C-c RET*.

When typing text into a field, Org treats **DEL**, **Backspace**, and all character keys in a special way, so that inserting and deleting avoids shifting other fields. Also, when typing *immediately after the cursor was moved into a new field with* **TAB**, *S-TAB or* **RET**, the field is automatically made blank. If this behavior is too unpredictable for you, configure the options `org-enable-table-editor` and `org-table-auto-blank-field`.

Creation and conversion

C-c | `org-table-create-or-convert-from-region`

Convert the active region to a table. If every line contains at least one TAB character, the function assumes that the material is tab separated. If every line contains a comma, comma-separated values (CSV) are assumed. If not, lines are split at whitespace into fields. You can use a prefix argument to force a specific separator: *C-u* forces CSV, *C-u C-u* forces TAB, *C-u C-u C-u* will prompt for a regular expression to match the separator, and a numeric argument N indicates that at least N consecutive spaces, or alternatively a TAB will be the separator. If there is no active region, this command creates an empty Org table. But it is easier just to start typing, like |*Name*|*Phone*|*Age RET* |*- TAB*.

Re-aligning and field motion

C-c C-c   `org-table-align`

Re-align the table and don't move to another field.

---

[1] To insert a vertical bar into a table field, use `\vert` or, inside a word `abc\vert{}def`.

<TAB>   org-table-next-field

Re-align the table, move to the next field. Creates a new row if necessary.

S-TAB   org-table-previous-field

Re-align, move to previous field.

RET   org-table-next-row

Re-align the table and move down to next row. Creates a new row if necessary.
At the beginning or end of a line, RET still does NEWLINE, so it can be used
to split a table.

M-a   org-table-beginning-of-field

Move to beginning of the current table field, or on to the previous field.

M-e   org-table-end-of-field

Move to end of the current table field, or on to the next field.

Column and row editing

M-left   org-table-move-column-left
M-right   org-table-move-column-right

Move the current column left/right.

M-S-left   org-table-delete-column

Kill the current column.

M-S-right   org-table-insert-column

Insert a new column to the left of the cursor position.

M-up   org-table-move-row-up
M-down   org-table-move-row-down

Move the current row up/down.

M-S-up   org-table-kill-row

Kill the current row or horizontal line.

M-S-down   org-table-insert-row

Insert a new row above the current row. With a prefix argument, the line is
created below the current one.

C-c -   org-table-insert-hline

Insert a horizontal line below current row. With a prefix argument, the line is
created above the current line.

C-c RET   org-table-hline-and-move

Insert a horizontal line below current row, and move the cursor into the row
below that line.

C-c ^   org-table-sort-lines

Sort the table lines in the region. The position of point indicates the column
to be used for sorting, and the range of lines is the range between the nearest
horizontal separator lines, or the entire table. If point is before the first column,
you will be prompted for the sorting column. If there is an active region, the
mark specifies the first line and the sorting column, while point should be in
the last line to be included into the sorting. The command prompts for the

sorting type (alphabetically, numerically, or by time). When called with a prefix argument, alphabetic sorting will be case-sensitive.

Regions

`C-c C-x M-w`   `org-table-copy-region`
Copy a rectangular region from a table to a special clipboard. Point and mark determine edge fields of the rectangle. If there is no active region, copy just the current field. The process ignores horizontal separator lines.

`C-c C-x C-w`   `org-table-cut-region`
Copy a rectangular region from a table to a special clipboard, and blank all fields in the rectangle. So this is the "cut" operation.

`C-c C-x C-y`   `org-table-paste-rectangle`
Paste a rectangular region into a table. The upper left corner ends up in the current field. All involved fields will be overwritten. If the rectangle does not fit into the present table, the table is enlarged as needed. The process ignores horizontal separator lines.

`M-RET`   `org-table-wrap-region`
Split the current field at the cursor position and move the rest to the line below. If there is an active region, and both point and mark are in the same column, the text in the column is wrapped to minimum width for the given number of lines. A numeric prefix argument may be used to change the number of desired lines. If there is no region, but you specify a prefix argument, the current field is made blank, and the content is appended to the field above.

Calculations

`C-c +`   `org-table-sum`
Sum the numbers in the current column, or in the rectangle defined by the active region. The result is shown in the echo area and can be inserted with `C-y`.

`S-RET`   `org-table-copy-down`
When current field is empty, copy from first non-empty field above. When not empty, copy current field down to next row and move cursor along with it. Depending on the option `org-table-copy-increment`, integer field values will be incremented during copy. Integers that are too large will not be incremented. Also, a `0` prefix argument temporarily disables the increment. This key is also used by shift-selection and related modes (see Section 15.10.2 [Conflicts], page 222).

Miscellaneous

`C-c '`   `org-table-edit-field`
Edit the current field in a separate window. This is useful for fields that are not fully visible (see Section 3.2 [Column width and alignment], page 22). When called with a `C-u` prefix, just make the full field visible, so that it can be edited in place. When called with two `C-u` prefixes, make the editor window follow the cursor through the table and always show the current field. The follow mode exits automatically when the cursor leaves the table, or when you repeat this command with `C-u C-u C-c '`.

M-x org-table-import RET

> Import a file as a table. The table should be TAB or whitespace separated. Use, for example, to import a spreadsheet table or data from a database, because these programs generally can write TAB-separated text files. This command works by inserting the file into the buffer and then converting the region to a table. Any prefix argument is passed on to the converter, which uses it to determine the separator.

C-c | org-table-create-or-convert-from-region

> Tables can also be imported by pasting tabular text into the Org buffer, selecting the pasted text with *C-x C-x* and then using the *C-c |* command (see above under *Creation and conversion*).

M-x org-table-export RET

> Export the table, by default as a TAB-separated file. Use for data exchange with, for example, spreadsheet or database programs. The format used to export the file can be configured in the option `org-table-export-default-format`. You may also use properties `TABLE_EXPORT_FILE` and `TABLE_EXPORT_FORMAT` to specify the file name and the format for table export in a subtree. Org supports quite general formats for exported tables. The exporter format is the same as the format used by Orgtbl radio tables, see Section A.6.3 [Translator functions], page 231, for a detailed description.

If you don't like the automatic table editor because it gets in your way on lines which you would like to start with '|', you can turn it off with

(setq org-enable-table-editor nil)

Then the only table command that still works is *C-c C-c* to do a manual re-align.

3.2 Column width and alignment

The width of columns is automatically determined by the table editor. And also the alignment of a column is determined automatically from the fraction of number-like versus non-number fields in the column.

Sometimes a single field or a few fields need to carry more text, leading to inconveniently wide columns. Or maybe you want to make a table with several columns having a fixed width, regardless of content. To set[2] the width of a column, one field anywhere in the column may contain just the string '<N>' where 'N' is an integer specifying the width of the column in characters. The next re-align will then set the width of this column to this value.

```
|---+---------------------------|                    |---+--------|
|   |                           |                    |   | <6>    |
| 1 | one                       |                    | 1 | one    |
| 2 | two                       |        ----\       | 2 | two    |
| 3 | This is a long chunk of text |     ----/       | 3 | This=> |
| 4 | four                      |                    | 4 | four   |
|---+---------------------------|                    |---+--------|
```

Fields that are wider become clipped and end in the string '=>'. Note that the full text is still in the buffer but is hidden. To see the full text, hold the mouse over the field—a

---

[2] This feature does not work on XEmacs.

tool-tip window will show the full content. To edit such a field, use the command *C-c `* (that is *C-c* followed by the backquote). This will open a new window with the full field. Edit it and finish with *C-c C-c*.

When visiting a file containing a table with narrowed columns, the necessary character hiding has not yet happened, and the table needs to be aligned before it looks nice. Setting the option `org-startup-align-all-tables` will realign all tables in a file upon visiting, but also slow down startup. You can also set this option on a per-file basis with:

```
#+STARTUP: align
#+STARTUP: noalign
```

If you would like to overrule the automatic alignment of number-rich columns to the right and of string-rich column to the left, you can use '<r>', '<c>'[3] or '<l>' in a similar fashion. You may also combine alignment and field width like this: '<r10>'.

Lines which only contain these formatting cookies will be removed automatically when exporting the document.

3.3 Column groups

When Org exports tables, it does so by default without vertical lines because that is visually more satisfying in general. Occasionally however, vertical lines can be useful to structure a table into groups of columns, much like horizontal lines can do for groups of rows. In order to specify column groups, you can use a special row where the first field contains only '/'. The further fields can either contain '<' to indicate that this column should start a group, '>' to indicate the end of a column, or '<>' (no space between '<' and '>') to make a column a group of its own. Boundaries between column groups will upon export be marked with vertical lines. Here is an example:

```
| N | N^2 | N^3 | N^4 | sqrt(n) | sqrt[4](N) |
|---+-----+-----+-----+---------+------------|
| / |  <  |     |  >  |    <    |          > |
| 1 |  1  |  1  |  1  |    1    |          1 |
| 2 |  4  |  8  | 16  | 1.4142  |     1.1892 |
| 3 |  9  | 27  | 81  | 1.7321  |     1.3161 |
|---+-----+-----+-----+---------+------------|
#+TBLFM: $2=$1^2::$3=$1^3::$4=$1^4::$5=sqrt($1)::$6=sqrt(sqrt(($1)))
```

It is also sufficient to just insert the column group starters after every vertical line you would like to have:

```
|  N | N^2 | N^3 | N^4 | sqrt(n) | sqrt[4](N) |
|----+-----+-----+-----+---------+------------|
| /  | <   |     |     | <       |            |
```

3.4 The Orgtbl minor mode

If you like the intuitive way the Org table editor works, you might also want to use it in other modes like Text mode or Mail mode. The minor mode Orgtbl mode makes this possible. You can always toggle the mode with *M-x orgtbl-mode RET*. To turn it on by default, for example in Message mode, use

---

[3] Centering does not work inside Emacs, but it does have an effect when exporting to HTML.

(add-hook 'message-mode-hook 'turn-on-orgtbl)

Furthermore, with some special setup, it is possible to maintain tables in arbitrary syntax with Orgtbl mode. For example, it is possible to construct LaTeX tables with the underlying ease and power of Orgtbl mode, including spreadsheet capabilities. For details, see Section A.6 [Tables in arbitrary syntax], page 229.

3.5 The spreadsheet

The table editor makes use of the Emacs `calc` package to implement spreadsheet-like capabilities. It can also evaluate Emacs Lisp forms to derive fields from other fields. While fully featured, Org's implementation is not identical to other spreadsheets. For example, Org knows the concept of a *column formula* that will be applied to all non-header fields in a column without having to copy the formula to each relevant field. There is also a formula debugger, and a formula editor with features for highlighting fields in the table corresponding to the references at the point in the formula, moving these references by arrow keys

3.5.1 References

To compute fields in the table from other fields, formulas must reference other fields or ranges. In Org, fields can be referenced by name, by absolute coordinates, and by relative coordinates. To find out what the coordinates of a field are, press `C-c ?` in that field, or press `C-c }` to toggle the display of a grid.

Field references

Formulas can reference the value of another field in two ways. Like in any other spreadsheet, you may reference fields with a letter/number combination like `B3`, meaning the 2nd field in the 3rd row. However, Org prefers[4] to use another, more general representation that looks like this:

> `@row$column`

Column specifications can be absolute like `$1`, `$2`,...`$N`, or relative to the current column (i.e., the column of the field which is being computed) like `$+1` or `$-2`. `$<` and `$>` are immutable references to the first and last column, respectively, and you can use `$>>>` to indicate the third column from the right.

The row specification only counts data lines and ignores horizontal separator lines (hlines). Like with columns, you can use absolute row numbers `@1`, `@2`,...`@N`, and row numbers relative to the current row like `@+3` or `@-1`. `@<` and `@>` are immutable references the first and last[5] row in the table, respectively. You may also specify the row relative to one of the hlines: `@I` refers to the first hline, `@II` to the second, etc. `@-I` refers to the first such line above the current line, `@+I` to the first such line below the current line. You can also write `@III+2` which is the second data line after the third hline in the table.

---

[4] Org will understand references typed by the user as 'B4', but it will not use this syntax when offering a formula for editing. You can customize this behavior using the option `org-table-use-standard-references`.

[5] For backward compatibility you can also use special names like `$LR5` and `$LR12` to refer in a stable way to the 5th and 12th field in the last row of the table. However, this syntax is deprecated, it should not be used for new documents. Use `@>$` instead.

@0 and $0 refer to the current row and column, respectively, i.e., to the row/column for the field being computed. Also, if you omit either the column or the row part of the reference, the current row/column is implied.

Org's references with *unsigned* numbers are fixed references in the sense that if you use the same reference in the formula for two different fields, the same field will be referenced each time. Org's references with *signed* numbers are floating references because the same reference operator can reference different fields depending on the field being calculated by the formula.

Here are a few examples:

@2$3	2nd row, 3rd column (same as C2)
$5	column 5 in the current row (same as E&)
@2	current column, row 2
@-1$-3	the field one row up, three columns to the left
@-I$2	field just under hline above current row, column 2
@>$5	field in the last row, in column 5

Range references

You may reference a rectangular range of fields by specifying two field references connected by two dots '..'. If both fields are in the current row, you may simply use '$2..$7', but if at least one field is in a different row, you need to use the general @row$column format at least for the first field (i.e the reference must start with '@' in order to be interpreted correctly). Examples:

$1..$3	first three fields in the current row
$P..$Q	range, using column names (see under Advanced)
$<<<..$>>	start in third column, continue to the last but one
@2$1..@4$3	6 fields between these two fields (same as A2..C4)
@-1$-2..@-1	3 fields in the row above, starting from 2 columns on the left
@I..II	between first and second hline, short for @I..@II

Range references return a vector of values that can be fed into Calc vector functions. Empty fields in ranges are normally suppressed, so that the vector contains only the non-empty fields. For other options with the mode switches 'E', 'N' and examples see Section 3.5.2 [Formula syntax for Calc], page 26.

Field coordinates in formulas

One of the very first actions during evaluation of Calc formulas and Lisp formulas is to substitute @# and $# in the formula with the row or column number of the field where the current result will go to. The traditional Lisp formula equivalents are org-table-current-dline and org-table-current-column. Examples:

```
if(@# % 2, $#, string(""))
```
Insert column number on odd rows, set field to empty on even rows.

```
$2 = '(identity remote(FOO, @@#$1))
```
Copy text or values of each row of column 1 of the table named FOO into column 2 of the current table.

```
@3 = 2 * remote(FOO, @1$$#)
```
        Insert the doubled value of each column of row 1 of the table named `FOO` into row 3 of the current table.

For the second/third example, the table named `FOO` must have at least as many rows/columns as the current table. Note that this is inefficient[6] for large number of rows/columns.

Named references

'`$name`' is interpreted as the name of a column, parameter or constant. Constants are defined globally through the option `org-table-formula-constants`, and locally (for the file) through a line like

```
#+CONSTANTS: c=299792458. pi=3.14 eps=2.4e-6
```

Also properties (see Chapter 7 [Properties and columns], page 62) can be used as constants in table formulas: for a property '`:Xyz:`' use the name '`$PROP_Xyz`', and the property will be searched in the current outline entry and in the hierarchy above it. If you have the `constants.el` package, it will also be used to resolve constants, including natural constants like '`$h`' for Planck's constant, and units like '`$km`' for kilometers[7]. Column names and parameters can be specified in special table lines. These are described below, see Section 3.5.10 [Advanced features], page 34. All names must start with a letter, and further consist of letters and numbers.

Remote references

You may also reference constants, fields and ranges from a different table, either in the current file or even in a different file. The syntax is

```
remote(NAME-OR-ID,REF)
```

where NAME can be the name of a table in the current file as set by a `#+NAME: Name` line before the table. It can also be the ID of an entry, even in a different file, and the reference then refers to the first table in that entry. REF is an absolute field or range reference as described above for example `@3$3` or `$somename`, valid in the referenced table.

Indirection of NAME-OR-ID: When NAME-OR-ID has the format `@ROW$COLUMN` it will be substituted with the name or ID found in this field of the current table. For example `remote($1, @>$2)` => `remote(year_2013, @>$1)`. The format B3 is not supported because it can not be distinguished from a plain table name or ID.

3.5.2 Formula syntax for Calc

A formula can be any algebraic expression understood by the Emacs `Calc` package. Note that `calc` has the non-standard convention that '`/`' has lower precedence than '`*`', so that '`a/b*c`' is interpreted as '`a/(b*c)`'. Before evaluation by `calc-eval` (see Section "Calling Calc from Your Lisp Programs" in *GNU Emacs Calc Manual*), variable substitution takes place according to the rules described above. The range vectors can be directly fed into the Calc vector functions like '`vmean`' and '`vsum`'.

---

[6] The computation time scales as O(N^2) because the table named `FOO` is parsed for each field to be read.

[7] `constants.el` can supply the values of constants in two different unit systems, `SI` and `cgs`. Which one is used depends on the value of the variable `constants-unit-system`. You can use the `#+STARTUP` options `constSI` and `constcgs` to set this value for the current buffer.

A formula can contain an optional mode string after a semicolon. This string consists of flags to influence Calc and other modes during execution. By default, Org uses the standard Calc modes (precision 12, angular units degrees, fraction and symbolic modes off). The display format, however, has been changed to (`float 8`) to keep tables compact. The default settings can be configured using the option `org-calc-default-modes`.

List of modes:

p20   Set the internal Calc calculation precision to 20 digits.

n3, s3, e2, f4
              Normal, scientific, engineering or fixed format of the result of Calc passed back to Org. Calc formatting is unlimited in precision as long as the Calc calculation precision is greater.

D, R   Degree and radian angle modes of Calc.

F, S   Fraction and symbolic modes of Calc.

T, t   Duration computations in Calc or Lisp, see Section 3.5.4 [Durations and time values], page 29.

E   If and how to consider empty fields. Without 'E' empty fields in range references are suppressed so that the Calc vector or Lisp list contains only the non-empty fields. With 'E' the empty fields are kept. For empty fields in ranges or empty field references the value 'nan' (not a number) is used in Calc formulas and the empty string is used for Lisp formulas. Add 'N' to use 0 instead for both formula types. For the value of a field the mode 'N' has higher precedence than 'E'.

N   Interpret all fields as numbers, use 0 for non-numbers. See the next section to see how this is essential for computations with Lisp formulas. In Calc formulas it is used only occasionally because there number strings are already interpreted as numbers without 'N'.

L   Literal, for Lisp formulas only. See the next section.

Unless you use large integer numbers or high-precision-calculation and -display for floating point numbers you may alternatively provide a 'printf' format specifier to reformat the Calc result after it has been passed back to Org instead of letting Calc already do the formatting[8]. A few examples:

$1+$2	Sum of first and second field
$1+$2;%.2f	Same, format result to two decimals
exp($2)+exp($1)	Math functions can be used
$0;%.1f	Reformat current cell to 1 decimal
($3-32)*5/9	Degrees F -> C conversion
$c/$1/$cm	Hz -> cm conversion, using constants.el
tan($1);Dp3s1	Compute in degrees, precision 3, display SCI 1
sin($1);Dp3%.1e	Same, but use printf specifier for display

---

[8] The 'printf' reformatting is limited in precision because the value passed to it is converted into an 'integer' or 'double'. The 'integer' is limited in size by truncating the signed value to 32 bits. The 'double' is limited in precision to 64 bits overall which leaves approximately 16 significant decimal digits.

```
taylor($3,x=7,2)
```
            Taylor series of $3, at x=7, second degree

Calc also contains a complete set of logical operations, (see Section "Logical Operations" in *GNU Emacs Calc Manual*). For example

```
if($1 < 20, teen, string(""))
```
> "teen" if age $1 is less than 20, else the Org table result field is set to empty with the empty string.

```
if("$1" == "nan" || "$2" == "nan", string(""), $1 + $2); E f-1
```
> Sum of the first two columns. When at least one of the input fields is empty the Org table result field is set to empty. 'E' is required to not convert empty fields to 0. 'f-1' is an optional Calc format string similar to '%.1f' but leaves empty results empty.

```
if(typeof(vmean($1..$7)) == 12, string(""), vmean($1..$7); E
```
> Mean value of a range unless there is any empty field. Every field in the range that is empty is replaced by 'nan' which lets 'vmean' result in 'nan'. Then 'typeof == 12' detects the 'nan' from 'vmean' and the Org table result field is set to empty. Use this when the sample set is expected to never have missing values.

```
if("$1..$7" == "[]", string(""), vmean($1..$7))
```
> Mean value of a range with empty fields skipped. Every field in the range that is empty is skipped. When all fields in the range are empty the mean value is not defined and the Org table result field is set to empty. Use this when the sample set can have a variable size.

```
vmean($1..$7); EN
```
> To complete the example before: Mean value of a range with empty fields counting as samples with value 0. Use this only when incomplete sample sets should be padded with 0 to the full size.

You can add your own Calc functions defined in Emacs Lisp with `defmath` and use them in formula syntax for Calc.

3.5.3 Emacs Lisp forms as formulas

It is also possible to write a formula in Emacs Lisp. This can be useful for string manipulation and control structures, if Calc's functionality is not enough.

If a formula starts with a single-quote followed by an opening parenthesis, then it is evaluated as a Lisp form. The evaluation should return either a string or a number. Just as with `calc` formulas, you can specify modes and a printf format after a semicolon.

With Emacs Lisp forms, you need to be conscious about the way field references are interpolated into the form. By default, a reference will be interpolated as a Lisp string (in double-quotes) containing the field. If you provide the 'N' mode switch, all referenced elements will be numbers (non-number fields will be zero) and interpolated as Lisp numbers, without quotes. If you provide the 'L' flag, all fields will be interpolated literally, without quotes. I.e., if you want a reference to be interpreted as a string by the Lisp form, enclose the reference operator itself in double-quotes, like `"$3"`. Ranges are inserted as space-separated fields, so you can embed them in list or vector syntax.

Here are a few examples—note how the 'N' mode is used when we do computations in Lisp:

```
'(concat (substring $1 1 2) (substring $1 0 1) (substring $1 2))
```
>   Swap the first two characters of the content of column 1.

```
'(+ $1 $2);N
```
>   Add columns 1 and 2, equivalent to Calc's $1+$2.

```
'(apply '+ '($1..$4));N
```
>   Compute the sum of columns 1 to 4, like Calc's vsum($1..$4).

3.5.4 Durations and time values

If you want to compute time values use the T flag, either in Calc formulas or Elisp formulas:

```
| Task 1 |  Task 2 |   Total |
|---------+---------+---------|
|    2:12 |    1:47 | 03:59:00 |
| 3:02:20 | -2:07:00 |    0.92 |
#+TBLFM: @2$3=$1+$2;T::@3$3=$1+$2;t
```

Input duration values must be of the form HH:MM[:SS], where seconds are optional. With the T flag, computed durations will be displayed as HH:MM:SS (see the first formula above). With the t flag, computed durations will be displayed according to the value of the option org-table-duration-custom-format, which defaults to 'hours and will display the result as a fraction of hours (see the second formula in the example above).

Negative duration values can be manipulated as well, and integers will be considered as seconds in addition and subtraction.

3.5.5 Field and range formulas

To assign a formula to a particular field, type it directly into the field, preceded by ':=', for example ':=vsum(@II..III)'. When you press TAB or RET or *C-c C-c* with the cursor still in the field, the formula will be stored as the formula for this field, evaluated, and the current field will be replaced with the result.

Formulas are stored in a special line starting with '#+TBLFM:' directly below the table. If you type the equation in the 4th field of the 3rd data line in the table, the formula will look like '@3$4=$1+$2'. When inserting/deleting/swapping columns and rows with the appropriate commands, *absolute references* (but not relative ones) in stored formulas are modified in order to still reference the same field. To avoid this, in particular in range references, anchor ranges at the table borders (using @<, @>, $<, $>), or at hlines using the @I notation. Automatic adaptation of field references does of course not happen if you edit the table structure with normal editing commands—then you must fix the equations yourself.

Instead of typing an equation into the field, you may also use the following command

C-u C-c =   org-table-eval-formula
>   Install a new formula for the current field. The command prompts for a formula
>   with default taken from the '#+TBLFM:' line, applies it to the current field, and
>   stores it.

The left-hand side of a formula can also be a special expression in order to assign the formula to a number of different fields. There is no keyboard shortcut to enter such range formulas. To add them, use the formula editor (see Section 3.5.8 [Editing and debugging formulas], page 31) or edit the `#+TBLFM:` line directly.

`$2=`   Column formula, valid for the entire column. This is so common that Org treats these formulas in a special way, see Section 3.5.6 [Column formulas], page 30.

`@3=`   Row formula, applies to all fields in the specified row. `@>=` means the last row.

`@1$2..@4$3=`
            Range formula, applies to all fields in the given rectangular range. This can also be used to assign a formula to some but not all fields in a row.

`$name=`   Named field, see Section 3.5.10 [Advanced features], page 34.

3.5.6 Column formulas

When you assign a formula to a simple column reference like `$3=`, the same formula will be used in all fields of that column, with the following very convenient exceptions: (i) If the table contains horizontal separator hlines with rows above and below, everything before the first such hline is considered part of the table *header* and will not be modified by column formulas. Therefore a header is mandatory when you use column formulas and want to add hlines to group rows, like for example to separate a total row at the bottom from the summand rows above. (ii) Fields that already get a value from a field/range formula will be left alone by column formulas. These conditions make column formulas very easy to use.

To assign a formula to a column, type it directly into any field in the column, preceded by an equal sign, like '`=$1+$2`'. When you press `TAB` or `RET` or *C-c C-c* with the cursor still in the field, the formula will be stored as the formula for the current column, evaluated and the current field replaced with the result. If the field contains only '`=`', the previously stored formula for this column is used. For each column, Org will only remember the most recently used formula. In the '`#+TBLFM:`' line, column formulas will look like '`$4=$1+$2`'. The left-hand side of a column formula cannot be the name of column, it must be the numeric column reference or `$>`.

Instead of typing an equation into the field, you may also use the following command:

C-c =   org-table-eval-formula
            Install a new formula for the current column and replace current field with the result of the formula. The command prompts for a formula, with default taken from the '`#+TBLFM`' line, applies it to the current field and stores it. With a numeric prefix argument(e.g., *C-5 C-c =*) the command will apply it to that many consecutive fields in the current column.

3.5.7 Lookup functions

Org has three predefined Emacs Lisp functions for lookups in tables.

`(org-lookup-first VAL S-LIST R-LIST &optional PREDICATE)`
            Searches for the first element `S` in list `S-LIST` for which

            (PREDICATE VAL S)

            is `t`; returns the value from the corresponding position in list `R-LIST`. The default `PREDICATE` is `equal`. Note that the parameters `VAL` and `S` are passed to `PREDICATE` in the same order as the corresponding parameters are in the call to `org-lookup-first`, where `VAL` precedes `S-LIST`. If `R-LIST` is `nil`, the matching element `S` of `S-LIST` is returned.

`(org-lookup-last VAL S-LIST R-LIST &optional PREDICATE)`

> Similar to `org-lookup-first` above, but searches for the *last* element for which `PREDICATE` is `t`.

`(org-lookup-all VAL S-LIST R-LIST &optional PREDICATE)`

> Similar to `org-lookup-first`, but searches for *all* elements for which `PREDICATE` is `t`, and returns *all* corresponding values. This function can not be used by itself in a formula, because it returns a list of values. However, powerful lookups can be built when this function is combined with other Emacs Lisp functions.

If the ranges used in these functions contain empty fields, the `E` mode for the formula should usually be specified: otherwise empty fields will not be included in `S-LIST` and/or `R-LIST` which can, for example, result in an incorrect mapping from an element of `S-LIST` to the corresponding element of `R-LIST`.

These three functions can be used to implement associative arrays, count matching cells, rank results, group data etc. For practical examples see this tutorial on Worg.

3.5.8 Editing and debugging formulas

You can edit individual formulas in the minibuffer or directly in the field. Org can also prepare a special buffer with all active formulas of a table. When offering a formula for editing, Org converts references to the standard format (like `B3` or `D&`) if possible. If you prefer to only work with the internal format (like `@3$2` or `$4`), configure the option `org-table-use-standard-references`.

`C-c =` or `C-u C-c =`   org-table-eval-formula

> Edit the formula associated with the current column/field in the minibuffer. See Section 3.5.6 [Column formulas], page 30, and Section 3.5.5 [Field and range formulas], page 29.

`C-u C-u C-c =`   org-table-eval-formula

> Re-insert the active formula (either a field formula, or a column formula) into the current field, so that you can edit it directly in the field. The advantage over editing in the minibuffer is that you can use the command `C-c ?`.

`C-c ?`   org-table-field-info

> While editing a formula in a table field, highlight the field(s) referenced by the reference at the cursor position in the formula.

`C-c }`

> Toggle the display of row and column numbers for a table, using overlays (`org-table-toggle-coordinate-overlays`). These are updated each time the table is aligned; you can force it with `C-c C-c`.

`C-c {`

> Toggle the formula debugger on and off (`org-table-toggle-formula-debugger`). See below.

`C-c '`   org-table-edit-formulas

> Edit all formulas for the current table in a special buffer, where the formulas will be displayed one per line. If the current field has an active formula, the

cursor in the formula editor will mark it. While inside the special buffer, Org will automatically highlight any field or range reference at the cursor position. You may edit, remove and add formulas, and use the following commands:

C-c C-c or *C-x C-s*   org-table-fedit-finish
> Exit the formula editor and store the modified formulas. With *C-u* prefix, also apply the new formulas to the entire table.

C-c C-q   org-table-fedit-abort
> Exit the formula editor without installing changes.

C-c C-r   org-table-fedit-toggle-ref-type
> Toggle all references in the formula editor between standard (like B3) and internal (like @3$2).

TAB   org-table-fedit-lisp-indent
> Pretty-print or indent Lisp formula at point. When in a line containing a Lisp formula, format the formula according to Emacs Lisp rules. Another **TAB** collapses the formula back again. In the open formula, **TAB** re-indents just like in Emacs Lisp mode.

M-TAB   lisp-complete-symbol
> Complete Lisp symbols, just like in Emacs Lisp mode.

S-up/down/left/right
> Shift the reference at point. For example, if the reference is B3 and you press *S-right*, it will become C3. This also works for relative references and for hline references.

M-S-up   org-table-fedit-line-up
M-S-down   org-table-fedit-line-down
> Move the test line for column formulas in the Org buffer up and down.

M-up   org-table-fedit-scroll-down
M-down   org-table-fedit-scroll-up
> Scroll the window displaying the table.

C-c }   Turn the coordinate grid in the table on and off.

Making a table field blank does not remove the formula associated with the field, because that is stored in a different line (the '#+TBLFM' line)—during the next recalculation the field will be filled again. To remove a formula from a field, you have to give an empty reply when prompted for the formula, or to edit the '#+TBLFM' line.

You may edit the '#+TBLFM' directly and re-apply the changed equations with *C-c C-c* in that line or with the normal recalculation commands in the table.

Using multiple #+TBLFM lines

You may apply the formula temporarily. This is useful when you switch the formula. Place multiple '#+TBLFM' lines right after the table, and then press *C-c C-c* on the formula to apply. Here is an example:

```
| x | y |
|---+---|
| 1 |   |
| 2 |   |
#+TBLFM: $2=$1*1
#+TBLFM: $2=$1*2
```

Pressing *C-c C-c* in the line of '#+TBLFM: $2=$1*2' yields:

```
| x | y |
|---+---|
| 1 | 2 |
| 2 | 4 |
#+TBLFM: $2=$1*1
#+TBLFM: $2=$1*2
```

Note: If you recalculate this table (with *C-u C-c *, for example), you will get the following result of applying only the first '#+TBLFM' line.

```
| x | y |
|---+---|
| 1 | 1 |
| 2 | 2 |
#+TBLFM: $2=$1*1
#+TBLFM: $2=$1*2
```

Debugging formulas

When the evaluation of a formula leads to an error, the field content becomes the string '#ERROR'. If you would like see what is going on during variable substitution and calculation in order to find a bug, turn on formula debugging in the **Tbl** menu and repeat the calculation, for example by pressing *C-u C-u C-c = RET* in a field. Detailed information will be displayed.

3.5.9 Updating the table

Recalculation of a table is normally not automatic, but needs to be triggered by a command. See Section 3.5.10 [Advanced features], page 34, for a way to make recalculation at least semi-automatic.

In order to recalculate a line of a table or the entire table, use the following commands:

*C-c **   `org-table-recalculate`
> Recalculate the current row by first applying the stored column formulas from left to right, and all field/range formulas in the current row.

*C-u C-c **
C-u C-c C-c
> Recompute the entire table, line by line. Any lines before the first hline are left alone, assuming that these are part of the table header.

*C-u C-u C-c * or C-u C-u C-c C-c*   `org-table-iterate`
> Iterate the table by recomputing it until no further changes occur. This may be necessary if some computed fields use the value of other fields that are computed *later* in the calculation sequence.

M-x org-table-recalculate-buffer-tables RET
>   Recompute all tables in the current buffer.

M-x org-table-iterate-buffer-tables RET
>   Iterate all tables in the current buffer, in order to converge table-to-table dependencies.

3.5.10 Advanced features

If you want the recalculation of fields to happen automatically, or if you want to be able to assign *names*[9] to fields and columns, you need to reserve the first column of the table for special marking characters.

C-#   org-table-rotate-recalc-marks
>   Rotate the calculation mark in first column through the states ' ', '#', '*', '!', '$'. When there is an active region, change all marks in the region.

Here is an example of a table that collects exam results of students and makes use of these features:

```
|---+---------+--------+--------+--------+-------+------|
|   | Student | Prob 1 | Prob 2 | Prob 3 | Total | Note |
|---+---------+--------+--------+--------+-------+------|
| ! |         |        | P1     | P2     | P3    | Tot  |      |
| # | Maximum |        | 10     | 15     | 25    | 50    | 10.0 |
| ^ |         |        | m1     | m2     | m3    | mt    |      |
|---+---------+--------+--------+--------+-------+------|
| # | Peter   | 10     | 8      | 23     | 41    | 8.2  |
| # | Sam     | 2      | 4      | 3      | 9     | 1.8  |
|---+---------+--------+--------+--------+-------+------|
|   | Average |        |        |        | 25.0  |      |
| ^ |         |        |        |        | at    |      |
| $ | max=50  |        |        |        |       |      |
|---+---------+--------+--------+--------+-------+------|
#+TBLFM: $6=vsum($P1..$P3)::$7=10*$Tot/$max;%.1f::$at=vmean(@-II..@-I);%.1f
```

Important: please note that for these special tables, recalculating the table with *C-u C-c ** will only affect rows that are marked '#' or '*', and fields that have a formula assigned to the field itself. The column formulas are not applied in rows with empty first field.

The marking characters have the following meaning:

'!'
>   The fields in this line define names for the columns, so that you may refer to a column as '$Tot' instead of '$6'.

'^'
>   This row defines names for the fields *above* the row. With such a definition, any formula in the table may use '$m1' to refer to the value '10'. Also, if you assign a formula to a names field, it will be stored as '$name=...'.

'_'
>   Similar to '^', but defines names for the fields in the row *below*.

---

[9] Such names must start by an alphabetic character and use only alphanumeric/underscore characters.

'$'   Fields in this row can define *parameters* for formulas. For example, if a field in
           a '$' row contains 'max=50', then formulas in this table can refer to the value
           50 using '$max'. Parameters work exactly like constants, only that they can be
           defined on a per-table basis.

'#'   Fields in this row are automatically recalculated when pressing TAB or RET or
           S-TAB in this row. Also, this row is selected for a global recalculation with C-u
           C-c *. Unmarked lines will be left alone by this command.

'*'   Selects this line for global recalculation with C-u C-c *, but not for automatic
           recalculation. Use this when automatic recalculation slows down editing too
           much.

' '   Unmarked lines are exempt from recalculation with C-u C-c *. All lines that
           should be recalculated should be marked with '#' or '*'.

'/'   Do not export this line. Useful for lines that contain the narrowing '<N>' markers
           or column group markers.

Finally, just to whet your appetite for what can be done with the fantastic `calc.el`
package, here is a table that computes the Taylor series of degree n at location x for a
couple of functions.

```
|---+------------+---+-----+-----------------------------------|
|   | Func       | n | x   | Result                            |
|---+------------+---+-----+-----------------------------------|
| # | exp(x)     | 1 | x   | 1 + x                             |
| # | exp(x)     | 2 | x   | 1 + x + x^2 / 2                   |
| # | exp(x)     | 3 | x   | 1 + x + x^2 / 2 + x^3 / 6         |
| # | x^2+sqrt(x)| 2 | x=0 | x*(0.5 / 0) + x^2 (2 - 0.25 / 0) / 2 |
| # | x^2+sqrt(x)| 2 | x=1 | 2 + 2.5 x - 2.5 + 0.875 (x - 1)^2 |
| * | tan(x)     | 3 | x   | 0.0175 x + 1.77e-6 x^3            |
|---+------------+---+-----+-----------------------------------|
#+TBLFM: $5=taylor($2,$4,$3);n3
```

3.6 Org-Plot

Org-Plot can produce 2D and 3D graphs of information stored in org tables using `Gnuplot`
`http://www.gnuplot.info/` and **gnuplot-mode** `http://xafs.org/BruceRavel/`
`GnuplotMode`. To see this in action, ensure that you have both Gnuplot and Gnuplot
mode installed on your system, then call **org-plot/gnuplot** on the following table.

```
#+PLOT: title:"Citas" ind:1 deps:(3) type:2d with:histograms set:"yrange [0:]"
| Sede      | Max cites | H-index |
|-----------+-----------+---------|
| Chile     |    257.72 |   21.39 |
| Leeds     |    165.77 |   19.68 |
| Sao Paolo |     71.00 |   11.50 |
| Stockholm |    134.19 |   14.33 |
| Morelia   |    257.56 |   17.67 |
```

Notice that Org Plot is smart enough to apply the table's headers as labels. Further
control over the labels, type, content, and appearance of plots can be exercised through

the `#+PLOT:` lines preceding a table. See below for a complete list of Org-plot options. For more information and examples see the Org-plot tutorial at `http://orgmode.org/worg/org-tutorials/org-plot.html`.

Plot Options

`set`	Specify any `gnuplot` option to be set when graphing.
`title`	Specify the title of the plot.
`ind`	Specify which column of the table to use as the `x` axis.
`deps`	Specify the columns to graph as a Lisp style list, surrounded by parentheses and separated by spaces for example `dep:(3 4)` to graph the third and fourth columns (defaults to graphing all other columns aside from the `ind` column).
`type`	Specify whether the plot will be `2d`, `3d`, or `grid`.
`with`	Specify a `with` option to be inserted for every col being plotted (e.g., `lines`, `points`, `boxes`, `impulses`, etc...). Defaults to `lines`.
`file`	If you want to plot to a file, specify `"path/to/desired/output-file"`.
`labels`	List of labels to be used for the `deps` (defaults to the column headers if they exist).
`line`	Specify an entire line to be inserted in the Gnuplot script.
`map`	When plotting `3d` or `grid` types, set this to `t` to graph a flat mapping rather than a `3d` slope.
`timefmt`	Specify format of Org mode timestamps as they will be parsed by Gnuplot. Defaults to '`%Y-%m-%d-%H:%M:%S`'.
`script`	If you want total control, you can specify a script file (place the file name between double-quotes) which will be used to plot. Before plotting, every instance of `$datafile` in the specified script will be replaced with the path to the generated data file. Note: even if you set this option, you may still want to specify the plot type, as that can impact the content of the data file.

4 Hyperlinks

Like HTML, Org provides links inside a file, external links to other files, Usenet articles, emails, and much more.

4.1 Link format

Org will recognize plain URL-like links and activate them as clickable links. The general link format, however, looks like this:

[[link][description]]   or alternatively   [[link]]

Once a link in the buffer is complete (all brackets present), Org will change the display so that 'description' is displayed instead of '[[link][description]]' and 'link' is displayed instead of '[[link]]'. Links will be highlighted in the face org-link, which by default is an underlined face. You can directly edit the visible part of a link. Note that this can be either the 'link' part (if there is no description) or the 'description' part. To edit also the invisible 'link' part, use *C-c C-l* with the cursor on the link.

If you place the cursor at the beginning or just behind the end of the displayed text and press BACKSPACE, you will remove the (invisible) bracket at that location. This makes the link incomplete and the internals are again displayed as plain text. Inserting the missing bracket hides the link internals again. To show the internal structure of all links, use the menu entry Org->Hyperlinks->Literal links.

4.2 Internal links

If the link does not look like a URL, it is considered to be internal in the current file. The most important case is a link like '[[#my-custom-id]]' which will link to the entry with the CUSTOM_ID property 'my-custom-id'. You are responsible yourself to make sure these custom IDs are unique in a file.

Links such as '[[My Target]]' or '[[My Target][Find my target]]' lead to a text search in the current file.

The link can be followed with *C-c C-o* when the cursor is on the link, or with a mouse click (see Section 4.4 [Handling links], page 40). Links to custom IDs will point to the corresponding headline. The preferred match for a text link is a *dedicated target*: the same string in double angular brackets, like '<<My Target>>'.

If no dedicated target exists, the link will then try to match the exact name of an element within the buffer. Naming is done with the #+NAME keyword, which has to be put in the line before the element it refers to, as in the following example

```
#+NAME: My Target
| a  | table       |
|----+-------------|
| of | four cells  |
```

If none of the above succeeds, Org will search for a headline that is exactly the link text but may also include a TODO keyword and tags[1].

---

[1] To insert a link targeting a headline, in-buffer completion can be used. Just type a star followed by a few optional letters into the buffer and press *M-TAB*. All headlines in the current buffer will be offered as completions.

During export, internal links will be used to mark objects and assign them a number. Marked objects will then be referenced by links pointing to them. In particular, links without a description will appear as the number assigned to the marked object[2]. In the following excerpt from an Org buffer

```
- one item
- <<target>>another item
Here we refer to item [[target]].
```

The last sentence will appear as 'Here we refer to item 2' when exported.

In non-Org files, the search will look for the words in the link text. In the above example the search would be for 'my target'.

Following a link pushes a mark onto Org's own mark ring. You can return to the previous position with `C-c &`. Using this command several times in direct succession goes back to positions recorded earlier.

4.2.1 Radio targets

Org can automatically turn any occurrences of certain target names in normal text into a link. So without explicitly creating a link, the text connects to the target radioing its position. Radio targets are enclosed by triple angular brackets. For example, a target '`<<My Target>>`' causes each occurrence of 'my target' in normal text to become activated as a link. The Org file is scanned automatically for radio targets only when the file is first loaded into Emacs. To update the target list during editing, press `C-c C-c` with the cursor on or at a target.

4.3 External links

Org supports links to files, websites, Usenet and email messages, BBDB database entries and links to both IRC conversations and their logs. External links are URL-like locators. They start with a short identifying string followed by a colon. There can be no space after the colon. The following list shows examples for each link type.

`http://www.astro.uva.nl/~dominik`	on the web
`doi:10.1000/182`	DOI for an electronic resource
`file:/home/dominik/images/jupiter.jpg`	file, absolute path
`/home/dominik/images/jupiter.jpg`	same as above
`file:papers/last.pdf`	file, relative path
`./papers/last.pdf`	same as above
`file:/myself@some.where:papers/last.pdf`	file, path on remote machine
`/myself@some.where:papers/last.pdf`	same as above
`file:sometextfile::NNN`	file, jump to line number
`file:projects.org`	another Org file
`file:projects.org::some words`	text search in Org file[3]

---

[2] When targeting a `#+NAME` keyword, `#+CAPTION` keyword is mandatory in order to get proper numbering (see Section 11.2 [Images and tables], page 129).

[3]

The actual behavior of the search will depend on the value of the option `org-link-search-must-match-exact-headline`. If its value is `nil`, then a fuzzy text search will be done. If it is t, then only the

`file:projects.org::*task title`	heading search in Org file
`file+sys:/path/to/file`	open via OS, like double-click
`file+emacs:/path/to/file`	force opening by Emacs
`docview:papers/last.pdf::NNN`	open in doc-view mode at page
`id:B7423F4D-2E8A-471B-8810-C40F074717E9`	Link to heading by ID
`news:comp.emacs`	Usenet link
`mailto:adent@galaxy.net`	Mail link
`mhe:folder`	MH-E folder link
`mhe:folder#id`	MH-E message link
`rmail:folder`	RMAIL folder link
`rmail:folder#id`	RMAIL message link
`gnus:group`	Gnus group link
`gnus:group#id`	Gnus article link
`bbdb:R.*Stallman`	BBDB link (with regexp)
`irc:/irc.com/#emacs/bob`	IRC link
`info:org#External links`	Info node link
`shell:ls *.org`	A shell command
`elisp:org-agenda`	Interactive Elisp command
`elisp:(find-file-other-frame "Elisp.org")`	Elisp form to evaluate

On top of these built-in link types, some are available through the `contrib/` directory (see Section 1.2 [Installation], page 2). For example, these links to VM or Wanderlust messages are available when you load the corresponding libraries from the `contrib/` directory:

`vm:folder`	VM folder link
`vm:folder#id`	VM message link
`vm://myself@some.where.org/folder#id`	VM on remote machine
`vm-imap:account:folder`	VM IMAP folder link
`vm-imap:account:folder#id`	VM IMAP message link
`wl:folder`	WANDERLUST folder link
`wl:folder#id`	WANDERLUST message link

For customizing Org to add new link types Section A.3 [Adding hyperlink types], page 226.

A link should be enclosed in double brackets and may contain a descriptive text to be displayed instead of the URL (see Section 4.1 [Link format], page 37), for example:

    [[http://www.gnu.org/software/emacs/][GNU Emacs]]

If the description is a file name or URL that points to an image, HTML export (see Section 12.6 [HTML export], page 145) will inline the image as a clickable button. If there is no description at all and the link points to an image, that image will be inlined into the exported HTML file.

Org also finds external links in the normal text and activates them as links. If spaces must be part of the link (for example in 'bbdb:Richard Stallman'), or if you need to remove ambiguities about the end of the link, enclose them in square brackets.

---

exact headline will be matched. If the value is 'query-to-create, then an exact headline will be searched; if it is not found, then the user will be queried to create it.

4.4 Handling links

Org provides methods to create a link in the correct syntax, to insert it into an Org file, and to follow the link.

`C-c l`   `org-store-link`
> Store a link to the current location. This is a *global* command (you must create the key binding yourself) which can be used in any buffer to create a link. The link will be stored for later insertion into an Org buffer (see below). What kind of link will be created depends on the current buffer:
>
> **Org mode buffers**
> For Org files, if there is a '`<<target>>`' at the cursor, the link points to the target. Otherwise it points to the current headline, which will also be the description[4].
>
> If the headline has a `CUSTOM_ID` property, a link to this custom ID will be stored. In addition or alternatively (depending on the value of `org-id-link-to-org-use-id`), a globally unique `ID` property will be created and/or used to construct a link[5]. So using this command in Org buffers will potentially create two links: a human-readable from the custom ID, and one that is globally unique and works even if the entry is moved from file to file. Later, when inserting the link, you need to decide which one to use.
>
> **Email/News clients: VM, Rmail, Wanderlust, MH-E, Gnus**
> Pretty much all Emacs mail clients are supported. The link will point to the current article, or, in some GNUS buffers, to the group. The description is constructed from the author and the subject.
>
> **Web browsers: W3 and W3M**
> Here the link will be the current URL, with the page title as description.
>
> **Contacts: BBDB**
> Links created in a BBDB buffer will point to the current entry.
>
> **Chat: IRC**
> For IRC links, if you set the option `org-irc-link-to-logs` to `t`, a '`file:/`' style link to the relevant point in the logs for the current conversation is created. Otherwise an '`irc:/`' style link to the user/channel/server under the point will be stored.
>
> **Other files**
> For any other files, the link will point to the file, with a search string (see Section 4.7 [Search options], page 43) pointing to the contents of the current line. If there is an active region, the selected words will form the basis of the search string. If the automatically created link is not working correctly or accurately enough, you can write custom functions to select the search string and to do the search for particular file types—see Section 4.8 [Custom searches], page 44. The key binding `C-c l` is only a suggestion—see Section 1.2 [Installation], page 2.

---

[4] If the headline contains a timestamp, it will be removed from the link and result in a wrong link—you should avoid putting timestamp in the headline.

[5] The library `org-id.el` must first be loaded, either through `org-customize` by enabling `org-id` in `org-modules`, or by adding `(require 'org-id)` in your `.emacs`.

Agenda view

When the cursor is in an agenda view, the created link points to the entry referenced by the current line.

`C-c C-l`   org-insert-link

Insert a link[6]. This prompts for a link to be inserted into the buffer. You can just type a link, using text for an internal link, or one of the link type prefixes mentioned in the examples above. The link will be inserted into the buffer[7], along with a descriptive text. If some text was selected when this command is called, the selected text becomes the default description.

Inserting stored links

All links stored during the current session are part of the history for this prompt, so you can access them with `up` and `down` (or `M-p/n`).

Completion support

Completion with `TAB` will help you to insert valid link prefixes like 'http:' or 'ftp:', including the prefixes defined through link abbreviations (see Section 4.6 [Link abbreviations], page 43). If you press `RET` after inserting only the *prefix*, Org will offer specific completion support for some link types[8] For example, if you type *file RET*, file name completion (alternative access: `C-u C-c C-l`, see below) will be offered, and after *bbdb RET* you can complete contact names.

`C-u C-c C-l`

When `C-c C-l` is called with a `C-u` prefix argument, a link to a file will be inserted and you may use file name completion to select the name of the file. The path to the file is inserted relative to the directory of the current Org file, if the linked file is in the current directory or in a sub-directory of it, or if the path is written relative to the current directory using '../'. Otherwise an absolute path is used, if possible with '~/' for your home directory. You can force an absolute path with two `C-u` prefixes.

`C-c C-l` (with cursor on existing link)

When the cursor is on an existing link, `C-c C-l` allows you to edit the link and description parts of the link.

`C-c C-o`   org-open-at-point

Open link at point. This will launch a web browser for URLs (using `browse-url-at-point`), run VM/MH-E/Wanderlust/Rmail/Gnus/BBDB for the corresponding links, and execute the command in a shell link. When the cursor is on an internal link, this command runs the corresponding search. When the cursor is on a TAG list in a headline, it creates the corresponding TAGS view. If the cursor is on a timestamp, it compiles the agenda for that date. Furthermore, it will visit text and remote files in 'file:' links with

---

[6] Note that you don't have to use this command to insert a link. Links in Org are plain text, and you can type or paste them straight into the buffer. By using this command, the links are automatically enclosed in double brackets, and you will be asked for the optional descriptive text.

[7] After insertion of a stored link, the link will be removed from the list of stored links. To keep it in the list later use, use a triple `C-u` prefix argument to `C-c C-l`, or configure the option `org-keep-stored-link-after-insertion`.

[8] This works by calling a special function `org-PREFIX-complete-link`.

Emacs and select a suitable application for local non-text files. Classification of files is based on file extension only. See option `org-file-apps`. If you want to override the default application and visit the file with Emacs, use a *C-u* prefix. If you want to avoid opening in Emacs, use a *C-u C-u* prefix.

If the cursor is on a headline, but not on a link, offer all links in the headline and entry text. If you want to setup the frame configuration for following links, customize `org-link-frame-setup`.

RET   When `org-return-follows-link` is set, RET will also follow the link at point.

mouse-2

mouse-1   On links, *mouse-2* will open the link just as *C-c C-o* would. Under Emacs 22 and later, *mouse-1* will also follow a link.

mouse-3   Like *mouse-2*, but force file links to be opened with Emacs, and internal links to be displayed in another window[9].

C-c C-x C-v   `org-toggle-inline-images`
                     Toggle the inline display of linked images. Normally this will only inline images that have no description part in the link, i.e., images that will also be inlined during export. When called with a prefix argument, also display images that do have a link description. You can ask for inline images to be displayed at startup by configuring the variable `org-startup-with-inline-images`[10].

C-c %   `org-mark-ring-push`
                     Push the current position onto the mark ring, to be able to return easily. Commands following an internal link do this automatically.

C-c &   `org-mark-ring-goto`
                     Jump back to a recorded position. A position is recorded by the commands following internal links, and by *C-c %*. Using this command several times in direct succession moves through a ring of previously recorded positions.

C-c C-x C-n   `org-next-link`
C-c C-x C-p   `org-previous-link`
                     Move forward/backward to the next link in the buffer. At the limit of the buffer, the search fails once, and then wraps around. The key bindings for this are really too long; you might want to bind this also to *C-n* and *C-p*

                     (add-hook 'org-load-hook
                       (lambda ()
                         (define-key org-mode-map "\C-n" 'org-next-link)
                         (define-key org-mode-map "\C-p" 'org-previous-link)))

4.5 Using links outside Org

You can insert and follow links that have Org syntax not only in Org, but in any Emacs buffer. For this, you should create two global commands, like this (please select suitable global keys yourself):

---

[9] See the option `org-display-internal-link-with-indirect-buffer`

[10] with corresponding `#+STARTUP` keywords `inlineimages` and `noinlineimages`

```
(global-set-key "\C-c L" 'org-insert-link-global)
(global-set-key "\C-c o" 'org-open-at-point-global)
```

4.6 Link abbreviations

Long URLs can be cumbersome to type, and often many similar links are needed in a document. For this you can use link abbreviations. An abbreviated link looks like this

```
[[linkword:tag][description]]
```

where the tag is optional. The *linkword* must be a word, starting with a letter, followed by letters, numbers, '-', and '_'. Abbreviations are resolved according to the information in the variable `org-link-abbrev-alist` that relates the linkwords to replacement text. Here is an example:

```
(setq org-link-abbrev-alist
 '(("bugzilla"  . "http://10.1.2.9/bugzilla/show_bug.cgi?id=")
   ("url-to-ja" . "http://translate.google.fr/translate?sl=en&tl=ja&u=%h")
   ("google"    . "http://www.google.com/search?q=")
   ("gmap"      . "http://maps.google.com/maps?q=%s")
   ("omap"      . "http://nominatim.openstreetmap.org/search?q=%s&polygon=1")
   ("ads"       . "http://adsabs.harvard.edu/cgi-bin/nph-abs_connect?author=%s&db_key=AST")))
```

If the replacement text contains the string '%s', it will be replaced with the tag. Using '%h' instead of '%s' will url-encode the tag (see the example above, where we need to encode the URL parameter.) Using '%(my-function)' will pass the tag to a custom function, and replace it by the resulting string.

If the replacement text doesn't contain any specifier, it will simply be appended to the string in order to create the link.

Instead of a string, you may also specify a function that will be called with the tag as the only argument to create the link.

With the above setting, you could link to a specific bug with `[[bugzilla:129]]`, search the web for 'OrgMode' with `[[google:OrgMode]]`, show the map location of the Free Software Foundation `[[gmap:51 Franklin Street, Boston]]` or of Carsten office `[[omap:Science Park 904, Amsterdam, The Netherlands]]` and find out what the Org author is doing besides Emacs hacking with `[[ads:Dominik,C]]`.

If you need special abbreviations just for a single Org buffer, you can define them in the file with

```
#+LINK: bugzilla  http://10.1.2.9/bugzilla/show_bug.cgi?id=
#+LINK: google    http://www.google.com/search?q=%s
```

In-buffer completion (see Section 15.1 [Completion], page 212) can be used after '[' to complete link abbreviations. You may also define a function `org-PREFIX-complete-link` that implements special (e.g., completion) support for inserting such a link with `C-c C-l`. Such a function should not accept any arguments, and return the full link with prefix.

4.7 Search options in file links

File links can contain additional information to make Emacs jump to a particular location in the file when following a link. This can be a line number or a search option after a double[11]

---

[11] For backward compatibility, line numbers can also follow a single colon.

colon. For example, when the command `C-c l` creates a link (see Section 4.4 [Handling links], page 40) to a file, it encodes the words in the current line as a search string that can be used to find this line back later when following the link with `C-c C-o`.

Here is the syntax of the different ways to attach a search to a file link, together with an explanation:

```
[[file:~/code/main.c::255]]
[[file:~/xx.org::My Target]]
[[file:~/xx.org::*My Target]]
[[file:~/xx.org::#my-custom-id]]
[[file:~/xx.org::/regexp/]]
```

255   Jump to line 255.

My Target   Search for a link target '<<My Target>>', or do a text search for 'my target', similar to the search in internal links, see Section 4.2 [Internal links], page 37. In HTML export (see Section 12.6 [HTML export], page 145), such a file link will become an HTML reference to the corresponding named anchor in the linked file.

*My Target
        In an Org file, restrict search to headlines.

#my-custom-id
        Link to a heading with a `CUSTOM_ID` property

/regexp/   Do a regular expression search for `regexp`. This uses the Emacs command `occur` to list all matches in a separate window. If the target file is in Org mode, `org-occur` is used to create a sparse tree with the matches.

As a degenerate case, a file link with an empty file name can be used to search the current file. For example, `[[file:::find me]]` does a search for 'find me' in the current file, just as '`[[find me]]`' would.

4.8 Custom Searches

The default mechanism for creating search strings and for doing the actual search related to a file link may not work correctly in all cases. For example, BibTEX database files have many entries like 'year="1993"' which would not result in good search strings, because the only unique identification for a BibTEX entry is the citation key.

If you come across such a problem, you can write custom functions to set the right search string for a particular file type, and to do the search for the string in the file. Using **add-hook**, these functions need to be added to the hook variables **org-create-file-search-functions** and **org-execute-file-search-functions**. See the docstring for these variables for more information. Org actually uses this mechanism for BibTEX database files, and you can use the corresponding code as an implementation example. See the file **org-bibtex.el**.

5 TODO items

Org mode does not maintain TODO lists as separate documents[1]. Instead, TODO items are an integral part of the notes file, because TODO items usually come up while taking notes! With Org mode, simply mark any entry in a tree as being a TODO item. In this way, information is not duplicated, and the entire context from which the TODO item emerged is always present.

Of course, this technique for managing TODO items scatters them throughout your notes file. Org mode compensates for this by providing methods to give you an overview of all the things that you have to do.

5.1 Basic TODO functionality

Any headline becomes a TODO item when it starts with the word 'TODO', for example:

```
*** TODO Write letter to Sam Fortune
```

The most important commands to work with TODO entries are:

`C-c C-t`   `org-todo`

> Rotate the TODO state of the current item among
>
> ```
> ,-> (unmarked) -> TODO -> DONE --.
> ,---------------------------------,
> ```
>
> If TODO keywords have fast access keys (see Section 5.2.4 [Fast access to TODO states], page 48), you will be prompted for a TODO keyword through the fast selection interface; this is the default behavior when **org-use-fast-todo-selection** is non-nil.
>
> The same rotation can also be done "remotely" from the timeline and agenda buffers with the *t* command key (see Section 10.5 [Agenda commands], page 111).

`C-u C-c C-t`

> When TODO keywords have no selection keys, select a specific keyword using completion; otherwise force cycling through TODO states with no prompt. When **org-use-fast-todo-selection** is set to **prefix**, use the fast selection interface.

`S-right / S-left`

> Select the following/preceding TODO state, similar to cycling. Useful mostly if more than two TODO states are possible (see Section 5.2 [TODO extensions], page 46). See also Section 15.10.2 [Conflicts], page 222, for a discussion of the interaction with **shift-selection-mode**. See also the variable **org-treat-S-cursor-todo-selection-as-state-change**.

`C-c / t`   `org-show-todo-tree`

> View TODO items in a *sparse tree* (see Section 2.6 [Sparse trees], page 11). Folds the entire buffer, but shows all TODO items (with not-DONE state) and

---

[1] Of course, you can make a document that contains only long lists of TODO items, but this is not required.

the headings hierarchy above them. With a prefix argument (or by using `C-c / T`), search for a specific TODO. You will be prompted for the keyword, and you can also give a list of keywords like `KWD1|KWD2|...` to list entries that match any one of these keywords. With a numeric prefix argument N, show the tree for the Nth keyword in the option `org-todo-keywords`. With two prefix arguments, find all TODO states, both un-done and done.

`C-c a t`   `org-todo-list`
> Show the global TODO list. Collects the TODO items (with not-DONE states) from all agenda files (see Chapter 10 [Agenda views], page 98) into a single buffer. The new buffer will be in **agenda-mode**, which provides commands to examine and manipulate the TODO entries from the new buffer (see Section 10.5 [Agenda commands], page 111). See Section 10.3.2 [Global TODO list], page 102, for more information.

`S-M-RET`   `org-insert-todo-heading`
> Insert a new TODO entry below the current one.

Changing a TODO state can also trigger tag changes. See the docstring of the option `org-todo-state-tags-triggers` for details.

5.2 Extended use of TODO keywords

By default, marked TODO entries have one of only two states: TODO and DONE. Org mode allows you to classify TODO items in more complex ways with *TODO keywords* (stored in `org-todo-keywords`). With special setup, the TODO keyword system can work differently in different files.

Note that *tags* are another way to classify headlines in general and TODO items in particular (see Chapter 6 [Tags], page 58).

5.2.1 TODO keywords as workflow states

You can use TODO keywords to indicate different *sequential* states in the process of working on an item, for example[2]:

```
(setq org-todo-keywords
  '((sequence "TODO" "FEEDBACK" "VERIFY" "|" "DONE" "DELEGATED")))
```

The vertical bar separates the TODO keywords (states that *need action*) from the DONE states (which need *no further action*). If you don't provide the separator bar, the last state is used as the DONE state. With this setup, the command `C-c C-t` will cycle an entry from TODO to FEEDBACK, then to VERIFY, and finally to DONE and DELEGATED. You may also use a numeric prefix argument to quickly select a specific state. For example `C-3 C-c C-t` will change the state immediately to VERIFY. Or you can use `S-left` to go backward through the sequence. If you define many keywords, you can use in-buffer completion (see Section 15.1 [Completion], page 212) or even a special one-key selection scheme (see Section 5.2.4 [Fast access to TODO states], page 48) to insert these words into the buffer. Changing a TODO state can be logged with a timestamp, see Section 5.3.2 [Tracking TODO state changes], page 51, for more information.

---

[2] Changing this variable only becomes effective after restarting Org mode in a buffer.

5.2.2 TODO keywords as types

The second possibility is to use TODO keywords to indicate different *types* of action items. For example, you might want to indicate that items are for "work" or "home". Or, when you work with several people on a single project, you might want to assign action items directly to persons, by using their names as TODO keywords. This would be set up like this:

(setq org-todo-keywords '((type "Fred" "Sara" "Lucy" "|" "DONE")))

In this case, different keywords do not indicate a sequence, but rather different types. So the normal work flow would be to assign a task to a person, and later to mark it DONE. Org mode supports this style by adapting the workings of the command *C-c C-t*[3]. When used several times in succession, it will still cycle through all names, in order to first select the right type for a task. But when you return to the item after some time and execute *C-c C-t* again, it will switch from any name directly to DONE. Use prefix arguments or completion to quickly select a specific name. You can also review the items of a specific TODO type in a sparse tree by using a numeric prefix to *C-c / t*. For example, to see all things Lucy has to do, you would use *C-3 C-c / t*. To collect Lucy's items from all agenda files into a single buffer, you would use the numeric prefix argument as well when creating the global TODO list: *C-3 C-c a t*.

5.2.3 Multiple keyword sets in one file

Sometimes you may want to use different sets of TODO keywords in parallel. For example, you may want to have the basic `TODO/DONE`, but also a workflow for bug fixing, and a separate state indicating that an item has been canceled (so it is not DONE, but also does not require action). Your setup would then look like this:

(setq org-todo-keywords
    '((sequence "TODO" "|" "DONE")
     (sequence "REPORT" "BUG" "KNOWNCAUSE" "|" "FIXED")
     (sequence "|" "CANCELED")))

The keywords should all be different, this helps Org mode to keep track of which subsequence should be used for a given entry. In this setup, *C-c C-t* only operates within a subsequence, so it switches from `DONE` to (nothing) to `TODO`, and from `FIXED` to (nothing) to `REPORT`. Therefore you need a mechanism to initially select the correct sequence. Besides the obvious ways like typing a keyword or using completion, you may also apply the following commands:

C-u C-u C-c C-t
C-S-right
C-S-left   These keys jump from one TODO subset to the next. In the above example, *C-u C-u C-c C-t* or *C-S-right* would jump from `TODO` or `DONE` to `REPORT`, and any of the words in the second row to `CANCELED`. Note that the *C-S-* key binding conflict with **shift-selection-mode** (see Section 15.10.2 [Conflicts], page 222).

---

[3] This is also true for the *t* command in the timeline and agenda buffers.

S-right

S-left   *S-left* and *S-right* and walk through *all* keywords from all sets, so for example
              S-right would switch from DONE to REPORT in the example above. See also
              Section 15.10.2 [Conflicts], page 222, for a discussion of the interaction with
              shift-selection-mode.

5.2.4 Fast access to TODO states

If you would like to quickly change an entry to an arbitrary TODO state instead of cycling
through the states, you can set up keys for single-letter access to the states. This is done
by adding the selection character after each keyword, in parentheses[4]. For example:

(setq org-todo-keywords
      '((sequence "TODO(t)" "|" "DONE(d)")
        (sequence "REPORT(r)" "BUG(b)" "KNOWNCAUSE(k)" "|" "FIXED(f)")
        (sequence "|" "CANCELED(c)")))

If you then press *C-c C-t* followed by the selection key, the entry will be switched to
this state. *SPC* can be used to remove any TODO keyword from an entry.[5]

5.2.5 Setting up keywords for individual files

It can be very useful to use different aspects of the TODO mechanism in different files.
For file-local settings, you need to add special lines to the file which set the keywords and
interpretation for that file only. For example, to set one of the two examples discussed
above, you need one of the following lines, starting in column zero anywhere in the file:

    #+TODO: TODO FEEDBACK VERIFY | DONE CANCELED

(you may also write #+SEQ_TODO to be explicit about the interpretation, but it means the
same as #+TODO), or

    #+TYP_TODO: Fred Sara Lucy Mike | DONE

A setup for using several sets in parallel would be:

    #+TODO: TODO | DONE
    #+TODO: REPORT BUG KNOWNCAUSE | FIXED
    #+TODO: | CANCELED

To make sure you are using the correct keyword, type '#+' into the buffer and then use
M-TAB completion.

Remember that the keywords after the vertical bar (or the last keyword if no bar is
there) must always mean that the item is DONE (although you may use a different word).
After changing one of these lines, use *C-c C-c* with the cursor still in the line to make the
changes known to Org mode[6].

---

[4] All characters are allowed except @^!, which have a special meaning here.

[5] Check also the option org-fast-tag-selection-include-todo, it allows you to change the TODO state
     through the tags interface (see Section 6.2 [Setting tags], page 58), in case you like to mingle the two
     concepts. Note that this means you need to come up with unique keys across both sets of keywords.

[6] Org mode parses these lines only when Org mode is activated after visiting a file. *C-c C-c* with the
     cursor in a line starting with '#+' is simply restarting Org mode for the current buffer.

5.2.6 Faces for TODO keywords

Org mode highlights TODO keywords with special faces: `org-todo` for keywords indicating that an item still has to be acted upon, and `org-done` for keywords indicating that an item is finished. If you are using more than 2 different states, you might want to use special faces for some of them. This can be done using the option `org-todo-keyword-faces`. For example:

(setq org-todo-keyword-faces
      '(("TODO" . org-warning) ("STARTED" . "yellow")
       ("CANCELED" . (:foreground "blue" :weight bold))))

While using a list with face properties as shown for CANCELED *should* work, this does not always seem to be the case. If necessary, define a special face and use that. A string is interpreted as a color. The option `org-faces-easy-properties` determines if that color is interpreted as a foreground or a background color.

5.2.7 TODO dependencies

The structure of Org files (hierarchy and lists) makes it easy to define TODO dependencies. Usually, a parent TODO task should not be marked DONE until all subtasks (defined as children tasks) are marked as DONE. And sometimes there is a logical sequence to a number of (sub)tasks, so that one task cannot be acted upon before all siblings above it are done. If you customize the option `org-enforce-todo-dependencies`, Org will block entries from changing state to DONE while they have children that are not DONE. Furthermore, if an entry has a property ORDERED, each of its children will be blocked until all earlier siblings are marked DONE. Here is an example:

```
* TODO Blocked until (two) is done
** DONE one
** TODO two

* Parent
  :PROPERTIES:
  :ORDERED: t
  :END:
** TODO a
** TODO b, needs to wait for (a)
** TODO c, needs to wait for (a) and (b)
```

C-c C-x o   `org-toggle-ordered-property`

        Toggle the ORDERED property of the current entry. A property is used for this behavior because this should be local to the current entry, not inherited like a tag. However, if you would like to *track* the value of this property with a tag for better visibility, customize the option `org-track-ordered-property-with-tag`.

C-u C-u C-u C-c C-t

        Change TODO state, circumventing any state blocking.

If you set the option `org-agenda-dim-blocked-tasks`, TODO entries that cannot be closed because of such dependencies will be shown in a dimmed font or even made invisible in agenda views (see Chapter 10 [Agenda views], page 98).

You can also block changes of TODO states by looking at checkboxes (see Section 5.6 [Checkboxes], page 55). If you set the option `org-enforce-todo-checkbox-dependencies`, an entry that has unchecked checkboxes will be blocked from switching to DONE.

If you need more complex dependency structures, for example dependencies between entries in different trees or files, check out the contributed module `org-depend.el`.

5.3 Progress logging

Org mode can automatically record a timestamp and possibly a note when you mark a TODO item as DONE, or even each time you change the state of a TODO item. This system is highly configurable; settings can be on a per-keyword basis and can be localized to a file or even a subtree. For information on how to clock working time for a task, see Section 8.4 [Clocking work time], page 78.

5.3.1 Closing items

The most basic logging is to keep track of *when* a certain TODO item was finished. This is achieved with[1]

(setq org-log-done 'time)

Then each time you turn an entry from a TODO (not-done) state into any of the DONE states, a line 'CLOSED: [timestamp]' will be inserted just after the headline. If you turn the entry back into a TODO item through further state cycling, that line will be removed again. If you turn the entry back to a non-TODO state (by pressing C-c C-t SPC for example), that line will also be removed, unless you set org-closed-keep-when-no-todo to non-nil. If you want to record a note along with the timestamp, use[2]

(setq org-log-done 'note)

You will then be prompted for a note, and that note will be stored below the entry with a 'Closing Note' heading.

In the timeline (see Section 10.3.4 [Timeline], page 106) and in the agenda (see Section 10.3.1 [Weekly/daily agenda], page 100), you can then use the *l* key to display the TODO items with a 'CLOSED' timestamp on each day, giving you an overview of what has been done.

5.3.2 Tracking TODO state changes

When TODO keywords are used as workflow states (see Section 5.2.1 [Workflow states], page 46), you might want to keep track of when a state change occurred and maybe take a note about this change. You can either record just a timestamp, or a time-stamped note for a change. These records will be inserted after the headline as an itemized list, newest first[3]. When taking a lot of notes, you might want to get the notes out of the way into a drawer (see Section 2.8 [Drawers], page 15). Customize org-log-into-drawer to get this behavior—the recommended drawer for this is called LOGBOOK[4]. You can also overrule the setting of this variable for a subtree by setting a LOG_INTO_DRAWER property.

Since it is normally too much to record a note for every state, Org mode expects configuration on a per-keyword basis for this. This is achieved by adding special markers '!' (for a timestamp) or '@' (for a note with timestamp) in parentheses after each keyword. For example, with the setting

(setq org-todo-keywords

---

[1] The corresponding in-buffer setting is: #+STARTUP: logdone

[2] The corresponding in-buffer setting is: #+STARTUP: lognotedone.

[3] See the option org-log-states-order-reversed

[4] Note that the LOGBOOK drawer is unfolded when pressing SPC in the agenda to show an entry—use C-u SPC to keep it folded here

```
'((sequence "TODO(t)" "WAIT(w@/!)" "|" "DONE(d!)" "CANCELED(c@)")))
```

To record a timestamp without a note for TODO keywords configured with '@', just type `C-c C-c` to enter a blank note when prompted.

You not only define global TODO keywords and fast access keys, but also request that a time is recorded when the entry is set to DONE[5], and that a note is recorded when switching to WAIT or CANCELED. The setting for WAIT is even more special: the '!' after the slash means that in addition to the note taken when entering the state, a timestamp should be recorded when *leaving* the WAIT state, if and only if the *target* state does not configure logging for entering it. So it has no effect when switching from WAIT to DONE, because DONE is configured to record a timestamp only. But when switching from WAIT back to TODO, the '/!' in the WAIT setting now triggers a timestamp even though TODO has no logging configured.

You can use the exact same syntax for setting logging preferences local to a buffer:

```
#+TODO: TODO(t) WAIT(w@/!) | DONE(d!) CANCELED(c@)
```

In order to define logging settings that are local to a subtree or a single item, define a LOGGING property in this entry. Any non-empty LOGGING property resets all logging settings to `nil`. You may then turn on logging for this specific tree using STARTUP keywords like `lognotedone` or `logrepeat`, as well as adding state specific settings like `TODO(!)`. For example

```
* TODO Log each state with only a time
  :PROPERTIES:
  :LOGGING: TODO(!) WAIT(!) DONE(!) CANCELED(!)
  :END:
* TODO Only log when switching to WAIT, and when repeating
  :PROPERTIES:
  :LOGGING: WAIT(@) logrepeat
  :END:
* TODO No logging at all
  :PROPERTIES:
  :LOGGING: nil
  :END:
```

5.3.3 Tracking your habits

Org has the ability to track the consistency of a special category of TODOs, called "habits". A habit has the following properties:

1. You have enabled the `habits` module by customizing `org-modules`.

2. The habit is a TODO item, with a TODO keyword representing an open state.

3. The property `STYLE` is set to the value `habit`.

4. The TODO has a scheduled date, usually with a `.+` style repeat interval. A `++` style may be appropriate for habits with time constraints, e.g., must be done on weekends, or a `+` style for an unusual habit that can have a backlog, e.g., weekly reports.

---

[5] It is possible that Org mode will record two timestamps when you are using both `org-log-done` and state change logging. However, it will never prompt for two notes—if you have configured both, the state change recording note will take precedence and cancel the 'Closing Note'.

5. The TODO may also have minimum and maximum ranges specified by using the syntax '.+2d/3d', which says that you want to do the task at least every three days, but at most every two days.

6. You must also have state logging for the **DONE** state enabled (see Section 5.3.2 [Tracking TODO state changes], page 51), in order for historical data to be represented in the consistency graph. If it is not enabled it is not an error, but the consistency graphs will be largely meaningless.

To give you an idea of what the above rules look like in action, here's an actual habit with some history:

```
** TODO Shave
   SCHEDULED: <2009-10-17 Sat .+2d/4d>
   - State "DONE"        from "TODO"       [2009-10-15 Thu]
   - State "DONE"        from "TODO"       [2009-10-12 Mon]
   - State "DONE"        from "TODO"       [2009-10-10 Sat]
   - State "DONE"        from "TODO"       [2009-10-04 Sun]
   - State "DONE"        from "TODO"       [2009-10-02 Fri]
   - State "DONE"        from "TODO"       [2009-09-29 Tue]
   - State "DONE"        from "TODO"       [2009-09-25 Fri]
   - State "DONE"        from "TODO"       [2009-09-19 Sat]
   - State "DONE"        from "TODO"       [2009-09-16 Wed]
   - State "DONE"        from "TODO"       [2009-09-12 Sat]
   :PROPERTIES:
   :STYLE:     habit
   :LAST_REPEAT: [2009-10-19 Mon 00:36]
   :END:
```

What this habit says is: I want to shave at most every 2 days (given by the **SCHEDULED** date and repeat interval) and at least every 4 days. If today is the 15th, then the habit first appears in the agenda on Oct 17, after the minimum of 2 days has elapsed, and will appear overdue on Oct 19, after four days have elapsed.

What's really useful about habits is that they are displayed along with a consistency graph, to show how consistent you've been at getting that task done in the past. This graph shows every day that the task was done over the past three weeks, with colors for each day. The colors used are:

Blue   If the task wasn't to be done yet on that day.

Green   If the task could have been done on that day.

Yellow   If the task was going to be overdue the next day.

Red   If the task was overdue on that day.

In addition to coloring each day, the day is also marked with an asterisk if the task was actually done that day, and an exclamation mark to show where the current day falls in the graph.

There are several configuration variables that can be used to change the way habits are displayed in the agenda.

`org-habit-graph-column`

> The buffer column at which the consistency graph should be drawn. This will overwrite any text in that column, so it is a good idea to keep your habits' titles brief and to the point.

`org-habit-preceding-days`

> The amount of history, in days before today, to appear in consistency graphs.

`org-habit-following-days`

> The number of days after today that will appear in consistency graphs.

`org-habit-show-habits-only-for-today`

> If non-`nil`, only show habits in today's agenda view. This is set to true by default.

Lastly, pressing *K* in the agenda buffer will cause habits to temporarily be disabled and they won't appear at all. Press *K* again to bring them back. They are also subject to tag filtering, if you have habits which should only be done in certain contexts, for example.

5.4 Priorities

If you use Org mode extensively, you may end up with enough TODO items that it starts to make sense to prioritize them. Prioritizing can be done by placing a *priority cookie* into the headline of a TODO item, like this

```
*** TODO [#A] Write letter to Sam Fortune
```

By default, Org mode supports three priorities: 'A', 'B', and 'C'. 'A' is the highest priority. An entry without a cookie is treated just like priority 'B'. Priorities make a difference only for sorting in the agenda (see Section 10.3.1 [Weekly/daily agenda], page 100); outside the agenda, they have no inherent meaning to Org mode. The cookies can be highlighted with special faces by customizing `org-priority-faces`.

Priorities can be attached to any outline node; they do not need to be TODO items.

C-c ,   Set the priority of the current headline (`org-priority`). The command prompts for a priority character 'A', 'B' or 'C'. When you press SPC instead, the priority cookie is removed from the headline. The priorities can also be changed "remotely" from the timeline and agenda buffer with the , command (see Section 10.5 [Agenda commands], page 111).

S-up   `org-priority-up`
S-down   `org-priority-down`
           Increase/decrease priority of current headline[6]. Note that these keys are also used to modify timestamps (see Section 8.2 [Creating timestamps], page 72). See also Section 15.10.2 [Conflicts], page 222, for a discussion of the interaction with `shift-selection-mode`.

You can change the range of allowed priorities by setting the options `org-highest-priority`, `org-lowest-priority`, and `org-default-priority`. For an individual buffer, you may set these values (highest, lowest, default) like this (please make sure that the highest priority is earlier in the alphabet than the lowest priority):

```
#+PRIORITIES: A C B
```

---

[6] See also the option `org-priority-start-cycle-with-default`.

5.5 Breaking tasks down into subtasks

It is often advisable to break down large tasks into smaller, manageable subtasks. You can do this by creating an outline tree below a TODO item, with detailed subtasks on the tree[7]. To keep the overview over the fraction of subtasks that are already completed, insert either '[/]' or '[%]' anywhere in the headline. These cookies will be updated each time the TODO status of a child changes, or when pressing *C-c C-c* on the cookie. For example:

```
* Organize Party [33%]
** TODO Call people [1/2]
*** TODO Peter
*** DONE Sarah
** TODO Buy food
** DONE Talk to neighbor
```

If a heading has both checkboxes and TODO children below it, the meaning of the statistics cookie become ambiguous. Set the property COOKIE_DATA to either 'checkbox' or 'todo' to resolve this issue.

If you would like to have the statistics cookie count any TODO entries in the subtree (not just direct children), configure org-hierarchical-todo-statistics. To do this for a single subtree, include the word 'recursive' into the value of the COOKIE_DATA property.

```
* Parent capturing statistics [2/20]
  :PROPERTIES:
  :COOKIE_DATA: todo recursive
  :END:
```

If you would like a TODO entry to automatically change to DONE when all children are done, you can use the following setup:

```
(defun org-summary-todo (n-done n-not-done)
  "Switch entry to DONE when all subentries are done, to TODO otherwise."
  (let (org-log-done org-log-states)   ; turn off logging
    (org-todo (if (= n-not-done 0) "DONE" "TODO"))))

(add-hook 'org-after-todo-statistics-hook 'org-summary-todo)
```

Another possibility is the use of checkboxes to identify (a hierarchy of) a large number of subtasks (see Section 5.6 [Checkboxes], page 55).

5.6 Checkboxes

Every item in a plain list[8] (see Section 2.7 [Plain lists], page 12) can be made into a checkbox by starting it with the string '[ ]'. This feature is similar to TODO items (see Chapter 5 [TODO items], page 45), but is more lightweight. Checkboxes are not included in the global TODO list, so they are often great to split a task into a number of simple steps. Or you can use them in a shopping list. To toggle a checkbox, use *C-c C-c*, or use the mouse (thanks to Piotr Zielinski's org-mouse.el).

Here is an example of a checkbox list.

---

[7] To keep subtasks out of the global TODO list, see the org-agenda-todo-list-sublevels.

[8] With the exception of description lists. But you can allow it by modifying org-list-automatic-rules accordingly.

```
* TODO Organize party [2/4]
  - [-] call people [1/3]
    - [ ] Peter
    - [X] Sarah
    - [ ] Sam
  - [X] order food
  - [ ] think about what music to play
  - [X] talk to the neighbors
```

Checkboxes work hierarchically, so if a checkbox item has children that are checkboxes, toggling one of the children checkboxes will make the parent checkbox reflect if none, some, or all of the children are checked.

The '[2/4]' and '[1/3]' in the first and second line are cookies indicating how many checkboxes present in this entry have been checked off, and the total number of checkboxes present. This can give you an idea on how many checkboxes remain, even without opening a folded entry. The cookies can be placed into a headline or into (the first line of) a plain list item. Each cookie covers checkboxes of direct children structurally below the headline/item on which the cookie appears[9]. You have to insert the cookie yourself by typing either '[/]' or '[%]'. With '[/]' you get an 'n out of m' result, as in the examples above. With '[%]' you get information about the percentage of checkboxes checked (in the above example, this would be '[50%]' and '[33%]', respectively). In a headline, a cookie can count either checkboxes below the heading or TODO states of children, and it will display whatever was changed last. Set the property COOKIE_DATA to either 'checkbox' or 'todo' to resolve this issue.

If the current outline node has an ORDERED property, checkboxes must be checked off in sequence, and an error will be thrown if you try to check off a box while there are unchecked boxes above it.

The following commands work with checkboxes:

C-c C-c   org-toggle-checkbox
> Toggle checkbox status or (with prefix arg) checkbox presence at point. With a single prefix argument, add an empty checkbox or remove the current one[10]. With a double prefix argument, set it to '[-]', which is considered to be an intermediate state.

C-c C-x C-b   org-toggle-checkbox
> Toggle checkbox status or (with prefix arg) checkbox presence at point. With double prefix argument, set it to '[-]', which is considered to be an intermediate state.
>
> − If there is an active region, toggle the first checkbox in the region and set all remaining boxes to the same status as the first. With a prefix arg, add or remove the checkbox for all items in the region.
>
> − If the cursor is in a headline, toggle checkboxes in the region between this headline and the next (so *not* the entire subtree).

---

[9] Set the option org-checkbox-hierarchical-statistics if you want such cookies to count all checkboxes below the cookie, not just those belonging to direct children.

[10] C-u C-c C-c on the *first* item of a list with no checkbox will add checkboxes to the rest of the list.

— If there is no active region, just toggle the checkbox at point.

M-S-RET   `org-insert-todo-heading`

Insert a new item with a checkbox. This works only if the cursor is already in a plain list item (see Section 2.7 [Plain lists], page 12).

C-c C-x o   `org-toggle-ordered-property`

Toggle the `ORDERED` property of the entry, to toggle if checkboxes must be checked off in sequence. A property is used for this behavior because this should be local to the current entry, not inherited like a tag. However, if you would like to *track* the value of this property with a tag for better visibility, customize `org-track-ordered-property-with-tag`.

C-c #   `org-update-statistics-cookies`

Update the statistics cookie in the current outline entry. When called with a *C-u* prefix, update the entire file. Checkbox statistic cookies are updated automatically if you toggle checkboxes with *C-c C-c* and make new ones with *M-S-RET*. TODO statistics cookies update when changing TODO states. If you delete boxes/entries or add/change them by hand, use this command to get things back into sync.

6 Tags

An excellent way to implement labels and contexts for cross-correlating information is to assign *tags* to headlines. Org mode has extensive support for tags.

Every headline can contain a list of tags; they occur at the end of the headline. Tags are normal words containing letters, numbers, '_', and '@'. Tags must be preceded and followed by a single colon, e.g., ':work:'. Several tags can be specified, as in ':work:urgent:'. Tags will by default be in bold face with the same color as the headline. You may specify special faces for specific tags using the option `org-tag-faces`, in much the same way as you can for TODO keywords (see Section 5.2.6 [Faces for TODO keywords], page 49).

6.1 Tag inheritance

Tags make use of the hierarchical structure of outline trees. If a heading has a certain tag, all subheadings will inherit the tag as well. For example, in the list

```
* Meeting with the French group        :work:
** Summary by Frank                     :boss:notes:
*** TODO Prepare slides for him         :action:
```

the final heading will have the tags ':work:', ':boss:', ':notes:', and ':action:' even though the final heading is not explicitly marked with those tags. You can also set tags that all entries in a file should inherit just as if these tags were defined in a hypothetical level zero that surrounds the entire file. Use a line like this[1]:

```
#+FILETAGS: :Peter:Boss:Secret:
```

To limit tag inheritance to specific tags, use `org-tags-exclude-from-inheritance`. To turn it off entirely, use `org-use-tag-inheritance`.

When a headline matches during a tags search while tag inheritance is turned on, all the sublevels in the same tree will (for a simple match form) match as well[2]. The list of matches may then become very long. If you only want to see the first tags match in a subtree, configure `org-tags-match-list-sublevels` (not recommended).

Tag inheritance is relevant when the agenda search tries to match a tag, either in the **tags** or **tags-todo** agenda types. In other agenda types, `org-use-tag-inheritance` has no effect. Still, you may want to have your tags correctly set in the agenda, so that tag filtering works fine, with inherited tags. Set `org-agenda-use-tag-inheritance` to control this: the default value includes all agenda types, but setting this to `nil` can really speed up agenda generation.

6.2 Setting tags

Tags can simply be typed into the buffer at the end of a headline. After a colon, *M-TAB* offers completion on tags. There is also a special command for inserting tags:

C-c C-q   `org-set-tags-command`
> Enter new tags for the current headline. Org mode will either offer completion or a special single-key interface for setting tags, see below. After pressing RET,

---

[1] As with all these in-buffer settings, pressing *C-c C-c* activates any changes in the line.

[2] This is only true if the search does not involve more complex tests including properties (see Section 7.3 [Property searches], page 64).

the tags will be inserted and aligned to `org-tags-column`. When called with a `C-u` prefix, all tags in the current buffer will be aligned to that column, just to make things look nice. TAGS are automatically realigned after promotion, demotion, and TODO state changes (see Section 5.1 [TODO basics], page 45).

`C-c C-c`   `org-set-tags-command`
> When the cursor is in a headline, this does the same as `C-c C-q`.

Org supports tag insertion based on a *list of tags*. By default this list is constructed dynamically, containing all tags currently used in the buffer. You may also globally specify a hard list of tags with the variable `org-tag-alist`. Finally you can set the default tags for a given file with lines like

```
#+TAGS: @work @home @tennisclub
#+TAGS: laptop car pc sailboat
```

If you have globally defined your preferred set of tags using the variable `org-tag-alist`, but would like to use a dynamic tag list in a specific file, add an empty TAGS option line to that file:

```
#+TAGS:
```

If you have a preferred set of tags that you would like to use in every file, in addition to those defined on a per-file basis by TAGS option lines, then you may specify a list of tags with the variable `org-tag-persistent-alist`. You may turn this off on a per-file basis by adding a STARTUP option line to that file:

```
#+STARTUP: noptag
```

By default Org mode uses the standard minibuffer completion facilities for entering tags. However, it also implements another, quicker, tag selection method called *fast tag selection*. This allows you to select and deselect tags with just a single key press. For this to work well you should assign unique letters to most of your commonly used tags. You can do this globally by configuring the variable `org-tag-alist` in your `.emacs` file. For example, you may find the need to tag many items in different files with ':@home:'. In this case you can set something like:

```
(setq org-tag-alist '(("@work" . ?w) ("@home" . ?h) ("laptop" . ?l)))
```

If the tag is only relevant to the file you are working on, then you can instead set the TAGS option line as:

```
#+TAGS: @work(w)  @home(h)  @tennisclub(t)  laptop(l)  pc(p)
```

The tags interface will show the available tags in a splash window. If you want to start a new line after a specific tag, insert '\n' into the tag list

```
#+TAGS: @work(w)  @home(h)  @tennisclub(t) \n laptop(l)  pc(p)
```

or write them in two lines:

```
#+TAGS: @work(w)  @home(h)  @tennisclub(t)
#+TAGS: laptop(l)  pc(p)
```

You can also group together tags that are mutually exclusive by using braces, as in:

```
#+TAGS: { @work(w)  @home(h)  @tennisclub(t) }  laptop(l)  pc(p)
```

you indicate that at most one of '@work', '@home', and '@tennisclub' should be selected. Multiple such groups are allowed.

Don't forget to press *C-c C-c* with the cursor in one of these lines to activate any changes.

To set these mutually exclusive groups in the variable **org-tag-alist**, you must use the dummy tags **:startgroup** and **:endgroup** instead of the braces. Similarly, you can use **:newline** to indicate a line break. The previous example would be set globally by the following configuration:

```
(setq org-tag-alist '((:startgroup . nil)
             ("@work" . ?w) ("@home" . ?h)
             ("@tennisclub" . ?t)
             (:endgroup . nil)
             ("laptop" . ?l) ("pc" . ?p)))
```

If at least one tag has a selection key then pressing *C-c C-c* will automatically present you with a special interface, listing inherited tags, the tags of the current headline, and a list of all valid tags with corresponding keys[3]. In this interface, you can use the following keys:

a-z...   Pressing keys assigned to tags will add or remove them from the list of tags in the current line. Selecting a tag in a group of mutually exclusive tags will turn off any other tags from that group.

TAB   Enter a tag in the minibuffer, even if the tag is not in the predefined list. You will be able to complete on all tags present in the buffer. You can also add several tags: just separate them with a comma.

SPC   Clear all tags for this line.

RET   Accept the modified set.

C-g   Abort without installing changes.

q   If *q* is not assigned to a tag, it aborts like *C-g*.

!   Turn off groups of mutually exclusive tags. Use this to (as an exception) assign several tags from such a group.

C-c   Toggle auto-exit after the next change (see below). If you are using expert mode, the first *C-c* will display the selection window.

This method lets you assign tags to a headline with very few keys. With the above setup, you could clear the current tags and set '@home', 'laptop' and 'pc' tags with just the following keys: *C-c C-c SPC h l p RET*. Switching from '@home' to '@work' would be done with *C-c C-c w RET* or alternatively with *C-c C-c C-c w*. Adding the non-predefined tag 'Sarah' could be done with *C-c C-c TAB S a r a h RET RET*.

If you find that most of the time you need only a single key press to modify your list of tags, set **org-fast-tag-selection-single-key**. Then you no longer have to press RET to exit fast tag selection—it will immediately exit after the first change. If you then occasionally need more keys, press *C-c* to turn off auto-exit for the current tag selection process (in effect: start selection with *C-c C-c C-c* instead of *C-c C-c*). If you set the variable to the value **expert**, the special window is not even shown for single-key tag selection, it comes up only when you press an extra *C-c*.

---

[3] Keys will automatically be assigned to tags which have no configured keys.

6.3 Tag groups

In a set of mutually exclusive tags, the first tag can be defined as a *group tag*. When you search for a group tag, it will return matches for all members in the group. In an agenda view, filtering by a group tag will display headlines tagged with at least one of the members of the group. This makes tag searches and filters even more flexible.

You can set group tags by inserting a colon between the group tag and other tags—beware that all whitespaces are mandatory so that Org can parse this line correctly:

```
#+TAGS: { @read : @read_book @read_ebook }
```

In this example, '`@read`' is a *group tag* for a set of three tags: '`@read`', '`@read_book`' and '`@read_ebook`'.

You can also use the `:grouptags` keyword directly when setting `org-tag-alist`:

```
(setq org-tag-alist '((:startgroup . nil)
                      ("@read" . nil)
                      (:grouptags . nil)
                      ("@read_book" . nil)
                      ("@read_ebook" . nil)
                      (:endgroup . nil)))
```

You cannot nest group tags or use a group tag as a tag in another group.

If you want to ignore group tags temporarily, toggle group tags support with `org-toggle-tags-groups`, bound to `C-c C-x q`. If you want to disable tag groups completely, set `org-group-tags` to `nil`.

6.4 Tag searches

Once a system of tags has been set up, it can be used to collect related information into special lists.

`C-c / m` or `C-c \`   org-match-sparse-tree

> Create a sparse tree with all headlines matching a tags/property/TODO search. With a `C-u` prefix argument, ignore headlines that are not a TODO line. See Section 10.3.3 [Matching tags and properties], page 103.

`C-c a m`   org-tags-view

> Create a global list of tag matches from all agenda files. See Section 10.3.3 [Matching tags and properties], page 103.

`C-c a M`   org-tags-view

> Create a global list of tag matches from all agenda files, but check only TODO items and force checking subitems (see the option `org-tags-match-list-sublevels`).

These commands all prompt for a match string which allows basic Boolean logic like '`+boss+urgent-project1`', to find entries with tags '`boss`' and '`urgent`', but not '`project1`', or '`Kathy|Sally`' to find entries which are tagged, like '`Kathy`' or '`Sally`'. The full syntax of the search string is rich and allows also matching against TODO keywords, entry levels and properties. For a complete description with many examples, see Section 10.3.3 [Matching tags and properties], page 103.

7 Properties and columns

A property is a key-value pair associated with an entry. Properties can be set so they are associated with a single entry, with every entry in a tree, or with every entry in an Org mode file.

There are two main applications for properties in Org mode. First, properties are like tags, but with a value. Imagine maintaining a file where you document bugs and plan releases for a piece of software. Instead of using tags like `:release_1:`, `:release_2:`, you can use a property, say `:Release:`, that in different subtrees has different values, such as `1.0` or `2.0`. Second, you can use properties to implement (very basic) database capabilities in an Org buffer. Imagine keeping track of your music CDs, where properties could be things such as the album, artist, date of release, number of tracks, and so on.

Properties can be conveniently edited and viewed in column view (see Section 7.5 [Column view], page 66).

7.1 Property syntax

Properties are key-value pairs. When they are associated with a single entry or with a tree they need to be inserted into a special drawer (see Section 2.8 [Drawers], page 15) with the name **PROPERTIES**. Each property is specified on a single line, with the key (surrounded by colons) first, and the value after it. Here is an example:

```
* CD collection
** Classic
*** Goldberg Variations
    :PROPERTIES:
    :Title:     Goldberg Variations
    :Composer:  J.S. Bach
    :Artist:    Glen Gould
    :Publisher: Deutsche Grammophon
    :NDisks:    1
    :END:
```

Depending on the value of `org-use-property-inheritance`, a property set this way will either be associated with a single entry, or the subtree defined by the entry, see Section 7.4 [Property inheritance], page 65.

You may define the allowed values for a particular property ‘`:Xyz:`’ by setting a property ‘`:Xyz_ALL:`’. This special property is *inherited*, so if you set it in a level 1 entry, it will apply to the entire tree. When allowed values are defined, setting the corresponding property becomes easier and is less prone to typing errors. For the example with the CD collection, we can predefine publishers and the number of disks in a box like this:

```
* CD collection
  :PROPERTIES:
  :NDisks_ALL:  1 2 3 4
  :Publisher_ALL: "Deutsche Grammophon" Philips EMI
  :END:
```

If you want to set properties that can be inherited by any entry in a file, use a line like

```
#+PROPERTY: NDisks_ALL 1 2 3 4
```

Contrary to properties set from a special drawer, you have to refresh the buffer with *C-c C-c* to activate this change.

If you want to add to the value of an existing property, append a + to the property name. The following results in the property **var** having the value "foo=1 bar=2".

```
#+PROPERTY: var  foo=1
#+PROPERTY: var+ bar=2
```

It is also possible to add to the values of inherited properties. The following results in the **genres** property having the value "Classic Baroque" under the **Goldberg Variations** subtree.

```
* CD collection
** Classic
   :PROPERTIES:
   :GENRES: Classic
   :END:
*** Goldberg Variations
    :PROPERTIES:
    :Title:     Goldberg Variations
    :Composer:  J.S. Bach
    :Artist:    Glen Gould
    :Publisher: Deutsche Grammophon
    :NDisks:    1
    :GENRES+:   Baroque
    :END:
```

Note that a property can only have one entry per Drawer.

Property values set with the global variable **org-global-properties** can be inherited by all entries in all Org files.

The following commands help to work with properties:

M-TAB   pcomplete
> After an initial colon in a line, complete property keys. All keys used in the current file will be offered as possible completions.

C-c C-x p   org-set-property
> Set a property. This prompts for a property name and a value. If necessary, the property drawer is created as well.

C-u M-x org-insert-drawer RET
> Insert a property drawer into the current entry. The drawer will be inserted early in the entry, but after the lines with planning information like deadlines.

C-c C-c   org-property-action
> With the cursor in a property drawer, this executes property commands.

C-c C-c s   org-set-property
> Set a property in the current entry. Both the property and the value can be inserted using completion.

S-right	`org-property-next-allowed-value`
S-left	`org-property-previous-allowed-value`

    Switch property at point to the next/previous allowed value.

C-c C-c d   `org-delete-property`

    Remove a property from the current entry.

C-c C-c D   `org-delete-property-globally`

    Globally remove a property, from all entries in the current file.

C-c C-c c   `org-compute-property-at-point`

    Compute the property at point, using the operator and scope from the nearest column format definition.

7.2 Special properties

Special properties provide an alternative access method to Org mode features, like the TODO state or the priority of an entry, discussed in the previous chapters. This interface exists so that you can include these states in a column view (see Section 7.5 [Column view], page 66), or to use them in queries. The following property names are special and (except for :CATEGORY:) should not be used as keys in the properties drawer:

ID	A globally unique ID used for synchronization during iCalendar or MobileOrg export.
TODO	The TODO keyword of the entry.
TAGS	The tags defined directly in the headline.
ALLTAGS	All tags, including inherited ones.
CATEGORY	The category of an entry.
PRIORITY	The priority of the entry, a string with a single letter.
DEADLINE	The deadline time string, without the angular brackets.
SCHEDULED	The scheduling timestamp, without the angular brackets.
CLOSED	When was this entry closed?
TIMESTAMP	The first keyword-less timestamp in the entry.
TIMESTAMP_IA	The first inactive timestamp in the entry.
CLOCKSUM	The sum of CLOCK intervals in the subtree. `org-clock-sum` must be run first to compute the values in the current buffer.
CLOCKSUM_T	The sum of CLOCK intervals in the subtree for today. `org-clock-sum-today` must be run first to compute the values in the current buffer.
BLOCKED	"t" if task is currently blocked by children or siblings
ITEM	The headline of the entry.
FILE	The filename the entry is located in.

7.3 Property searches

To create sparse trees and special lists with selection based on properties, the same commands are used as for tag searches (see Section 6.4 [Tag searches], page 61).

C-c / m or *C-c *   `org-match-sparse-tree`

    Create a sparse tree with all matching entries. With a *C-u* prefix argument, ignore headlines that are not a TODO line.

C-c a m   org-tags-view
> Create a global list of tag/property matches from all agenda files. See
> Section 10.3.3 [Matching tags and properties], page 103.

C-c a M   org-tags-view
> Create a global list of tag matches from all agenda files, but check only TODO
> items and force checking of subitems (see the option **org-tags-match-list-sublevels**).

The syntax for the search string is described in Section 10.3.3 [Matching tags and properties], page 103.

There is also a special command for creating sparse trees based on a single property:

C-c / p   Create a sparse tree based on the value of a property. This first prompts for
the name of a property, and then for a value. A sparse tree is created with all
entries that define this property with the given value. If you enclose the value
in curly braces, it is interpreted as a regular expression and matched against
the property values.

7.4 Property Inheritance

The outline structure of Org mode documents lends itself to an inheritance model of properties: if the parent in a tree has a certain property, the children can inherit this property. Org mode does not turn this on by default, because it can slow down property searches significantly and is often not needed. However, if you find inheritance useful, you can turn it on by setting the variable **org-use-property-inheritance**. It may be set to **t** to make all properties inherited from the parent, to a list of properties that should be inherited, or to a regular expression that matches inherited properties. If a property has the value **nil**, this is interpreted as an explicit undefine of the property, so that inheritance search will stop at this value and return **nil**.

Org mode has a few properties for which inheritance is hard-coded, at least for the special applications for which they are used:

COLUMNS   The :COLUMNS: property defines the format of column view (see Section 7.5
[Column view], page 66). It is inherited in the sense that the level where a
:COLUMNS: property is defined is used as the starting point for a column view
table, independently of the location in the subtree from where columns view is
turned on.

CATEGORY   For agenda view, a category set through a :CATEGORY: property applies to the
entire subtree.

ARCHIVE   For archiving, the :ARCHIVE: property may define the archive location for the
entire subtree (see Section 9.6.1 [Moving subtrees], page 96).

LOGGING   The LOGGING property may define logging settings for an entry or a subtree
(see Section 5.3.2 [Tracking TODO state changes], page 51).

7.5 Column view

A great way to view and edit properties in an outline tree is *column view*. In column view, each outline node is turned into a table row. Columns in this table provide access to properties of the entries. Org mode implements columns by overlaying a tabular structure over the headline of each item. While the headlines have been turned into a table row, you can still change the visibility of the outline tree. For example, you get a compact table by switching to CONTENTS view (*S-TAB S-TAB*, or simply *c* while column view is active), but you can still open, read, and edit the entry below each headline. Or, you can switch to column view after executing a sparse tree command and in this way get a table only for the selected items. Column view also works in agenda buffers (see Chapter 10 [Agenda views], page 98) where queries have collected selected items, possibly from a number of files.

7.5.1 Defining columns

Setting up a column view first requires defining the columns. This is done by defining a column format line.

7.5.1.1 Scope of column definitions

To define a column format for an entire file, use a line like

```
#+COLUMNS: %25ITEM %TAGS %PRIORITY %TODO
```

To specify a format that only applies to a specific tree, add a :COLUMNS: property to the top node of that tree, for example:

```
** Top node for columns view
   :PROPERTIES:
   :COLUMNS: %25ITEM %TAGS %PRIORITY %TODO
   :END:
```

If a :COLUMNS: property is present in an entry, it defines columns for the entry itself, and for the entire subtree below it. Since the column definition is part of the hierarchical structure of the document, you can define columns on level 1 that are general enough for all sublevels, and more specific columns further down, when you edit a deeper part of the tree.

7.5.1.2 Column attributes

A column definition sets the attributes of a column. The general definition looks like this:

```
%[width]property[(title)][{summary-type}]
```

Except for the percent sign and the property name, all items are optional. The individual parts have the following meaning:

width	An integer specifying the width of the column in characters. If omitted, the width will be determined automatically.
property	The property that should be edited in this column. Special properties representing meta data are allowed here as well (see Section 7.2 [Special properties], page 64)
title	The header text for the column. If omitted, the property name is used.
{summary-type}	The summary type. If specified, the column values for

parent nodes are computed from the children.

Supported summary types are:

`{+}`	Sum numbers in this column.
`{+;%.1f}`	Like '+', but format result with '%.1f'.
`{$}`	Currency, short for '+;%.2f'.
`{:}`	Sum times, HH:MM, plain numbers are hours.
`{X}`	Checkbox status, '`[X]`' if all children are '`[X]`'.
`{X/}`	Checkbox status, '`[n/m]`'.
`{X%}`	Checkbox status, '`[n%]`'.
`{min}`	Smallest number in column.
`{max}`	Largest number.
`{mean}`	Arithmetic mean of numbers.
`{:min}`	Smallest time value in column.
`{:max}`	Largest time value.
`{:mean}`	Arithmetic mean of time values.
`{@min}`	Minimum age (in days/hours/mins/seconds).
`{@max}`	Maximum age (in days/hours/mins/seconds).
`{@mean}`	Arithmetic mean of ages (in days/hours/mins/seconds).
`{est+}`	Add low-high estimates.

Be aware that you can only have one summary type for any property you include. Subsequent columns referencing the same property will all display the same summary information.

The `est+` summary type requires further explanation. It is used for combining estimates, expressed as low-high ranges. For example, instead of estimating a particular task will take 5 days, you might estimate it as 5–6 days if you're fairly confident you know how much work is required, or 1–10 days if you don't really know what needs to be done. Both ranges average at 5.5 days, but the first represents a more predictable delivery.

When combining a set of such estimates, simply adding the lows and highs produces an unrealistically wide result. Instead, `est+` adds the statistical mean and variance of the sub-tasks, generating a final estimate from the sum. For example, suppose you had ten tasks, each of which was estimated at 0.5 to 2 days of work. Straight addition produces an estimate of 5 to 20 days, representing what to expect if everything goes either extremely well or extremely poorly. In contrast, `est+` estimates the full job more realistically, at 10–15 days.

Numbers are right-aligned when a format specifier with an explicit width like `%5d` or `%5.1f` is used.

Here is an example for a complete columns definition, along with allowed values.

```
:COLUMNS:   %25ITEM %9Approved(Approved?){X} %Owner %11Status \¹
            %10Time_Estimate{:} %CLOCKSUM %CLOCKSUM_T
:Owner_ALL:     Tammy Mark Karl Lisa Don
:Status_ALL:    "In progress" "Not started yet" "Finished" ""
:Approved_ALL:  "[ ]" "[X]"
```

The first column, '`%25ITEM`', means the first 25 characters of the item itself, i.e., of the headline. You probably always should start the column definition with the 'ITEM' specifier. The

---

[1] Please note that the COLUMNS definition must be on a single line—it is wrapped here only because of formatting constraints.

other specifiers create columns 'Owner' with a list of names as allowed values, for 'Status' with four different possible values, and for a checkbox field 'Approved'. When no width is given after the '%' character, the column will be exactly as wide as it needs to be in order to fully display all values. The 'Approved' column does have a modified title ('Approved?', with a question mark). Summaries will be created for the 'Time_Estimate' column by adding time duration expressions like HH:MM, and for the 'Approved' column, by providing an '[X]' status if all children have been checked. The 'CLOCKSUM' and 'CLOCKSUM_T' columns are special, they lists the sums of CLOCK intervals in the subtree, either for all clocks or just for today.

7.5.2 Using column view

Turning column view on and off

C-c C-x C-c   org-columns

> Turn on column view. If the cursor is before the first headline in the file, column view is turned on for the entire file, using the #+COLUMNS definition. If the cursor is somewhere inside the outline, this command searches the hierarchy, up from point, for a :COLUMNS: property that defines a format. When one is found, the column view table is established for the tree starting at the entry that contains the :COLUMNS: property. If no such property is found, the format is taken from the #+COLUMNS line or from the variable org-columns-default-format, and column view is established for the current entry and its subtree.

r   org-columns-redo
> Recreate the column view, to include recent changes made in the buffer.

g   org-columns-redo
> Same as *r*.

q   org-columns-quit
> Exit column view.

Editing values

left right up down
> Move through the column view from field to field.

S-left/right
> Switch to the next/previous allowed value of the field. For this, you have to have specified allowed values for a property.

1..9,0   Directly select the Nth allowed value, *0* selects the 10th value.

n   org-columns-next-allowed-value
p   org-columns-previous-allowed-value
> Same as *S-left/right*

e   org-columns-edit-value
> Edit the property at point. For the special properties, this will invoke the same interface that you normally use to change that property. For example, when editing a TAGS property, the tag completion or fast selection interface will pop up.

C-c C-c   `org-columns-set-tags-or-toggle`
        When there is a checkbox at point, toggle it.

v   `org-columns-show-value`
        View the full value of this property. This is useful if the width of the column is
        smaller than that of the value.

a   `org-columns-edit-allowed`
        Edit the list of allowed values for this property. If the list is found in the
        hierarchy, the modified value is stored there. If no list is found, the new value
        is stored in the first entry that is part of the current column view.

Modifying the table structure

`<`   `org-columns-narrow`
`>`   `org-columns-widen`
        Make the column narrower/wider by one character.

S-M-right   `org-columns-new`
        Insert a new column, to the left of the current column.

S-M-left   `org-columns-delete`
        Delete the current column.

7.5.3 Capturing column view

Since column view is just an overlay over a buffer, it cannot be exported or printed directly.
If you want to capture a column view, use a **columnview** dynamic block (see Section A.7
[Dynamic blocks], page 233). The frame of this block looks like this:

```
* The column view
#+BEGIN: columnview :hlines 1 :id "label"


#+END:
```

This dynamic block has the following parameters:

`:id`   This is the most important parameter. Column view is a feature that is often
            localized to a certain (sub)tree, and the capture block might be at a different
            location in the file. To identify the tree whose view to capture, you can use 4
            values:

local	use the tree in which the capture block is located
global	make a global view, including all headings in the file
"file:*path-to-file*"	run column view at the top of this file
"*ID*"	call column view in the tree that has an :ID: property with the value *label*. You can use *M-x org-id-copy RET* to create a globally unique ID for the current entry and copy it to the kill-ring.

`:hlines`   When `t`, insert an hline after every line. When a number *N*, insert an hline
            before each headline with level `<=` *N*.

`:vlines`   When set to `t`, force column groups to get vertical lines.

`:maxlevel`
> When set to a number, don't capture entries below this level.

`:skip-empty-rows`
> When set to `t`, skip rows where the only non-empty specifier of the column view is `ITEM`.

The following commands insert or update the dynamic block:

`C-c C-x i`   org-insert-columns-dblock
> Insert a dynamic block capturing a column view. You will be prompted for the scope or ID of the view.

`C-c C-c` or `C-c C-x C-u`   org-dblock-update
> Update dynamic block at point. The cursor needs to be in the `#+BEGIN` line of the dynamic block.

`C-u C-c C-x C-u`   org-update-all-dblocks
> Update all dynamic blocks (see Section A.7 [Dynamic blocks], page 233). This is useful if you have several clock table blocks, column-capturing blocks or other dynamic blocks in a buffer.

You can add formulas to the column view table and you may add plotting instructions in front of the table—these will survive an update of the block. If there is a `#+TBLFM:` after the table, the table will actually be recalculated automatically after an update.

An alternative way to capture and process property values into a table is provided by Eric Schulte's `org-collector.el` which is a contributed package[2]. It provides a general API to collect properties from entries in a certain scope, and arbitrary Lisp expressions to process these values before inserting them into a table or a dynamic block.

7.6 The Property API

There is a full API for accessing and changing properties. This API can be used by Emacs Lisp programs to work with properties and to implement features based on them. For more information see Section A.11 [Using the property API], page 238.

---

[2] Contributed packages are not part of Emacs, but are distributed with the main distribution of Org (visit `http://orgmode.org`).

8 Dates and times

To assist project planning, TODO items can be labeled with a date and/or a time. The specially formatted string carrying the date and time information is called a *timestamp* in Org mode. This may be a little confusing because timestamp is often used to indicate when something was created or last changed. However, in Org mode this term is used in a much wider sense.

8.1 Timestamps, deadlines, and scheduling

A timestamp is a specification of a date (possibly with a time or a range of times) in a special format, either '<2003-09-16 Tue>'[1] or '<2003-09-16 Tue 09:39>' or '<2003-09-16 Tue 12:00-12:30>'[2]. A timestamp can appear anywhere in the headline or body of an Org tree entry. Its presence causes entries to be shown on specific dates in the agenda (see Section 10.3.1 [Weekly/daily agenda], page 100). We distinguish:

Plain timestamp; Event; Appointment

A simple timestamp just assigns a date/time to an item. This is just like writing down an appointment or event in a paper agenda. In the timeline and agenda displays, the headline of an entry associated with a plain timestamp will be shown exactly on that date.

```
* Meet Peter at the movies
  <2006-11-01 Wed 19:15>
* Discussion on climate change
  <2006-11-02 Thu 20:00-22:00>
```

Timestamp with repeater interval

A timestamp may contain a *repeater interval*, indicating that it applies not only on the given date, but again and again after a certain interval of N days (d), weeks (w), months (m), or years (y). The following will show up in the agenda every Wednesday:

```
* Pick up Sam at school
  <2007-05-16 Wed 12:30 +1w>
```

Diary-style sexp entries

For more complex date specifications, Org mode supports using the special sexp diary entries implemented in the Emacs calendar/diary package[3]. For example with optional time

---

[1] In this simplest form, the day name is optional when you type the date yourself. However, any dates inserted or modified by Org will add that day name, for reading convenience.

[2] This is inspired by the standard ISO 8601 date/time format. To use an alternative format, see Section 8.2.2 [Custom time format], page 75.

[3] When working with the standard diary sexp functions, you need to be very careful with the order of the arguments. That order depends evilly on the variable `calendar-date-style` (or, for older Emacs versions, `european-calendar-style`). For example, to specify a date December 12, 2005, the call might look like (diary-date 12 1 2005) or (diary-date 1 12 2005) or (diary-date 2005 12 1), depending on the settings. This has been the source of much confusion. Org mode users can resort to special versions of these functions like `org-date` or `org-anniversary`. These work just like the corresponding `diary`-functions, but with stable ISO order of arguments (year, month, day) wherever applicable, independent of the value of `calendar-date-style`.

```
* 22:00-23:00 The nerd meeting on every 2nd Thursday of the month
  <%%(diary-float t 4 2)>
```

Time/Date range

> Two timestamps connected by '--' denote a range. The headline will be shown on the first and last day of the range, and on any dates that are displayed and fall in the range. Here is an example:

```
** Meeting in Amsterdam
   <2004-08-23 Mon>--<2004-08-26 Thu>
```

Inactive timestamp

> Just like a plain timestamp, but with square brackets instead of angular ones. These timestamps are inactive in the sense that they do *not* trigger an entry to show up in the agenda.

```
* Gillian comes late for the fifth time
  [2006-11-01 Wed]
```

8.2 Creating timestamps

For Org mode to recognize timestamps, they need to be in the specific format. All commands listed below produce timestamps in the correct format.

`C-c .`   org-time-stamp

> Prompt for a date and insert a corresponding timestamp. When the cursor is at an existing timestamp in the buffer, the command is used to modify this timestamp instead of inserting a new one. When this command is used twice in succession, a time range is inserted.

`C-c !`   org-time-stamp-inactive

> Like `C-c .`, but insert an inactive timestamp that will not cause an agenda entry.

`C-u C-c .`
`C-u C-c !`   Like `C-c .` and `C-c !`, but use the alternative format which contains date and time. The default time can be rounded to multiples of 5 minutes, see the option `org-time-stamp-rounding-minutes`.

`C-c C-c`   Normalize timestamp, insert/fix day name if missing or wrong.

`C-c <`   org-date-from-calendar

> Insert a timestamp corresponding to the cursor date in the Calendar.

`C-c >`   org-goto-calendar

> Access the Emacs calendar for the current date. If there is a timestamp in the current line, go to the corresponding date instead.

`C-c C-o`   org-open-at-point

> Access the agenda for the date given by the timestamp or -range at point (see Section 10.3.1 [Weekly/daily agenda], page 100).

`S-left`   org-timestamp-down-day
`S-right`   org-timestamp-up-day

> Change date at cursor by one day. These key bindings conflict with shift-selection and related modes (see Section 15.10.2 [Conflicts], page 222).

S-up   org-timestamp-up
S-down   org-timestamp-down-down
> Change the item under the cursor in a timestamp. The cursor can be on a year, month, day, hour or minute. When the timestamp contains a time range like '15:30-16:30', modifying the first time will also shift the second, shifting the time block with constant length. To change the length, modify the second time. Note that if the cursor is in a headline and not at a timestamp, these same keys modify the priority of an item. (see Section 5.4 [Priorities], page 54). The key bindings also conflict with shift-selection and related modes (see Section 15.10.2 [Conflicts], page 222).

C-c C-y   org-evaluate-time-range
> Evaluate a time range by computing the difference between start and end. With a prefix argument, insert result after the time range (in a table: into the following column).

8.2.1 The date/time prompt

When Org mode prompts for a date/time, the default is shown in default date/time format, and the prompt therefore seems to ask for a specific format. But it will in fact accept date/time information in a variety of formats. Generally, the information should start at the beginning of the string. Org mode will find whatever information is in there and derive anything you have not specified from the *default date and time*. The default is usually the current date and time, but when modifying an existing timestamp, or when entering the second stamp of a range, it is taken from the stamp in the buffer. When filling in information, Org mode assumes that most of the time you will want to enter a date in the future: if you omit the month/year and the given day/month is *before* today, it will assume that you mean a future date[4]. If the date has been automatically shifted into the future, the time prompt will show this with '(=>F).'

For example, let's assume that today is **June 13, 2006**. Here is how various inputs will be interpreted, the items filled in by Org mode are in **bold**.

```
3-2-5           ⇒ 2003-02-05
2/5/3           ⇒ 2003-02-05
14              ⇒ 2006-06-14
12              ⇒ 2006-07-12
2/5             ⇒ 2007-02-05
Fri             ⇒ nearest Friday after the default date
sep 15          ⇒ 2006-09-15
feb 15          ⇒ 2007-02-15
sep 12 9        ⇒ 2009-09-12
12:45           ⇒ 2006-06-13 12:45
22 sept 0:34    ⇒ 2006-09-22 0:34
w4              ⇒ ISO week for of the current year 2006
2012 w4 fri     ⇒ Friday of ISO week 4 in 2012
2012-w04-5      ⇒ Same as above
```

---

[4] See the variable `org-read-date-prefer-future`. You may set that variable to the symbol `time` to even make a time before now shift the date to tomorrow.

Furthermore you can specify a relative date by giving, as the *first* thing in the input: a plus/minus sign, a number and a letter ([hdwmy]) to indicate change in hours, days, weeks, months, or years. With a single plus or minus, the date is always relative to today. With a double plus or minus, it is relative to the default date. If instead of a single letter, you use the abbreviation of day name, the date will be the Nth such day, e.g.:

```
+0              ⇒ today
.               ⇒ today
+4d             ⇒ four days from today
+4              ⇒ same as above
+2w             ⇒ two weeks from today
++5             ⇒ five days from default date
+2tue           ⇒ second Tuesday from now
-wed            ⇒ last Wednesday
```

The function understands English month and weekday abbreviations. If you want to use unabbreviated names and/or other languages, configure the variables `parse-time-months` and `parse-time-weekdays`.

Not all dates can be represented in a given Emacs implementation. By default Org mode forces dates into the compatibility range 1970–2037 which works on all Emacs implementations. If you want to use dates outside of this range, read the docstring of the variable `org-read-date-force-compatible-dates`.

You can specify a time range by giving start and end times or by giving a start time and a duration (in HH:MM format). Use one or two dash(es) as the separator in the former case and use '+' as the separator in the latter case, e.g.:

```
11am-1:15pm     ⇒ 11:00-13:15
11am--1:15pm    ⇒ same as above
11am+2:15       ⇒ same as above
```

Parallel to the minibuffer prompt, a calendar is popped up[5]. When you exit the date prompt, either by clicking on a date in the calendar, or by pressing RET, the date selected in the calendar will be combined with the information entered at the prompt. You can control the calendar fully from the minibuffer:

```
RET                 Choose date at cursor in calendar.
mouse-1             Select date by clicking on it.
S-right/left        One day forward/backward.
S-down/up           One week forward/backward.
M-S-right/left      One month forward/backward.
> / <               Scroll calendar forward/backward by one month.
M-v / C-v           Scroll calendar forward/backward by 3 months.
```

The actions of the date/time prompt may seem complex, but I assure you they will grow on you, and you will start getting annoyed by pretty much any other way of entering a date/time out there. To help you understand what is going on, the current interpretation of your input will be displayed live in the minibuffer[6].

---

[5] If you don't need/want the calendar, configure the variable `org-popup-calendar-for-date-prompt`.

[6] If you find this distracting, turn the display off with `org-read-date-display-live`.

8.2.2 Custom time format

Org mode uses the standard ISO notation for dates and times as it is defined in ISO 8601. If you cannot get used to this and require another representation of date and time to keep you happy, you can get it by customizing the options `org-display-custom-times` and `org-time-stamp-custom-formats`.

`C-c C-x C-t`   org-toggle-time-stamp-overlays
> Toggle the display of custom formats for dates and times.

Org mode needs the default format for scanning, so the custom date/time format does not *replace* the default format—instead it is put *over* the default format using text properties. This has the following consequences:

- You cannot place the cursor onto a timestamp anymore, only before or after.
- The *S-up/down* keys can no longer be used to adjust each component of a timestamp. If the cursor is at the beginning of the stamp, *S-up/down* will change the stamp by one day, just like *S-left/right*. At the end of the stamp, the time will be changed by one minute.
- If the timestamp contains a range of clock times or a repeater, these will not be overlaid, but remain in the buffer as they were.
- When you delete a timestamp character-by-character, it will only disappear from the buffer after *all* (invisible) characters belonging to the ISO timestamp have been removed.
- If the custom timestamp format is longer than the default and you are using dates in tables, table alignment will be messed up. If the custom format is shorter, things do work as expected.

8.3 Deadlines and scheduling

A timestamp may be preceded by special keywords to facilitate planning:

DEADLINE
> Meaning: the task (most likely a TODO item, though not necessarily) is supposed to be finished on that date.
>
> On the deadline date, the task will be listed in the agenda. In addition, the agenda for *today* will carry a warning about the approaching or missed deadline, starting `org-deadline-warning-days` before the due date, and continuing until the entry is marked DONE. An example:
>
> ```
> *** TODO write article about the Earth for the Guide
>     DEADLINE: <2004-02-29 Sun>
>     The editor in charge is [[bbdb:Ford Prefect]]
> ```
>
> You can specify a different lead time for warnings for a specific deadline using the following syntax. Here is an example with a warning period of 5 days `DEADLINE: <2004-02-29 Sun -5d>`. This warning is deactivated if the task gets scheduled and you set `org-agenda-skip-deadline-prewarning-if-scheduled` to `t`.

SCHEDULED
> Meaning: you are planning to start working on that task on the given date.

The headline will be listed under the given date[7]. In addition, a reminder that the scheduled date has passed will be present in the compilation for *today*, until the entry is marked DONE, i.e., the task will automatically be forwarded until completed.

```
*** TODO Call Trillian for a date on New Years Eve.
    SCHEDULED: <2004-12-25 Sat>
```

If you want to *delay* the display of this task in the agenda, use `SCHEDULED: <2004-12-25 Sat -2d>`: the task is still scheduled on the 25th but will appear two days later. In case the task contains a repeater, the delay is considered to affect all occurrences; if you want the delay to only affect the first scheduled occurrence of the task, use `--2d` instead. See `org-scheduled-delay-days` and `org-agenda-skip-scheduled-delay-if-deadline` for details on how to control this globally or per agenda.

Important: Scheduling an item in Org mode should *not* be understood in the same way that we understand *scheduling a meeting*. Setting a date for a meeting is just a simple appointment, you should mark this entry with a simple plain timestamp, to get this item shown on the date where it applies. This is a frequent misunderstanding by Org users. In Org mode, *scheduling* means setting a date when you want to start working on an action item.

You may use timestamps with repeaters in scheduling and deadline entries. Org mode will issue early and late warnings based on the assumption that the timestamp represents the *nearest instance* of the repeater. However, the use of diary sexp entries like `<%%(diary-float t 42)>` in scheduling and deadline timestamps is limited. Org mode does not know enough about the internals of each sexp function to issue early and late warnings. However, it will show the item on each day where the sexp entry matches.

8.3.1 Inserting deadlines or schedules

The following commands allow you to quickly insert[8] a deadline or to schedule an item:

`C-c C-d`   `org-deadline`

> Insert 'DEADLINE' keyword along with a stamp. The insertion will happen in the line directly following the headline. Any CLOSED timestamp will be removed. When called with a prefix arg, an existing deadline will be removed from the entry. Depending on the variable `org-log-redeadline`[9], a note will be taken when changing an existing deadline.

`C-c C-s`   `org-schedule`

> Insert 'SCHEDULED' keyword along with a stamp. The insertion will happen in the line directly following the headline. Any CLOSED timestamp will be removed. When called with a prefix argument, remove the scheduling date

---

[7] It will still be listed on that date after it has been marked DONE. If you don't like this, set the variable `org-agenda-skip-scheduled-if-done`.

[8] The 'SCHEDULED' and 'DEADLINE' dates are inserted on the line right below the headline. Don't put any text between this line and the headline.

[9] with corresponding `#+STARTUP` keywords `logredeadline`, `lognoteredeadline`, and `nologredeadline`

from the entry. Depending on the variable `org-log-reschedule`[10], a note will be taken when changing an existing scheduling time.

`C-c C-x C-k`   `org-mark-entry-for-agenda-action`
> Mark the current entry for agenda action. After you have marked the entry like this, you can open the agenda or the calendar to find an appropriate date. With the cursor on the selected date, press `k s` or `k d` to schedule the marked item.

`C-c / d`   `org-check-deadlines`
> Create a sparse tree with all deadlines that are either past-due, or which will become due within `org-deadline-warning-days`. With `C-u` prefix, show all deadlines in the file. With a numeric prefix, check that many days. For example, `C-1 C-c / d` shows all deadlines due tomorrow.

`C-c / b`   `org-check-before-date`
> Sparse tree for deadlines and scheduled items before a given date.

`C-c / a`   `org-check-after-date`
> Sparse tree for deadlines and scheduled items after a given date.

Note that `org-schedule` and `org-deadline` supports setting the date by indicating a relative time: e.g., +1d will set the date to the next day after today, and −1w will set the date to the previous week before any current timestamp.

8.3.2 Repeated tasks

Some tasks need to be repeated again and again. Org mode helps to organize such tasks using a so-called repeater in a DEADLINE, SCHEDULED, or plain timestamp. In the following example

```
** TODO Pay the rent
   DEADLINE: <2005-10-01 Sat +1m>
```

the `+1m` is a repeater; the intended interpretation is that the task has a deadline on <2005-10-01> and repeats itself every (one) month starting from that time. You can use yearly, monthly, weekly, daily and hourly repeat cookies by using the `y/w/m/d/h` letters. If you need both a repeater and a special warning period in a deadline entry, the repeater should come first and the warning period last: `DEADLINE: <2005-10-01 Sat +1m -3d>`.

Deadlines and scheduled items produce entries in the agenda when they are over-due, so it is important to be able to mark such an entry as completed once you have done so. When you mark a DEADLINE or a SCHEDULE with the TODO keyword DONE, it will no longer produce entries in the agenda. The problem with this is, however, that then also the *next* instance of the repeated entry will not be active. Org mode deals with this in the following way: When you try to mark such an entry DONE (using `C-c C-t`), it will shift the base date of the repeating timestamp by the repeater interval, and immediately set the entry state back to TODO[11]. In the example above, setting the state to DONE would actually switch the date like this:

---

[10] with corresponding `#+STARTUP` keywords `logreschedule`, `lognotereschedule`, and `nologreschedule`

[11] In fact, the target state is taken from, in this sequence, the `REPEAT_TO_STATE` property or the variable `org-todo-repeat-to-state`. If neither of these is specified, the target state defaults to the first state of the TODO state sequence.

```
** TODO Pay the rent
   DEADLINE: <2005-11-01 Tue +1m>
```

To mark a task with a repeater as DONE, use *C-- 1 C-c C-t* (i.e., org-todo with a numeric prefix argument of -1.)

A timestamp[12] will be added under the deadline, to keep a record that you actually acted on the previous instance of this deadline.

As a consequence of shifting the base date, this entry will no longer be visible in the agenda when checking past dates, but all future instances will be visible.

With the '+1m' cookie, the date shift will always be exactly one month. So if you have not paid the rent for three months, marking this entry DONE will still keep it as an overdue deadline. Depending on the task, this may not be the best way to handle it. For example, if you forgot to call your father for 3 weeks, it does not make sense to call him 3 times in a single day to make up for it. Finally, there are tasks like changing batteries which should always repeat a certain time *after* the last time you did it. For these tasks, Org mode has special repeaters '++' and '.+'. For example:

```
** TODO Call Father
   DEADLINE: <2008-02-10 Sun ++1w>
   Marking this DONE will shift the date by at least one week,
   but also by as many weeks as it takes to get this date into
   the future.  However, it stays on a Sunday, even if you called
   and marked it done on Saturday.
** TODO Check the batteries in the smoke detectors
   DEADLINE: <2005-11-01 Tue .+1m>
   Marking this DONE will shift the date to one month after
   today.
```

You may have both scheduling and deadline information for a specific task. If the repeater is set for the scheduling information only, you probably want the repeater to be ignored after the deadline. If so, set the variable org-agenda-skip-scheduled-if-deadline-is-shown to repeated-after-deadline. If you want both scheduling and deadline information to repeat after the same interval, set the same repeater for both timestamps.

An alternative to using a repeater is to create a number of copies of a task subtree, with dates shifted in each copy. The command *C-c C-x c* was created for this purpose, it is described in Section 2.5 [Structure editing], page 9.

8.4 Clocking work time

Org mode allows you to clock the time you spend on specific tasks in a project. When you start working on an item, you can start the clock. When you stop working on that task, or when you mark the task done, the clock is stopped and the corresponding time interval is recorded. It also computes the total time spent on each subtree[13] of a project. And it remembers a history or tasks recently clocked, so that you can jump quickly between a number of tasks absorbing your time.

---

[12] You can change this using the option org-log-repeat, or the #+STARTUP options logrepeat, lognoterepeat, and nologrepeat. With lognoterepeat, you will also be prompted for a note.

[13] Clocking only works if all headings are indented with less than 30 stars. This is a hardcoded limitation of 'lmax' in 'org-clock-sum'.

To save the clock history across Emacs sessions, use

(setq org-clock-persist 'history)
(org-clock-persistence-insinuate)

When you clock into a new task after resuming Emacs, the incomplete clock[14] will be found (see Section 8.4.3 [Resolving idle time], page 83) and you will be prompted about what to do with it.

8.4.1 Clocking commands

`C-c C-x C-i`   org-clock-in

> Start the clock on the current item (clock-in). This inserts the CLOCK keyword together with a timestamp. If this is not the first clocking of this item, the multiple CLOCK lines will be wrapped into a :LOGBOOK: drawer (see also the variable `org-clock-into-drawer`). You can also overrule the setting of this variable for a subtree by setting a `CLOCK_INTO_DRAWER` or `LOG_INTO_DRAWER` property. When called with a `C-u` prefix argument, select the task from a list of recently clocked tasks. With two `C-u C-u` prefixes, clock into the task at point and mark it as the default task; the default task will then always be available with letter `d` when selecting a clocking task. With three `C-u C-u C-u` prefixes, force continuous clocking by starting the clock when the last clock stopped.
>
> While the clock is running, the current clocking time is shown in the mode line, along with the title of the task. The clock time shown will be all time ever clocked for this task and its children. If the task has an effort estimate (see Section 8.5 [Effort estimates], page 84), the mode line displays the current clocking time against it[15] If the task is a repeating one (see Section 8.3.2 [Repeated tasks], page 77), only the time since the last reset of the task[16] will be shown. More control over what time is shown can be exercised with the `CLOCK_MODELINE_TOTAL` property. It may have the values `current` to show only the current clocking instance, `today` to show all time clocked on this tasks today (see also the variable `org-extend-today-until`), `all` to include all time, or `auto` which is the default[17].
>
> Clicking with `mouse-1` onto the mode line entry will pop up a menu with clocking options.

`C-c C-x C-o`   org-clock-out

> Stop the clock (clock-out). This inserts another timestamp at the same location where the clock was last started. It also directly computes the resulting time and inserts it after the time range as '=> HH:MM'. See the variable `org-log-note-clock-out` for the possibility to record an additional note together with the clock-out timestamp[18].

---

[14] To resume the clock under the assumption that you have worked on this task while outside Emacs, use (setq org-clock-persist t).

[15] To add an effort estimate "on the fly", hook a function doing this to `org-clock-in-prepare-hook`.

[16] as recorded by the `LAST_REPEAT` property

[17] See also the variable `org-clock-modeline-total`.

[18] The corresponding in-buffer setting is: `#+STARTUP: lognoteclock-out`

`C-c C-x C-x`   `org-clock-in-last`

> Reclock the last clocked task. With one `C-u` prefix argument, select the task from the clock history. With two `C-u` prefixes, force continuous clocking by starting the clock when the last clock stopped.

`C-c C-x C-e`   `org-clock-modify-effort-estimate`

> Update the effort estimate for the current clock task.

`C-c C-c` or `C-c C-y`   `org-evaluate-time-range`

> Recompute the time interval after changing one of the timestamps. This is only necessary if you edit the timestamps directly. If you change them with `S-cursor` keys, the update is automatic.

`C-S-up/down`   `org-clock-timestamps-up/down`

> On `CLOCK` log lines, increase/decrease both timestamps so that the clock duration keeps the same.

`S-M-up/down`   `org-timestamp-up/down`

> On `CLOCK` log lines, increase/decrease the timestamp at point and the one of the previous (or the next clock) timestamp by the same duration. For example, if you hit `S-M-up` to increase a clocked-out timestamp by five minutes, then the clocked-in timestamp of the next clock will be increased by five minutes.

`C-c C-t`   `org-todo`

> Changing the TODO state of an item to DONE automatically stops the clock if it is running in this same item.

`C-c C-x C-q`   `org-clock-cancel`

> Cancel the current clock. This is useful if a clock was started by mistake, or if you ended up working on something else.

`C-c C-x C-j`   `org-clock-goto`

> Jump to the headline of the currently clocked in task. With a `C-u` prefix arg, select the target task from a list of recently clocked tasks.

`C-c C-x C-d`   `org-clock-display`

> Display time summaries for each subtree in the current buffer. This puts overlays at the end of each headline, showing the total time recorded under that heading, including the time of any subheadings. You can use visibility cycling to study the tree, but the overlays disappear when you change the buffer (see variable `org-remove-highlights-with-change`) or press `C-c C-c`.

The `l` key may be used in the timeline (see Section 10.3.4 [Timeline], page 106) and in the agenda (see Section 10.3.1 [Weekly/daily agenda], page 100) to show which tasks have been worked on or closed during a day.

Important: note that both `org-clock-out` and `org-clock-in-last` can have a global keybinding and will not modify the window disposition.

8.4.2 The clock table

Org mode can produce quite complex reports based on the time clocking information. Such a report is called a *clock table*, because it is formatted as one or several Org tables.

`C-c C-x C-r`   `org-clock-report`

> Insert a dynamic block (see Section A.7 [Dynamic blocks], page 233) containing a clock report as an Org mode table into the current file. When the cursor is at an existing clock table, just update it. When called with a prefix argument, jump to the first clock report in the current document and update it. The clock table always includes also trees with `:ARCHIVE:` tag.

`C-c C-c` or `C-c C-x C-u`   `org-dblock-update`

> Update dynamic block at point. The cursor needs to be in the `#+BEGIN` line of the dynamic block.

`C-u C-c C-x C-u`

> Update all dynamic blocks (see Section A.7 [Dynamic blocks], page 233). This is useful if you have several clock table blocks in a buffer.

`S-left`
`S-right`   `org-clocktable-try-shift`

> Shift the current `:block` interval and update the table. The cursor needs to be in the `#+BEGIN: clocktable` line for this command. If `:block` is `today`, it will be shifted to `today-1` etc.

Here is an example of the frame for a clock table as it is inserted into the buffer with the `C-c C-x C-r` command:

```
#+BEGIN: clocktable :maxlevel 2 :emphasize nil :scope file
#+END: clocktable
```

The 'BEGIN' line specifies a number of options to define the scope, structure, and formatting of the report. Defaults for all these options can be configured in the variable `org-clocktable-defaults`.

First there are options that determine which clock entries are to be selected:

`:maxlevel`	Maximum level depth to which times are listed in the table. Clocks at deeper levels will be summed into the upper level.
`:scope`	The scope to consider. This can be any of the following:

`nil`	the current buffer or narrowed region
`file`	the full current buffer
`subtree`	the subtree where the clocktable is located
`tree`*N*	the surrounding level *N* tree, for example `tree3`
`tree`	the surrounding level 1 tree
`agenda`	all agenda files
`("file"..)`	scan these files
`file-with-archives`	current file and its archives
`agenda-with-archives`	all agenda files, including archives

`:block`	The time block to consider. This block is specified either absolutely, or relative to the current time and may be any of these formats:

`2007-12-31`	New year eve 2007
`2007-12`	December 2007
`2007-W50`	ISO-week 50 in 2007
`2007-Q2`	2nd quarter in 2007

	2007	the year 2007
	today, yesterday, today-*N*	a relative day
	thisweek, lastweek, thisweek-*N*	a relative week
	thismonth, lastmonth, thismonth-*N*	a relative month
	thisyear, lastyear, thisyear-*N*	a relative year
	Use *S-left/right* keys to shift the time interval.	
:tstart	A time string specifying when to start considering times. Relative times like "<-2w>" can also be used. See Section 10.3.3 [Matching tags and properties], page 103 for relative time syntax.	
:tend	A time string specifying when to stop considering times. Relative times like "<now>" can also be used. See Section 10.3.3 [Matching tags and properties], page 103 for relative time syntax.	
:wstart	The starting day of the week. The default is 1 for monday.	
:mstart	The starting day of the month. The default 1 is for the first day of the month.	
:step	week or day, to split the table into chunks. To use this, :block or :tstart, :tend are needed.	
:stepskip0	Do not show steps that have zero time.	
:fileskip0	Do not show table sections from files which did not contribute.	
:tags	A tags match to select entries that should contribute. See Section 10.3.3 [Matching tags and properties], page 103 for the match syntax.	

Then there are options which determine the formatting of the table. These options are interpreted by the function **org-clocktable-write-default**, but you can specify your own function using the :formatter parameter.

:emphasize	When t, emphasize level one and level two items.
:lang	Language[19] to use for descriptive cells like "Task".
:link	Link the item headlines in the table to their origins.
:narrow	An integer to limit the width of the headline column in the org table. If you write it like '50!', then the headline will also be shortened in export.
:indent	Indent each headline field according to its level.
:tcolumns	Number of columns to be used for times. If this is smaller than :maxlevel, lower levels will be lumped into one column.
:level	Should a level number column be included?
:sort	A cons cell like containing the column to sort and a sorting type. E.g., :sort (1 . ?a) sorts the first column alphabetically.
:compact	Abbreviation for :level nil :indent t :narrow 40! :tcolumns 1 All are overwritten except if there is an explicit :narrow
:timestamp	A timestamp for the entry, when available. Look for SCHEDULED, DEADLINE, TIMESTAMP and TIMESTAMP_IA, in this order.
:properties	List of properties that should be shown in the table. Each property will get its own column.
:inherit-props	When this flag is t, the values for :properties will be inherited.
:formula	Content of a #+TBLFM line to be added and evaluated. As a special case, ':formula %' adds a column with % time.

---

[19] Language terms can be set through the variable org-clock-clocktable-language-setup.

If you do not specify a formula here, any existing formula below the clock table will survive updates and be evaluated.

`:formatter`   A function to format clock data and insert it into the buffer.

To get a clock summary of the current level 1 tree, for the current day, you could write

```
#+BEGIN: clocktable :maxlevel 2 :block today :scope tree1 :link t
#+END: clocktable
```

and to use a specific time range you could write[20]

```
#+BEGIN: clocktable :tstart "<2006-08-10 Thu 10:00>"
                    :tend "<2006-08-10 Thu 12:00>"
#+END: clocktable
```

A range starting a week ago and ending right now could be written as

```
#+BEGIN: clocktable :tstart "<-1w>" :tend "<now>"
#+END: clocktable
```

A summary of the current subtree with % times would be

```
#+BEGIN: clocktable :scope subtree :link t :formula %
#+END: clocktable
```

A horizontally compact representation of everything clocked during last week would be

```
#+BEGIN: clocktable :scope agenda :block lastweek :compact t
#+END: clocktable
```

8.4.3 Resolving idle time and continuous clocking

Resolving idle time

If you clock in on a work item, and then walk away from your computer—perhaps to take a phone call—you often need to "resolve" the time you were away by either subtracting it from the current clock, or applying it to another one.

By customizing the variable `org-clock-idle-time` to some integer, such as 10 or 15, Emacs can alert you when you get back to your computer after being idle for that many minutes[21], and ask what you want to do with the idle time. There will be a question waiting for you when you get back, indicating how much idle time has passed (constantly updated with the current amount), as well as a set of choices to correct the discrepancy:

k   To keep some or all of the minutes and stay clocked in, press *k*. Org will ask how many of the minutes to keep. Press `RET` to keep them all, effectively changing nothing, or enter a number to keep that many minutes.

K   If you use the shift key and press *K*, it will keep however many minutes you request and then immediately clock out of that task. If you keep all of the minutes, this is the same as just clocking out of the current task.

---

[20] Note that all parameters must be specified in a single line—the line is broken here only to fit it into the manual.

[21] On computers using Mac OS X, idleness is based on actual user idleness, not just Emacs' idle time. For X11, you can install a utility program `x11idle.c`, available in the `contrib/scripts` directory of the Org git distribution, or install the `xprintidle` package and set it to the variable `org-clock-x11idle-program-name` if you are running Debian, to get the same general treatment of idleness. On other systems, idle time refers to Emacs idle time only.

s   To keep none of the minutes, use *s* to subtract all the away time from the clock, and then check back in from the moment you returned.

S   To keep none of the minutes and just clock out at the start of the away time, use the shift key and press *S*. Remember that using shift will always leave you clocked out, no matter which option you choose.

C   To cancel the clock altogether, use *C*. Note that if instead of canceling you subtract the away time, and the resulting clock amount is less than a minute, the clock will still be canceled rather than clutter up the log with an empty entry.

What if you subtracted those away minutes from the current clock, and now want to apply them to a new clock? Simply clock in to any task immediately after the subtraction. Org will notice that you have subtracted time "on the books", so to speak, and will ask if you want to apply those minutes to the next task you clock in on.

There is one other instance when this clock resolution magic occurs. Say you were clocked in and hacking away, and suddenly your cat chased a mouse who scared a hamster that crashed into your UPS's power button! You suddenly lose all your buffers, but thanks to auto-save you still have your recent Org mode changes, including your last clock in.

If you restart Emacs and clock into any task, Org will notice that you have a dangling clock which was never clocked out from your last session. Using that clock's starting time as the beginning of the unaccounted-for period, Org will ask how you want to resolve that time. The logic and behavior is identical to dealing with away time due to idleness; it is just happening due to a recovery event rather than a set amount of idle time.

You can also check all the files visited by your Org agenda for dangling clocks at any time using *M-x org-resolve-clocks RET* (or *C-c C-x C-z*).

Continuous clocking

You may want to start clocking from the time when you clocked out the previous task. To enable this systematically, set `org-clock-continuously` to `t`. Each time you clock in, Org retrieves the clock-out time of the last clocked entry for this session, and start the new clock from there.

If you only want this from time to time, use three universal prefix arguments with `org-clock-in` and two *C-u C-u* with `org-clock-in-last`.

8.5 Effort estimates

If you want to plan your work in a very detailed way, or if you need to produce offers with quotations of the estimated work effort, you may want to assign effort estimates to entries. If you are also clocking your work, you may later want to compare the planned effort with the actual working time, a great way to improve planning estimates. Effort estimates are stored in a special property 'Effort'[22]. You can set the effort for an entry with the following commands:

---

[22] You may change the property being used with the variable `org-effort-property`.

`C-c C-x e`   org-set-effort
> Set the effort estimate for the current entry. With a numeric prefix argument, set it to the Nth allowed value (see below). This command is also accessible from the agenda with the `e` key.

`C-c C-x C-e`   org-clock-modify-effort-estimate
> Modify the effort estimate of the item currently being clocked.

Clearly the best way to work with effort estimates is through column view (see Section 7.5 [Column view], page 66). You should start by setting up discrete values for effort estimates, and a `COLUMNS` format that displays these values together with clock sums (if you want to clock your time). For a specific buffer you can use

```
#+PROPERTY: Effort_ALL 0 0:10 0:30 1:00 2:00 3:00 4:00 5:00 6:00 7:00
#+COLUMNS: %40ITEM(Task) %17Effort(Estimated Effort){:} %CLOCKSUM
```

or, even better, you can set up these values globally by customizing the variables `org-global-properties` and `org-columns-default-format`. In particular if you want to use this setup also in the agenda, a global setup may be advised.

The way to assign estimates to individual items is then to switch to column mode, and to use `S-right` and `S-left` to change the value. The values you enter will immediately be summed up in the hierarchy. In the column next to it, any clocked time will be displayed.

If you switch to column view in the daily/weekly agenda, the effort column will summarize the estimated work effort for each day[23], and you can use this to find space in your schedule. To get an overview of the entire part of the day that is committed, you can set the option `org-agenda-columns-add-appointments-to-effort-sum`. The appointments on a day that take place over a specified time interval will then also be added to the load estimate of the day.

Effort estimates can be used in secondary agenda filtering that is triggered with the `/` key in the agenda (see Section 10.5 [Agenda commands], page 111). If you have these estimates defined consistently, two or three key presses will narrow down the list to stuff that fits into an available time slot.

8.6 Taking notes with a relative timer

When taking notes during, for example, a meeting or a video viewing, it can be useful to have access to times relative to a starting time. Org provides such a relative timer and make it easy to create timed notes.

`C-c C-x .`   org-timer
> Insert a relative time into the buffer. The first time you use this, the timer will be started. When called with a prefix argument, the timer is restarted.

`C-c C-x -`   org-timer-item
> Insert a description list item with the current relative time. With a prefix argument, first reset the timer to 0.

---

[23] Please note the pitfalls of summing hierarchical data in a flat list (see Section 10.8 [Agenda column view], page 125).

M-RET   `org-insert-heading`
>   Once the timer list is started, you can also use *M-RET* to insert new timer items.

C-c C-x ,   Pause the timer, or continue it if it is already paused (`org-timer-pause-or-continue`).

C-u C-c C-x ,
>   Stop the timer. After this, you can only start a new timer, not continue the old one. This command also removes the timer from the mode line.

C-c C-x 0   `org-timer-start`
>   Reset the timer without inserting anything into the buffer. By default, the timer is reset to 0. When called with a *C-u* prefix, reset the timer to specific starting offset. The user is prompted for the offset, with a default taken from a timer string at point, if any, So this can be used to restart taking notes after a break in the process. When called with a double prefix argument *C-u C-u*, change all timer strings in the active region by a certain amount. This can be used to fix timer strings if the timer was not started at exactly the right moment.

8.7 Countdown timer

Calling `org-timer-set-timer` from an Org mode buffer runs a countdown timer. Use *;* from agenda buffers, *C-c C-x ;* everywhere else.

   `org-timer-set-timer` prompts the user for a duration and displays a countdown timer in the modeline. `org-timer-default-timer` sets the default countdown value. Giving a prefix numeric argument overrides this default value.

9 Capture - Refile - Archive

An important part of any organization system is the ability to quickly capture new ideas and tasks, and to associate reference material with them. Org does this using a process called *capture*. It also can store files related to a task (*attachments*) in a special directory. Once in the system, tasks and projects need to be moved around. Moving completed project trees to an archive file keeps the system compact and fast.

9.1 Capture

Capture lets you quickly store notes with little interruption of your work flow. Org's method for capturing new items is heavily inspired by John Wiegley excellent `remember.el` package. Up to version 6.36, Org used a special setup for `remember.el`, then replaced it with `org-remember.el`. As of version 8.0, `org-remember.el` has been completely replaced by `org-capture.el`.

If your configuration depends on `org-remember.el`, you need to update it and use the setup described below. To convert your `org-remember-templates`, run the command

>   M-x org-capture-import-remember-templates RET

and then customize the new variable with *M-x customize-variable org-capture-templates*, check the result, and save the customization.

9.1.1 Setting up capture

The following customization sets a default target file for notes, and defines a global key[1] for capturing new material.

```
(setq org-default-notes-file (concat org-directory "/notes.org"))
(define-key global-map "\C-cc" 'org-capture)
```

9.1.2 Using capture

`C-c c`   org-capture
> Call the command **org-capture**. Note that this keybinding is global and not active by default: you need to install it. If you have templates defined see Section 9.1.3 [Capture templates], page 88, it will offer these templates for selection or use a new Org outline node as the default template. It will insert the template into the target file and switch to an indirect buffer narrowed to this new node. You may then insert the information you want.

`C-c C-c`   org-capture-finalize
> Once you have finished entering information into the capture buffer, `C-c C-c` will return you to the window configuration before the capture process, so that you can resume your work without further distraction. When called with a prefix arg, finalize and then jump to the captured item.

`C-c C-w`   org-capture-refile
> Finalize the capture process by refiling (see Section 9.5 [Refile and copy], page 94) the note to a different place. Please realize that this is a normal

---

[1] Please select your own key, `C-c c` is only a suggestion.

refiling command that will be executed—so the cursor position at the moment you run this command is important. If you have inserted a tree with a parent and children, first move the cursor back to the parent. Any prefix argument given to this command will be passed on to the **org-refile** command.

C-c C-k   **org-capture-kill**
> Abort the capture process and return to the previous state.

You can also call **org-capture** in a special way from the agenda, using the *k c* key combination. With this access, any timestamps inserted by the selected capture template will default to the cursor date in the agenda, rather than to the current date.

To find the locations of the last stored capture, use **org-capture** with prefix commands:

C-u C-c c
> Visit the target location of a capture template. You get to select the template in the usual way.

C-u C-u C-c c
> Visit the last stored capture item in its buffer.

You can also jump to the bookmark **org-capture-last-stored**, which will automatically be created unless you set **org-capture-bookmark** to nil.

To insert the capture at point in an Org buffer, call **org-capture** with a C-0 prefix argument.

9.1.3 Capture templates

You can use templates for different types of capture items, and for different target locations. The easiest way to create such templates is through the customize interface.

C-c c C   Customize the variable **org-capture-templates**.

Before we give the formal description of template definitions, let's look at an example. Say you would like to use one template to create general TODO entries, and you want to put these entries under the heading 'Tasks' in your file ~/org/gtd.org. Also, a date tree in the file journal.org should capture journal entries. A possible configuration would look like:

```
(setq org-capture-templates
 '(("t" "Todo" entry (file+headline "~/org/gtd.org" "Tasks")
      "* TODO %?\n  %i\n  %a")
   ("j" "Journal" entry (file+datetree "~/org/journal.org")
      "* %?\nEntered on %U\n  %i\n  %a")))
```

If you then press *C-c c t*, Org will prepare the template for you like this:

```
* TODO
  [[file:link to where you initiated capture]]
```

During expansion of the template, %a has been replaced by a link to the location from where you called the capture command. This can be extremely useful for deriving tasks from emails, for example. You fill in the task definition, press *C-c C-c* and Org returns you to the same place where you started the capture process.

To define special keys to capture to a particular template without going through the interactive template selection, you can create your key binding like this:

```
(define-key global-map "\C-cx"
  (lambda () (interactive) (org-capture nil "x")))
```

9.1.3.1 Template elements

Now lets look at the elements of a template definition. Each entry in `org-capture-templates` is a list with the following items:

keys
> The keys that will select the template, as a string, characters only, for example `"a"` for a template to be selected with a single key, or `"bt"` for selection with two keys. When using several keys, keys using the same prefix key must be sequential in the list and preceded by a 2-element entry explaining the prefix key, for example
>
> > `("b" "Templates for marking stuff to buy")`
>
> If you do not define a template for the `C` key, this key will be used to open the customize buffer for this complex variable.

description
> A short string describing the template, which will be shown during selection.

type
> The type of entry, a symbol. Valid values are:
>
> `entry`
> > An Org mode node, with a headline. Will be filed as the child of the target entry or as a top-level entry. The target file should be an Org mode file.
>
> `item`
> > A plain list item, placed in the first plain list at the target location. Again the target file should be an Org file.
>
> `checkitem`
> > A checkbox item. This only differs from the plain list item by the default template.
>
> `table-line`
> > a new line in the first table at the target location. Where exactly the line will be inserted depends on the properties `:prepend` and `:table-line-pos` (see below).
>
> `plain`
> > Text to be inserted as it is.

target
> Specification of where the captured item should be placed. In Org mode files, targets usually define a node. Entries will become children of this node. Other types will be added to the table or list in the body of this node. Most target specifications contain a file name. If that file name is the empty string, it defaults to `org-default-notes-file`. A file can also be given as a variable, function, or Emacs Lisp form.
>
> Valid values are:
>
> `(file "path/to/file")`
> > Text will be placed at the beginning or end of that file.
>
> `(id "id of existing org entry")`
> > Filing as child of this entry, or in the body of the entry.

`(file+headline "path/to/file" "node headline")`
>   Fast configuration if the target heading is unique in the file.

`(file+olp "path/to/file" "Level 1 heading" "Level 2" ...)`
>   For non-unique headings, the full path is safer.

`(file+regexp "path/to/file" "regexp to find location")`
>   Use a regular expression to position the cursor.

`(file+datetree "path/to/file")`
>   Will create a heading in a date tree for today's date[2].

`(file+datetree+prompt "path/to/file")`
>   Will create a heading in a date tree, but will prompt for the date.

`(file+function "path/to/file" function-finding-location)`
>   A function to find the right location in the file.

`(clock)`   File to the entry that is currently being clocked.

`(function function-finding-location)`
>   Most general way, write your own function to find both file and location.

template   The template for creating the capture item. If you leave this empty, an appropriate default template will be used. Otherwise this is a string with escape codes, which will be replaced depending on time and context of the capture call. The string with escapes may be loaded from a template file, using the special syntax (`file "path/to/template"`). See below for more details.

properties   The rest of the entry is a property list of additional options. Recognized properties are:

`:prepend`   Normally new captured information will be appended at the target location (last child, last table line, last list item...). Setting this property will change that.

`:immediate-finish`
>   When set, do not offer to edit the information, just file it away immediately. This makes sense if the template only needs information that can be added automatically.

`:empty-lines`
>   Set this to the number of lines to insert before and after the new item. Default 0, only common other value is 1.

`:clock-in`
>   Start the clock in this item.

`:clock-keep`
>   Keep the clock running when filing the captured entry.

---

[2] Datetree headlines for years accept tags, so if you use both `* 2013 :noexport:` and `* 2013` in your file, the capture will refile the note to the first one matched.

:clock-resume

> If starting the capture interrupted a clock, restart that clock when finished with the capture. Note that :clock-keep has precedence over :clock-resume. When setting both to t, the current clock will run and the previous one will not be resumed.

:unnarrowed

> Do not narrow the target buffer, simply show the full buffer. Default is to narrow it so that you only see the new material.

:table-line-pos

> Specification of the location in the table where the new line should be inserted. It can be a string, a variable holding a string or a function returning a string. The string should look like "II-3" meaning that the new line should become the third line before the second horizontal separator line.

:kill-buffer

> If the target file was not yet visited when capture was invoked, kill the buffer again after capture is completed.

9.1.3.2 Template expansion

In the template itself, special %-escapes[3] allow dynamic insertion of content. The templates are expanded in the order given here:

%[file]	Insert the contents of the file given by *file*.
%(sexp)	Evaluate Elisp *sexp* and replace with the result. For convenience, %:keyword (see below) placeholders within the expression will be expanded prior to this. The sexp must return a string.
%<...>	The result of format-time-string on the ... format specification.
%t	Timestamp, date only.
%T	Timestamp, with date and time.
%u, %U	Like the above, but inactive timestamps.
%i	Initial content, the region when capture is called while the region is active. The entire text will be indented like %i itself.
%a	Annotation, normally the link created with org-store-link.
%A	Like %a, but prompt for the description part.
%l	Like %a, but only insert the literal link.
%c	Current kill ring head.
%x	Content of the X clipboard.
%k	Title of the currently clocked task.
%K	Link to the currently clocked task.
%n	User name (taken from user-full-name).
%f	File visited by current buffer when org-capture was called.
%F	Full path of the file or directory visited by current buffer.
%:keyword	Specific information for certain link types, see below.
%^g	Prompt for tags, with completion on tags in target file.
%^G	Prompt for tags, with completion all tags in all agenda files.
%^t	Like %t, but prompt for date. Similarly %^T, %^u, %^U. You may define a prompt like %^{Birthday}t.
%^C	Interactive selection of which kill or clip to use.

---

[3] If you need one of these sequences literally, escape the % with a backslash.

`%^L`	Like `%^C`, but insert as link.
`%^{prop}p`	Prompt the user for a value for property *prop*.
`%^{prompt}`	prompt the user for a string and replace this sequence with it. You may specify a default value and a completion table with `%^{prompt|default|completion2|completion3...}`. The arrow keys access a prompt-specific history.
`%\n`	Insert the text entered at the nth `%^{prompt}`, where `n` is a number, starting from 1.
`%?`	After completing the template, position cursor here.

For specific link types, the following keywords will be defined[4]:

```
Link type                         | Available keywords
----------------------------------+---------------------------------------------
bbdb                              | %:name %:company
irc                               | %:server %:port %:nick
vm, vm-imap, wl, mh, mew, rmail   | %:type %:subject %:message-id
                                  | %:from %:fromname %:fromaddress
                                  | %:to   %:toname    %:toaddress
                                  | %:date (message date header field)
                                  | %:date-timestamp (date as active timestamp)
                                  | %:date-timestamp-inactive (date as inactive timestamp)
                                  | %:fromto (either "to NAME" or "from NAME")[5]
gnus                              | %:group, for messages also all email fields
w3, w3m                           | %:url
info                              | %:file %:node
calendar                          | %:date
```

To place the cursor after template expansion use:

`%?`	After completing the template, position cursor here.

9.1.3.3 Templates in contexts

To control whether a capture template should be accessible from a specific context, you can customize `org-capture-templates-contexts`. Let's say for example that you have a capture template `"p"` for storing Gnus emails containing patches. Then you would configure this option like this:

```
(setq org-capture-templates-contexts
      '(("p" (in-mode . "message-mode"))))
```

You can also tell that the command key `"p"` should refer to another template. In that case, add this command key like this:

```
(setq org-capture-templates-contexts
      '(("p" "q" (in-mode . "message-mode"))))
```

See the docstring of the variable for more information.

9.2 Attachments

It is often useful to associate reference material with an outline node/task. Small chunks of plain text can simply be stored in the subtree of a project. Hyperlinks (see Chapter 4 [Hyperlinks], page 37) can establish associations with files that live elsewhere on your computer or in the cloud, like emails or source code files belonging to a project. Another method is

---

[4] If you define your own link types (see Section A.3 [Adding hyperlink types], page 226), any property you store with `org-store-link-props` can be accessed in capture templates in a similar way.

[5] This will always be the other, not the user. See the variable `org-from-is-user-regexp`.

attachments, which are files located in a directory belonging to an outline node. Org uses directories named by the unique ID of each entry. These directories are located in the `data` directory which lives in the same directory where your Org file lives[6]. If you initialize this directory with `git init`, Org will automatically commit changes when it sees them. The attachment system has been contributed to Org by John Wiegley.

In cases where it seems better to do so, you can also attach a directory of your choice to an entry. You can also make children inherit the attachment directory from a parent, so that an entire subtree uses the same attached directory.

The following commands deal with attachments:

`C-c C-a`   `org-attach`

> The dispatcher for commands related to the attachment system. After these keys, a list of commands is displayed and you must press an additional key to select a command:
>
> `a`   `org-attach-attach`
> > Select a file and move it into the task's attachment directory. The file will be copied, moved, or linked, depending on `org-attach-method`. Note that hard links are not supported on all systems.
>
> `c/m/l`   Attach a file using the copy/move/link method. Note that hard links are not supported on all systems.
>
> `n`   `org-attach-new`
> > Create a new attachment as an Emacs buffer.
>
> `z`   `org-attach-sync`
> > Synchronize the current task with its attachment directory, in case you added attachments yourself.
>
> `o`   `org-attach-open`
> > Open current task's attachment. If there is more than one, prompt for a file name first. Opening will follow the rules set by `org-file-apps`. For more details, see the information on following hyperlinks (see Section 4.4 [Handling links], page 40).
>
> `O`   `org-attach-open-in-emacs`
> > Also open the attachment, but force opening the file in Emacs.
>
> `f`   `org-attach-reveal`
> > Open the current task's attachment directory.
>
> `F`   `org-attach-reveal-in-emacs`
> > Also open the directory, but force using `dired` in Emacs.
>
> `d`   `org-attach-delete-one`
> > Select and delete a single attachment.
>
> `D`   `org-attach-delete-all`
> > Delete all of a task's attachments. A safer way is to open the directory in `dired` and delete from there.

---

[6] If you move entries or Org files from one directory to another, you may want to configure `org-attach-directory` to contain an absolute path.

s	`org-attach-set-directory`

Set a specific directory as the entry's attachment directory. This works by putting the directory path into the `ATTACH_DIR` property.

i	`org-attach-set-inherit`

Set the `ATTACH_DIR_INHERIT` property, so that children will use the same directory for attachments as the parent does.

9.3 RSS feeds

Org can add and change entries based on information found in RSS feeds and Atom feeds. You could use this to make a task out of each new podcast in a podcast feed. Or you could use a phone-based note-creating service on the web to import tasks into Org. To access feeds, configure the variable `org-feed-alist`. The docstring of this variable has detailed information. Here is just an example:

```
(setq org-feed-alist
      '(("Slashdot"
         "http://rss.slashdot.org/Slashdot/slashdot"
         "~/txt/org/feeds.org" "Slashdot Entries")))
```

will configure that new items from the feed provided by `rss.slashdot.org` will result in new entries in the file `~/org/feeds.org` under the heading 'Slashdot Entries', whenever the following command is used:

C-c C-x g	`org-feed-update-all`

C-c C-x g Collect items from the feeds configured in `org-feed-alist` and act upon them.

C-c C-x G	`org-feed-goto-inbox`

Prompt for a feed name and go to the inbox configured for this feed.

Under the same headline, Org will create a drawer 'FEEDSTATUS' in which it will store information about the status of items in the feed, to avoid adding the same item several times.

For more information, including how to read atom feeds, see `org-feed.el` and the docstring of `org-feed-alist`.

9.4 Protocols for external access

You can set up Org for handling protocol calls from outside applications that are passed to Emacs through the **emacsserver**. For example, you can configure bookmarks in your web browser to send a link to the current page to Org and create a note from it using capture (see Section 9.1 [Capture], page 87). Or you could create a bookmark that will tell Emacs to open the local source file of a remote website you are looking at with the browser. See `http://orgmode.org/worg/org-contrib/org-protocol.php` for detailed documentation and setup instructions.

9.5 Refile and copy

When reviewing the captured data, you may want to refile or to copy some of the entries into a different list, for example into a project. Cutting, finding the right location, and then pasting the note is cumbersome. To simplify this process, you can use the following special command:

`C-c M-w`   `org-copy`
> Copying works like refiling, except that the original note is not deleted.

`C-c C-w`   `org-refile`
> Refile the entry or region at point. This command offers possible locations for refiling the entry and lets you select one with completion. The item (or all items in the region) is filed below the target heading as a subitem. Depending on **org-reverse-note-order**, it will be either the first or last subitem.
> By default, all level 1 headlines in the current buffer are considered to be targets, but you can have more complex definitions across a number of files. See the variable **org-refile-targets** for details. If you would like to select a location via a file-path-like completion along the outline path, see the variables **org-refile-use-outline-path** and **org-outline-path-complete-in-steps**. If you would like to be able to create new nodes as new parents for refiling on the fly, check the variable **org-refile-allow-creating-parent-nodes**. When the variable **org-log-refile**[7] is set, a timestamp or a note will be recorded when an entry has been refiled.

`C-u C-c C-w`
> Use the refile interface to jump to a heading.

`C-u C-u C-c C-w`   `org-refile-goto-last-stored`
> Jump to the location where **org-refile** last moved a tree to.

`C-2 C-c C-w`
> Refile as the child of the item currently being clocked.

`C-3 C-c C-w`
> Refile and keep the entry in place. Also see **org-refile-keep** to make this the default behavior, and beware that this may result in duplicated `ID` properties.

`C-0 C-c C-w` or `C-u C-u C-u C-c C-w`   `org-refile-cache-clear`
> Clear the target cache. Caching of refile targets can be turned on by setting **org-refile-use-cache**. To make the command see new possible targets, you have to clear the cache with this command.

9.6 Archiving

When a project represented by a (sub)tree is finished, you may want to move the tree out of the way and to stop it from contributing to the agenda. Archiving is important to keep your working files compact and global searches like the construction of agenda views fast.

`C-c C-x C-a`   `org-archive-subtree-default`
> Archive the current entry using the command specified in the variable **org-archive-default-command**.

---

[7] with corresponding `#+STARTUP` keywords `logrefile`, `lognoterefile`, and `nologrefile`

9.6.1 Moving a tree to the archive file

The most common archiving action is to move a project tree to another file, the archive file.

`C-c C-x C-s` or short `C-c $`   org-archive-subtree
>   Archive the subtree starting at the cursor position to the location given by
>   `org-archive-location`.

`C-u C-c C-x C-s`
>   Check if any direct children of the current headline could be moved to the
>   archive. To do this, each subtree is checked for open TODO entries. If none
>   are found, the command offers to move it to the archive location. If the cursor
>   is *not* on a headline when this command is invoked, the level 1 trees will be
>   checked.

The default archive location is a file in the same directory as the current file, with the
name derived by appending `_archive` to the current file name. You can also choose what
heading to file archived items under, with the possibility to add them to a datetree in a
file. For information and examples on how to specify the file and the heading, see the
documentation string of the variable `org-archive-location`.

There is also an in-buffer option for setting this variable, for example[8]:

```
#+ARCHIVE: %s_done::
```

If you would like to have a special ARCHIVE location for a single entry or a (sub)tree, give
the entry an `:ARCHIVE:` property with the location as the value (see Chapter 7 [Properties
and columns], page 62).

When a subtree is moved, it receives a number of special properties that record context
information like the file from where the entry came, its outline path the archiving time
etc. Configure the variable `org-archive-save-context-info` to adjust the amount of
information added.

9.6.2 Internal archiving

If you want to just switch off (for agenda views) certain subtrees without moving them to
a different file, you can use the `ARCHIVE tag`.

A headline that is marked with the ARCHIVE tag (see Chapter 6 [Tags], page 58) stays
at its location in the outline tree, but behaves in the following way:

— It does not open when you attempt to do so with a visibility cycling command (see
  Section 2.3 [Visibility cycling], page 6). You can force cycling archived subtrees with `C-TAB`, or by setting the option `org-cycle-open-archived-trees`. Also normal outline
  commands like `show-all` will open archived subtrees.

— During sparse tree construction (see Section 2.6 [Sparse trees], page 11), matches in
  archived subtrees are not exposed, unless you configure the option `org-sparse-tree-open-archived-trees`.

---

[8]   For backward compatibility, the following also works: If there are several such lines in a file, each specifies
      the archive location for the text below it. The first such line also applies to any text before its definition.
      However, using this method is *strongly* deprecated as it is incompatible with the outline structure of the
      document. The correct method for setting multiple archive locations in a buffer is using properties.

— During agenda view construction (see Chapter 10 [Agenda views], page 98), the content of archived trees is ignored unless you configure the option `org-agenda-skip-archived-trees`, in which case these trees will always be included. In the agenda you can press `v a` to get archives temporarily included.

— Archived trees are not exported (see Chapter 12 [Exporting], page 137), only the headline is. Configure the details using the variable `org-export-with-archived-trees`.

— Archived trees are excluded from column view unless the variable `org-columns-skip-archived-trees` is configured to `nil`.

The following commands help manage the ARCHIVE tag:

`C-c C-x a`   `org-toggle-archive-tag`
> Toggle the ARCHIVE tag for the current headline. When the tag is set, the headline changes to a shadowed face, and the subtree below it is hidden.

`C-u C-c C-x a`
> Check if any direct children of the current headline should be archived. To do this, each subtree is checked for open TODO entries. If none are found, the command offers to set the ARCHIVE tag for the child. If the cursor is *not* on a headline when this command is invoked, the level 1 trees will be checked.

`C-TAB`   `org-force-cycle-archived`
> Cycle a tree even if it is tagged with ARCHIVE.

`C-c C-x A`   `org-archive-to-archive-sibling`
> Move the current entry to the *Archive Sibling*. This is a sibling of the entry with the heading 'Archive' and the tag 'ARCHIVE'. The entry becomes a child of that sibling and in this way retains a lot of its original context, including inherited tags and approximate position in the outline.

10 Agenda views

Due to the way Org works, TODO items, time-stamped items, and tagged headlines can be scattered throughout a file or even a number of files. To get an overview of open action items, or of events that are important for a particular date, this information must be collected, sorted and displayed in an organized way.

Org can select items based on various criteria and display them in a separate buffer. Seven different view types are provided:

- an *agenda* that is like a calendar and shows information for specific dates,
- a *TODO list* that covers all unfinished action items,
- a *match view*, showings headlines based on the tags, properties, and TODO state associated with them,
- a *timeline view* that shows all events in a single Org file, in time-sorted view,
- a *text search view* that shows all entries from multiple files that contain specified keywords,
- a *stuck projects view* showing projects that currently don't move along, and
- *custom views* that are special searches and combinations of different views.

The extracted information is displayed in a special *agenda buffer*. This buffer is read-only, but provides commands to visit the corresponding locations in the original Org files, and even to edit these files remotely.

Two variables control how the agenda buffer is displayed and whether the window configuration is restored when the agenda exits: `org-agenda-window-setup` and `org-agenda-restore-windows-after-quit`.

10.1 Agenda files

The information to be shown is normally collected from all *agenda files*, the files listed in the variable `org-agenda-files`[1]. If a directory is part of this list, all files with the extension `.org` in this directory will be part of the list.

Thus, even if you only work with a single Org file, that file should be put into the list[2]. You can customize `org-agenda-files`, but the easiest way to maintain it is through the following commands

`C-c [`   `org-agenda-file-to-front`
> Add current file to the list of agenda files. The file is added to the front of the list. If it was already in the list, it is moved to the front. With a prefix argument, file is added/moved to the end.

`C-c ]`   `org-remove-file`
> Remove current file from the list of agenda files.

---

[1] If the value of that variable is not a list, but a single file name, then the list of agenda files will be maintained in that external file.

[2] When using the dispatcher, pressing `<` before selecting a command will actually limit the command to the current file, and ignore `org-agenda-files` until the next dispatcher command.

```
C-'                                                            org-cycle-agenda-files
C-,           Cycle through agenda file list, visiting one file after the other.
```

`M-x org-iswitchb RET`
> Command to use an `iswitchb`-like interface to switch to and between Org buffers.

The Org menu contains the current list of files and can be used to visit any of them.

If you would like to focus the agenda temporarily on a file not in this list, or on just one file in the list, or even on only a subtree in a file, then this can be done in different ways. For a single agenda command, you may press < once or several times in the dispatcher (see Section 10.2 [Agenda dispatcher], page 99). To restrict the agenda scope for an extended period, use the following commands:

```
C-c C-x <                                         org-agenda-set-restriction-lock
```
> Permanently restrict the agenda to the current subtree. When with a prefix argument, or with the cursor before the first headline in a file, the agenda scope is set to the entire file. This restriction remains in effect until removed with `C-c C-x >`, or by typing either < or > in the agenda dispatcher. If there is a window displaying an agenda view, the new restriction takes effect immediately.

```
C-c C-x >                                      org-agenda-remove-restriction-lock
```
> Remove the permanent restriction created by `C-c C-x <`.

When working with **speedbar.el**, you can use the following commands in the Speedbar frame:

```
< in the speedbar frame                       org-speedbar-set-agenda-restriction
```
> Permanently restrict the agenda to the item—either an Org file or a subtree in such a file—at the cursor in the Speedbar frame. If there is a window displaying an agenda view, the new restriction takes effect immediately.

```
> in the speedbar frame                       org-agenda-remove-restriction-lock
```
> Lift the restriction.

10.2 The agenda dispatcher

The views are created through a dispatcher, which should be bound to a global key—for example `C-c a` (see Section 1.3 [Activation], page 3). In the following we will assume that `C-c a` is indeed how the dispatcher is accessed and list keyboard access to commands accordingly. After pressing `C-c a`, an additional letter is required to execute a command. The dispatcher offers the following default commands:

a
> Create the calendar-like agenda (see Section 10.3.1 [Weekly/daily agenda], page 100).

`t / T`
> Create a list of all TODO items (see Section 10.3.2 [Global TODO list], page 102).

`m / M`
> Create a list of headlines matching a TAGS expression (see Section 10.3.3 [Matching tags and properties], page 103).

L
> Create the timeline view for the current buffer (see Section 10.3.4 [Timeline], page 106).

s	Create a list of entries selected by a boolean expression of keywords and/or regular expressions that must or must not occur in the entry.
/	Search for a regular expression in all agenda files and additionally in the files listed in `org-agenda-text-search-extra-files`. This uses the Emacs command `multi-occur`. A prefix argument can be used to specify the number of context lines for each match, default is 1.
# / !	Create a list of stuck projects (see Section 10.3.6 [Stuck projects], page 106).
<	Restrict an agenda command to the current buffer[3]. After pressing *<*, you still need to press the character selecting the command.
< <	If there is an active region, restrict the following agenda command to the region. Otherwise, restrict it to the current subtree[4]. After pressing *< <*, you still need to press the character selecting the command.
***	Toggle sticky agenda views. By default, Org maintains only a single agenda buffer and rebuilds it each time you change the view, to make sure everything is always up to date. If you often switch between agenda views and the build time bothers you, you can turn on sticky agenda buffers or make this the default by customizing the variable `org-agenda-sticky`. With sticky agendas, the agenda dispatcher will not recreate agenda views from scratch, it will only switch to the selected one, and you need to update the agenda by hand with *r* or *g* when needed. You can toggle sticky agenda view any time with `org-toggle-sticky-agenda`.

You can also define custom commands that will be accessible through the dispatcher, just like the default commands. This includes the possibility to create extended agenda buffers that contain several blocks together, for example the weekly agenda, the global TODO list and a number of special tags matches. See Section 10.6 [Custom agenda views], page 120.

10.3 The built-in agenda views

In this section we describe the built-in views.

10.3.1 The weekly/daily agenda

The purpose of the weekly/daily *agenda* is to act like a page of a paper agenda, showing all the tasks for the current week or day.

C-c a a   org-agenda-list

Compile an agenda for the current week from a list of Org files. The agenda shows the entries for each day. With a numeric prefix[5] (like *C-u 2 1 C-c a a*) you may set the number of days to be displayed.

The default number of days displayed in the agenda is set by the variable `org-agenda-span` (or the obsolete `org-agenda-ndays`). This variable can be set to any number of

---

[3] For backward compatibility, you can also press *1* to restrict to the current buffer.

[4] For backward compatibility, you can also press *0* to restrict to the current region/subtree.

[5] For backward compatibility, the universal prefix *C-u* causes all TODO entries to be listed before the agenda. This feature is deprecated, use the dedicated TODO list, or a block agenda instead (see Section 10.6.2 [Block agenda], page 122).

days you want to see by default in the agenda, or to a span name, such as `day`, `week`, `month` or `year`. For weekly agendas, the default is to start on the previous monday (see `org-agenda-start-on-weekday`). You can also set the start date using a date shift: `(setq org-agenda-start-day "+10d")` will start the agenda ten days from today in the future.

Remote editing from the agenda buffer means, for example, that you can change the dates of deadlines and appointments from the agenda buffer. The commands available in the Agenda buffer are listed in Section 10.5 [Agenda commands], page 111.

Calendar/Diary integration

Emacs contains the calendar and diary by Edward M. Reingold. The calendar displays a three-month calendar with holidays from different countries and cultures. The diary allows you to keep track of anniversaries, lunar phases, sunrise/set, recurrent appointments (weekly, monthly) and more. In this way, it is quite complementary to Org. It can be very useful to combine output from Org with the diary.

In order to include entries from the Emacs diary into Org mode's agenda, you only need to customize the variable

(setq org-agenda-include-diary t)

After that, everything will happen automatically. All diary entries including holidays, anniversaries, etc., will be included in the agenda buffer created by Org mode. `SPC`, `TAB`, and `RET` can be used from the agenda buffer to jump to the diary file in order to edit existing diary entries. The `i` command to insert new entries for the current date works in the agenda buffer, as well as the commands `S`, `M`, and `C` to display Sunrise/Sunset times, show lunar phases and to convert to other calendars, respectively. `c` can be used to switch back and forth between calendar and agenda.

If you are using the diary only for sexp entries and holidays, it is faster to not use the above setting, but instead to copy or even move the entries into an Org file. Org mode evaluates diary-style sexp entries, and does it faster because there is no overhead for first creating the diary display. Note that the sexp entries must start at the left margin, no whitespace is allowed before them. For example, the following segment of an Org file will be processed and entries will be made in the agenda:

```
* Birthdays and similar stuff
#+CATEGORY: Holiday
%%(org-calendar-holiday)   ; special function for holiday names
#+CATEGORY: Ann
%%(org-anniversary 1956  5 14)⁶ Arthur Dent is %d years old
%%(org-anniversary 1869 10  2) Mahatma Gandhi would be %d years old
```

Anniversaries from BBDB

If you are using the Big Brothers Database to store your contacts, you will very likely prefer to store anniversaries in BBDB rather than in a separate Org or diary file. Org supports this and will show BBDB anniversaries as part of the agenda. All you need to do is to add the following to one of your agenda files:

---

⁶ `org-anniversary` is just like `diary-anniversary`, but the argument order is always according to ISO and therefore independent of the value of `calendar-date-style`.

```
* Anniversaries
  :PROPERTIES:
  :CATEGORY: Anniv
  :END:
%%(org-bbdb-anniversaries)
```

You can then go ahead and define anniversaries for a BBDB record. Basically, you need to press *C-o anniversary RET* with the cursor in a BBDB record and then add the date in the format YYYY-MM-DD or MM-DD, followed by a space and the class of the anniversary ('birthday' or 'wedding', or a format string). If you omit the class, it will default to 'birthday'. Here are a few examples, the header for the file **org-bbdb.el** contains more detailed information.

```
1973-06-22
06-22
1955-08-02 wedding
2008-04-14 %s released version 6.01 of org mode, %d years ago
```

After a change to BBDB, or for the first agenda display during an Emacs session, the agenda display will suffer a short delay as Org updates its hash with anniversaries. However, from then on things will be very fast—much faster in fact than a long list of '%%(diary-anniversary)' entries in an Org or Diary file.

Appointment reminders

Org can interact with Emacs appointments notification facility. To add the appointments of your agenda files, use the command **org-agenda-to-appt**. This command lets you filter through the list of your appointments and add only those belonging to a specific category or matching a regular expression. It also reads a **APPT_WARNTIME** property which will then override the value of **appt-message-warning-time** for this appointment. See the docstring for details.

10.3.2 The global TODO list

The global TODO list contains all unfinished TODO items formatted and collected into a single place.

C-c a t   org-todo-list
> Show the global TODO list. This collects the TODO items from all agenda files (see Chapter 10 [Agenda views], page 98) into a single buffer. By default, this lists items with a state the is not a DONE state. The buffer is in **agenda-mode**, so there are commands to examine and manipulate the TODO entries directly from that buffer (see Section 10.5 [Agenda commands], page 111).

C-c a T   org-todo-list
> Like the above, but allows selection of a specific TODO keyword. You can also do this by specifying a prefix argument to *C-c a t*. You are prompted for a keyword, and you may also specify several keywords by separating them with '|' as the boolean OR operator. With a numeric prefix, the Nth keyword in **org-todo-keywords** is selected. The *r* key in the agenda buffer regenerates it, and you can give a prefix argument to this command to change the selected TODO keyword, for example *3 r*. If you often need a search for a specific

keyword, define a custom command for it (see Section 10.2 [Agenda dispatcher], page 99).

Matching specific TODO keywords can also be done as part of a tags search (see Section 6.4 [Tag searches], page 61).

Remote editing of TODO items means that you can change the state of a TODO entry with a single key press. The commands available in the TODO list are described in Section 10.5 [Agenda commands], page 111.

Normally the global TODO list simply shows all headlines with TODO keywords. This list can become very long. There are two ways to keep it more compact:

— Some people view a TODO item that has been *scheduled* for execution or have a *deadline* (see Section 8.1 [Timestamps], page 71) as no longer *open*. Configure the variables `org-agenda-todo-ignore-scheduled`, `org-agenda-todo-ignore-deadlines`, `org-agenda-todo-ignore-timestamp` and/or `org-agenda-todo-ignore-with-date` to exclude such items from the global TODO list.

— TODO items may have sublevels to break up the task into subtasks. In such cases it may be enough to list only the highest level TODO headline and omit the sublevels from the global list. Configure the variable `org-agenda-todo-list-sublevels` to get this behavior.

10.3.3 Matching tags and properties

If headlines in the agenda files are marked with *tags* (see Chapter 6 [Tags], page 58), or have properties (see Chapter 7 [Properties and columns], page 62), you can select headlines based on this metadata and collect them into an agenda buffer. The match syntax described here also applies when creating sparse trees with `C-c / m`.

`C-c a m`   org-tags-view
    Produce a list of all headlines that match a given set of tags. The command prompts for a selection criterion, which is a boolean logic expression with tags, like '+work+urgent-withboss' or 'work|home' (see Chapter 6 [Tags], page 58). If you often need a specific search, define a custom command for it (see Section 10.2 [Agenda dispatcher], page 99).

`C-c a M`   org-tags-view
    Like `C-c a m`, but only select headlines that are also TODO items in a not-DONE state and force checking subitems (see variable `org-tags-match-list-sublevels`). To exclude scheduled/deadline items, see the variable `org-agenda-tags-todo-honor-ignore-options`. Matching specific TODO keywords together with a tags match is also possible, see Section 6.4 [Tag searches], page 61.

The commands available in the tags list are described in Section 10.5 [Agenda commands], page 111.

Match syntax

A search string can use Boolean operators '&' for AND and '|' for OR. '&' binds more strongly than '|'. Parentheses are not implemented. Each element in the search is either a tag, a regular expression matching tags, or an expression like `PROPERTY OPERATOR VALUE` with a comparison operator, accessing a property value. Each element may be preceded by '-', to select against it, and '+' is syntactic sugar for positive selection. The `AND` operator '&' is optional when '+' or '-' is present. Here are some examples, using only tags.

'`work`'   Select headlines tagged '`:work:`'.

'`work&boss`'

       Select headlines tagged '`:work:`' and '`:boss:`'.

'`+work-boss`'

       Select headlines tagged '`:work:`', but discard those also tagged '`:boss:`'.

'`work|laptop`'

       Selects lines tagged '`:work:`' or '`:laptop:`'.

'`work|laptop+night`'

       Like before, but require the '`:laptop:`' lines to be tagged also '`:night:`'.

Instead of a tag, you may also specify a regular expression enclosed in curly braces. For example, '`work+{^boss.*}`' matches headlines that contain the tag '`:work:`' and any tag *starting* with '`boss`'.

Group tags (see Section 6.3 [Tag groups], page 61) are expanded as regular expressions. E.g., if '`:work:`' is a group tag for the group '`:work:lab:conf:`', then searching for '`work`' will search for '`{\(?:work\|lab\|conf\)}`' and searching for '`-work`' will search for all headlines but those with one of the tags in the group (i.e., '`-{\(?:work\|lab\|conf\)}`').

You may also test for properties (see Chapter 7 [Properties and columns], page 62) at the same time as matching tags. The properties may be real properties, or special properties that represent other metadata (see Section 7.2 [Special properties], page 64). For example, the "property" `TODO` represents the TODO keyword of the entry and the "property" `PRIORITY` represents the PRIORITY keyword of the entry. The ITEM special property cannot currently be used in tags/property searches[7].

In addition to the see Section 7.2 [Special properties], page 64, one other "property" can also be used. `LEVEL` represents the level of an entry. So a search '`+LEVEL=3+boss-TODO="DONE"`' lists all level three headlines that have the tag '`boss`' and are *not* marked with the TODO keyword DONE. In buffers with `org-odd-levels-only` set, '`LEVEL`' does not count the number of stars, but '`LEVEL=2`' will correspond to 3 stars etc.

Here are more examples:

'`work+TODO="WAITING"`'

       Select '`:work:`'-tagged TODO lines with the specific TODO keyword '`WAITING`'.

'`work+TODO="WAITING"|home+TODO="WAITING"`'

       Waiting tasks both at work and at home.

When matching properties, a number of different operators can be used to test the value of a property. Here is a complex example:

---

[7] But see [skipping entries based on regexp], page 235.

```
+work-boss+PRIORITY="A"+Coffee="unlimited"+Effort<2            \
      +With={Sarah\|Denny}+SCHEDULED>="<2008-10-11>"
```

The type of comparison will depend on how the comparison value is written:

— If the comparison value is a plain number, a numerical comparison is done, and the allowed operators are '<', '=', '>', '<=', '>=', and '<>'.

— If the comparison value is enclosed in double-quotes, a string comparison is done, and the same operators are allowed.

— If the comparison value is enclosed in double-quotes *and* angular brackets (like 'DEADLINE<="<2008-12-24 18:30>"'), both values are assumed to be date/time specifications in the standard Org way, and the comparison will be done accordingly. Special values that will be recognized are "<now>" for now (including time), and "<today>", and "<tomorrow>" for these days at 0:00 hours, i.e., without a time specification. Also strings like "<+5d>" or "<-2m>" with units d, w, m, and y for day, week, month, and year, respectively, can be used.

— If the comparison value is enclosed in curly braces, a regexp match is performed, with '=' meaning that the regexp matches the property value, and '<>' meaning that it does not match.

So the search string in the example finds entries tagged ':work:' but not ':boss:', which also have a priority value 'A', a ':Coffee:' property with the value 'unlimited', an 'Effort' property that is numerically smaller than 2, a ':With:' property that is matched by the regular expression 'Sarah\|Denny', and that are scheduled on or after October 11, 2008.

Accessing TODO, LEVEL, and CATEGORY during a search is fast. Accessing any other properties will slow down the search. However, once you have paid the price by accessing one property, testing additional properties is cheap again.

You can configure Org mode to use property inheritance during a search, but beware that this can slow down searches considerably. See Section 7.4 [Property inheritance], page 65, for details.

For backward compatibility, and also for typing speed, there is also a different way to test TODO states in a search. For this, terminate the tags/property part of the search string (which may include several terms connected with '|') with a '/' and then specify a Boolean expression just for TODO keywords. The syntax is then similar to that for tags, but should be applied with care: for example, a positive selection on several TODO keywords cannot meaningfully be combined with boolean AND. However, *negative selection* combined with AND can be meaningful. To make sure that only lines are checked that actually have any TODO keyword (resulting in a speed-up), use *C-c a M*, or equivalently start the TODO part after the slash with '!'. Using *C-c a M* or '/!' will not match TODO keywords in a DONE state. Examples:

'work/WAITING'
> Same as 'work+TODO="WAITING"'

'work/!-WAITING-NEXT'
> Select ':work:'-tagged TODO lines that are neither 'WAITING' nor 'NEXT'

'work/!+WAITING|+NEXT'
> Select ':work:'-tagged TODO lines that are either 'WAITING' or 'NEXT'.

10.3.4 Timeline for a single file

The timeline summarizes all time-stamped items from a single Org mode file in a *time-sorted view*. The main purpose of this command is to give an overview over events in a project.

`C-c a L`   `org-timeline`
> Show a time-sorted view of the Org file, with all time-stamped items. When called with a `C-u` prefix, all unfinished TODO entries (scheduled or not) are also listed under the current date.

The commands available in the timeline buffer are listed in Section 10.5 [Agenda commands], page 111.

10.3.5 Search view

This agenda view is a general text search facility for Org mode entries. It is particularly useful to find notes.

`C-c a s`   `org-search-view`
> This is a special search that lets you select entries by matching a substring or specific words using a boolean logic.

For example, the search string '`computer equipment`' will find entries that contain '`computer equipment`' as a substring. If the two words are separated by more space or a line break, the search will still match. Search view can also search for specific keywords in the entry, using Boolean logic. The search string '`+computer +wifi -ethernet -{8\.11[bg]}`' will search for note entries that contain the keywords `computer` and `wifi`, but not the keyword `ethernet`, and which are also not matched by the regular expression `8\.11[bg]`, meaning to exclude both 8.11b and 8.11g. The first '`+`' is necessary to turn on word search, other '`+`' characters are optional. For more details, see the docstring of the command `org-search-view`.

Note that in addition to the agenda files, this command will also search the files listed in `org-agenda-text-search-extra-files`.

10.3.6 Stuck projects

If you are following a system like David Allen's GTD to organize your work, one of the "duties" you have is a regular review to make sure that all projects move along. A *stuck* project is a project that has no defined next actions, so it will never show up in the TODO lists Org mode produces. During the review, you need to identify such projects and define next actions for them.

`C-c a #`   `org-agenda-list-stuck-projects`
> List projects that are stuck.

`C-c a !`   Customize the variable `org-stuck-projects` to define what a stuck project is and how to find it.

You almost certainly will have to configure this view before it will work for you. The built-in default assumes that all your projects are level-2 headlines, and that a project is not stuck if it has at least one entry marked with a TODO keyword TODO or NEXT or NEXTACTION.

Let's assume that you, in your own way of using Org mode, identify projects with a tag PROJECT, and that you use a TODO keyword MAYBE to indicate a project that should not be considered yet. Let's further assume that the TODO keyword DONE marks finished projects, and that NEXT and TODO indicate next actions. The tag @SHOP indicates shopping and is a next action even without the NEXT tag. Finally, if the project contains the special word IGNORE anywhere, it should not be listed either. In this case you would start by identifying eligible projects with a tags/todo match[8] '+PROJECT/-MAYBE-DONE', and then check for TODO, NEXT, @SHOP, and IGNORE in the subtree to identify projects that are not stuck. The correct customization for this is

```
(setq org-stuck-projects
      '("+PROJECT/-MAYBE-DONE" ("NEXT" "TODO") ("@SHOP")
        "\\<IGNORE\\>"))
```

Note that if a project is identified as non-stuck, the subtree of this entry will still be searched for stuck projects.

10.4 Presentation and sorting

Before displaying items in an agenda view, Org mode visually prepares the items and sorts them. Each item occupies a single line. The line starts with a *prefix* that contains the *category* (see Section 10.4.1 [Categories], page 107) of the item and other important information. You can customize in which column tags will be displayed through `org-agenda-tags-column`. You can also customize the prefix using the option `org-agenda-prefix-format`. This prefix is followed by a cleaned-up version of the outline headline associated with the item.

10.4.1 Categories

The category is a broad label assigned to each agenda item. By default, the category is simply derived from the file name, but you can also specify it with a special line in the buffer, like this[9]:

```
#+CATEGORY: Thesis
```

If you would like to have a special CATEGORY for a single entry or a (sub)tree, give the entry a `:CATEGORY:` property with the special category you want to apply as the value.

The display in the agenda buffer looks best if the category is not longer than 10 characters.

You can set up icons for category by customizing the `org-agenda-category-icon-alist` variable.

10.4.2 Time-of-day specifications

Org mode checks each agenda item for a time-of-day specification. The time can be part of the timestamp that triggered inclusion into the agenda, for example as in '<2005-05-10 Tue 19:00>'. Time ranges can be specified with two timestamps, like '<2005-05-10 Tue 20:30>--<2005-05-10 Tue 22:15>'.

---

[8] See Section 6.4 [Tag searches], page 61.

[9] For backward compatibility, the following also works: if there are several such lines in a file, each specifies the category for the text below it. The first category also applies to any text before the first CATEGORY line. However, using this method is *strongly* deprecated as it is incompatible with the outline structure of the document. The correct method for setting multiple categories in a buffer is using a property.

In the headline of the entry itself, a time(range) may also appear as plain text (like '`12:45`' or a '`8:30-1pm`'). If the agenda integrates the Emacs diary (see Section 10.3.1 [Weekly/daily agenda], page 100), time specifications in diary entries are recognized as well.

For agenda display, Org mode extracts the time and displays it in a standard 24 hour format as part of the prefix. The example times in the previous paragraphs would end up in the agenda like this:

```
 8:30-13:00 Arthur Dent lies in front of the bulldozer
12:45...... Ford Prefect arrives and takes Arthur to the pub
19:00...... The Vogon reads his poem
20:30-22:15 Marvin escorts the Hitchhikers to the bridge
```

If the agenda is in single-day mode, or for the display of today, the timed entries are embedded in a time grid, like

```
 8:00...... ------------------
 8:30-13:00 Arthur Dent lies in front of the bulldozer
10:00...... ------------------
12:00...... ------------------
12:45...... Ford Prefect arrives and takes Arthur to the pub
14:00...... ------------------
16:00...... ------------------
18:00...... ------------------
19:00...... The Vogon reads his poem
20:00...... ------------------
20:30-22:15 Marvin escorts the Hitchhikers to the bridge
```

The time grid can be turned on and off with the variable `org-agenda-use-time-grid`, and can be configured with `org-agenda-time-grid`.

10.4.3 Sorting agenda items

Before being inserted into a view, the items are sorted. How this is done depends on the type of view.

- For the daily/weekly agenda, the items for each day are sorted. The default order is to first collect all items containing an explicit time-of-day specification. These entries will be shown at the beginning of the list, as a *schedule* for the day. After that, items remain grouped in categories, in the sequence given by `org-agenda-files`. Within each category, items are sorted by priority (see Section 5.4 [Priorities], page 54), which is composed of the base priority (2000 for priority '`A`', 1000 for '`B`', and 0 for '`C`'), plus additional increments for overdue scheduled or deadline items.

- For the TODO list, items remain in the order of categories, but within each category, sorting takes place according to priority (see Section 5.4 [Priorities], page 54). The priority used for sorting derives from the priority cookie, with additions depending on how close an item is to its due or scheduled date.

- For tags matches, items are not sorted at all, but just appear in the sequence in which they are found in the agenda files.

Sorting can be customized using the variable org-agenda-sorting-strategy, and may also include criteria based on the estimated effort of an entry (see Section 8.5 [Effort estimates], page 84).

10.4.4 Filtering/limiting agenda items

Agenda built-in or customized commands are statically defined. Agenda filters and limits provide two ways of dynamically narrowing down the list of agenda entries: *filters* and *limits*. Filters only act on the display of the items, while limits take effect before the list of agenda entries is built. Filters are more often used interactively, while limits are mostly useful when defined as local variables within custom agenda commands.

Filtering in the agenda

/   org-agenda-filter-by-tag

Filter the agenda view with respect to a tag and/or effort estimates. The difference between this and a custom agenda command is that filtering is very fast, so that you can switch quickly between different filters without having to recreate the agenda.[10]

You will be prompted for a tag selection letter; SPC will mean any tag at all. Pressing TAB at that prompt will offer use completion to select a tag (including any tags that do not have a selection character). The command then hides all entries that do not contain or inherit this tag. When called with prefix arg, remove the entries that *do* have the tag. A second / at the prompt will turn off the filter and unhide any hidden entries. If the first key you press is either + or -, the previous filter will be narrowed by requiring or forbidding the selected additional tag. Instead of pressing + or - after /, you can also immediately use the \ command.

Org also supports automatic, context-aware tag filtering. If the variable org-agenda-auto-exclude-function is set to a user-defined function, that function can decide which tags should be excluded from the agenda automatically. Once this is set, the / command then accepts RET as a sub-option key and runs the auto exclusion logic. For example, let's say you use a Net tag to identify tasks which need network access, an Errand tag for errands in town, and a Call tag for making phone calls. You could auto-exclude these tags based on the availability of the Internet, and outside of business hours, with something like this:

---

[10] Custom commands can preset a filter by binding the variable org-agenda-tag-filter-preset as an option. This filter will then be applied to the view and persist as a basic filter through refreshes and more secondary filtering. The filter is a global property of the entire agenda view—in a block agenda, you should only set this in the global options section, not in the section of an individual block.

```
(defun org-my-auto-exclude-function (tag)
  (and (cond
         ((string= tag "Net")
          (/= 0 (call-process "/sbin/ping" nil nil nil
                              "-c1" "-q" "-t1" "mail.gnu.org")))
         ((or (string= tag "Errand") (string= tag "Call"))
          (let ((hour (nth 2 (decode-time))))
            (or (< hour 8) (> hour 21)))))
       (concat "-" tag)))

(setq org-agenda-auto-exclude-function 'org-my-auto-exclude-function)
```

\   `org-agenda-filter-by-tag-refine`

Narrow the current agenda filter by an additional condition. When called with prefix arg, remove the entries that *do* have the tag, or that do match the effort criterion. You can achieve the same effect by pressing + or - as the first key after the / command.

[ ] { }

in *search view*

add new search words ([and]) or new regular expressions ({ and }) to the query string. The opening bracket/brace will add a positive search term prefixed by '+', indicating that this search term *must* occur/match in the entry. The closing bracket/brace will add a negative search term which *must not* occur/match in the entry for it to be selected.

<   `org-agenda-filter-by-category`

Filter the current agenda view with respect to the category of the item at point. Pressing < another time will remove this filter. You can add a filter preset through the option **org-agenda-category-filter-preset** (see below.)

^   `org-agenda-filter-by-top-headline`

Filter the current agenda view and only display the siblings and the parent headline of the one at point.

=   `org-agenda-filter-by-regexp`

Filter the agenda view by a regular expression: only show agenda entries matching the regular expression the user entered. When called with a prefix argument, it will filter *out* entries matching the regexp. With two universal prefix arguments, it will remove all the regexp filters, which can be accumulated. You can add a filter preset through the option **org-agenda-category-filter-preset** (see below.)

_   `org-agenda-filter-by-effort`

Filter the agenda view with respect to effort estimates. You first need to set up allowed efforts globally, for example

(setq org-global-properties
      '(("Effort_ALL". "0 0:10 0:30 1:00 2:00 3:00 4:00")))

You can then filter for an effort by first typing an operator, one of <, >, and =, and then the one-digit index of an effort estimate in your array of allowed values, where *0* means the 10th value. The filter will then restrict to entries with effort smaller-or-equal, equal, or larger-or-equal than the selected value. For application of the operator, entries without a defined effort will be treated according to the value of `org-sort-agenda-noeffort-is-high`.

| `org-agenda-filter-remove-all`

Remove all filters in the current agenda view.

Setting limits for the agenda

Here is a list of options that you can set, either globally, or locally in your custom agenda viewssee Section 10.6 [Custom agenda views], page 120.

org-agenda-max-entries
> Limit the number of entries.

org-agenda-max-effort
> Limit the duration of accumulated efforts (as minutes).

org-agenda-max-todos
> Limit the number of entries with TODO keywords.

org-agenda-max-tags
> Limit the number of tagged entries.

When set to a positive integer, each option will exclude entries from other categories: for example, (setq `org-agenda-max-effort` 100) will limit the agenda to 100 minutes of effort and exclude any entry that has no effort property. If you want to include entries with no effort property, use a negative value for `org-agenda-max-effort`.

One useful setup is to use `org-agenda-max-entries` locally in a custom command. For example, this custom command will display the next five entries with a **NEXT** TODO keyword.

```
(setq org-agenda-custom-commands
      '(("n" todo "NEXT"
         ((org-agenda-max-entries 5)))))
```

Once you mark one of these five entry as **DONE**, rebuilding the agenda will again the next five entries again, including the first entry that was excluded so far.

You can also dynamically set temporary limits, which will be lost when rebuilding the agenda:

~   `org-agenda-limit-interactively`

This prompts for the type of limit to apply and its value.

10.5 Commands in the agenda buffer

Entries in the agenda buffer are linked back to the Org file or diary file where they originate. You are not allowed to edit the agenda buffer itself, but commands are provided to show and jump to the original entry location, and to edit the Org files "remotely" from the agenda buffer. In this way, all information is stored only once, removing the risk that your agenda and note files may diverge.

Some commands can be executed with mouse clicks on agenda lines. For the other commands, the cursor needs to be in the desired line.

Motion

n   `org-agenda-next-line`
> Next line (same as **down** and *C-n*).

p   `org-agenda-previous-line`
> Previous line (same as **up** and *C-p*).

N   `org-agenda-next-item`
> Next item: same as next line, but only consider items.

P   `org-agenda-previous-item`
> Previous item: same as previous line, but only consider items.

View/Go to Org file

SPC or *mouse-3*   `org-agenda-show-and-scroll-up`
> Display the original location of the item in another window. With prefix arg, make sure that the entire entry is made visible in the outline, not only the heading.

L   `org-agenda-recenter`
> Display original location and recenter that window.

TAB or *mouse-2*   `org-agenda-goto`
> Go to the original location of the item in another window.

RET   `org-agenda-switch-to`
> Go to the original location of the item and delete other windows.

F   `org-agenda-follow-mode`
> Toggle Follow mode. In Follow mode, as you move the cursor through the agenda buffer, the other window always shows the corresponding location in the Org file. The initial setting for this mode in new agenda buffers can be set with the variable `org-agenda-start-with-follow-mode`.

C-c C-x b   `org-agenda-tree-to-indirect-buffer`
> Display the entire subtree of the current item in an indirect buffer. With a numeric prefix argument N, go up to level N and then take that tree. If N is negative, go up that many levels. With a *C-u* prefix, do not remove the previously used indirect buffer.

C-c C-o   `org-agenda-open-link`
> Follow a link in the entry. This will offer a selection of any links in the text belonging to the referenced Org node. If there is only one link, it will be followed without a selection prompt.

Change display

A   Interactively select another agenda view and append it to the current view.

o   Delete other windows.

`v d` or short `d`	`org-agenda-day-view`
`v w` or short `w`	`org-agenda-week-view`
`v t`	`org-agenda-fortnight-view`
`v m`	`org-agenda-month-view`
`v y`	`org-agenda-year-view`
`v SPC`	`org-agenda-reset-view`

Switch to day/week/month/year view. When switching to day or week view, this setting becomes the default for subsequent agenda refreshes. Since month and year views are slow to create, they do not become the default. A numeric prefix argument may be used to jump directly to a specific day of the year, ISO week, month, or year, respectively. For example, *32 d* jumps to February 1st, *9 w* to ISO week number 9. When setting day, week, or month view, a year may be encoded in the prefix argument as well. For example, *200712 w* will jump to week 12 in 2007. If such a year specification has only one or two digits, it will be mapped to the interval 1938–2037. *v SPC* will reset to what is set in `org-agenda-span`.

f   `org-agenda-later`
Go forward in time to display the following `org-agenda-current-span` days. For example, if the display covers a week, switch to the following week. With prefix arg, go forward that many times `org-agenda-current-span` days.

b   `org-agenda-earlier`
Go backward in time to display earlier dates.

.   `org-agenda-goto-today`
Go to today.

j   `org-agenda-goto-date`
Prompt for a date and go there.

J   `org-agenda-clock-goto`
Go to the currently clocked-in task *in the agenda buffer.*

D   `org-agenda-toggle-diary`
Toggle the inclusion of diary entries. See Section 10.3.1 [Weekly/daily agenda], page 100.

v l or short *l*   `org-agenda-log-mode`
Toggle Logbook mode. In Logbook mode, entries that were marked DONE while logging was on (variable `org-log-done`) are shown in the agenda, as are entries that have been clocked on that day. You can configure the entry types that should be included in log mode using the variable `org-agenda-log-mode-items`. When called with a *C-u* prefix, show all possible logbook entries, including state changes. When called with two prefix arguments *C-u C-u*, show only logging information, nothing else. *v L* is equivalent to *C-u v l*.

v [or short *[*   `org-agenda-manipulate-query-add`
Include inactive timestamps into the current view. Only for weekly/daily agenda and timeline views.

`v a`   `org-agenda-archives-mode`
`v A`   `org-agenda-archives-mode 'files`
> Toggle Archives mode. In Archives mode, trees that are marked ARCHIVED are also scanned when producing the agenda. When you use the capital *A*, even all archive files are included. To exit archives mode, press *v a* again.

`v R`   or short   `R`   `org-agenda-clockreport-mode`
> Toggle Clockreport mode. In Clockreport mode, the daily/weekly agenda will always show a table with the clocked times for the time span and file scope covered by the current agenda view. The initial setting for this mode in new agenda buffers can be set with the variable `org-agenda-start-with-clockreport-mode`. By using a prefix argument when toggling this mode (i.e., *C-u R*), the clock table will not show contributions from entries that are hidden by agenda filtering[11]. See also the variable `org-clock-report-include-clocking-task`.

`v c`   Show overlapping clock entries, clocking gaps, and other clocking problems in the current agenda range. You can then visit clocking lines and fix them manually. See the variable `org-agenda-clock-consistency-checks` for information on how to customize the definition of what constituted a clocking problem. To return to normal agenda display, press *l* to exit Logbook mode.

`v E`   or short   `E`   `org-agenda-entry-text-mode`
> Toggle entry text mode. In entry text mode, a number of lines from the Org outline node referenced by an agenda line will be displayed below the line. The maximum number of lines is given by the variable `org-agenda-entry-text-maxlines`. Calling this command with a numeric prefix argument will temporarily modify that number to the prefix value.

`G`   `org-agenda-toggle-time-grid`
> Toggle the time grid on and off. See also the variables `org-agenda-use-time-grid` and `org-agenda-time-grid`.

`r`   `org-agenda-redo`
> Recreate the agenda buffer, for example to reflect the changes after modification of the timestamps of items with *S-left* and *S-right*. When the buffer is the global TODO list, a prefix argument is interpreted to create a selective list for a specific TODO keyword.

`g`   `org-agenda-redo`
> Same as *r*.

`C-x C-s`   or short   `s`   `org-save-all-org-buffers`
> Save all Org buffers in the current Emacs session, and also the locations of IDs.

`C-c C-x C-c`   `org-agenda-columns`
> Invoke column view (see Section 7.5 [Column view], page 66) in the agenda buffer. The column view format is taken from the entry at point, or (if there is no entry at point), from the first entry in the agenda view. So whatever the

---

[11] Only tags filtering will be respected here, effort filtering is ignored.

format for that entry would be in the original buffer (taken from a property, from a `#+COLUMNS` line, or from the default variable `org-columns-default-format`), will be used in the agenda.

`C-c C-x >`   org-agenda-remove-restriction-lock
Remove the restriction lock on the agenda, if it is currently restricted to a file or subtree (see Section 10.1 [Agenda files], page 98).

Secondary filtering and query editing

For a detailed description of these commands, see see Section 10.4.4 [Filtering/limiting agenda items], page 109.

`/`   org-agenda-filter-by-tag
Filter the agenda view with respect to a tag and/or effort estimates.

`\`   org-agenda-filter-by-tag-refine
Narrow the current agenda filter by an additional condition.

`<`   org-agenda-filter-by-category
Filter the current agenda view with respect to the category of the item at point. Pressing `<` another time will remove this filter.

`^`   org-agenda-filter-by-top-headline
Filter the current agenda view and only display the siblings and the parent headline of the one at point.

`=`   org-agenda-filter-by-regexp
Filter the agenda view by a regular expression: only show agenda entries matching the regular expression the user entered. When called with a prefix argument, it will filter *out* entries matching the regexp. With two universal prefix arguments, it will remove all the regexp filters, which can be accumulated. You can add a filter preset through the option `org-agenda-category-filter-preset` (see below.)

`|`   org-agenda-filter-remove-all
Remove all filters in the current agenda view.

Remote editing

`0--9`   Digit argument.

`C-_`   org-agenda-undo
Undo a change due to a remote editing command. The change is undone both in the agenda buffer and in the remote buffer.

`t`   org-agenda-todo
Change the TODO state of the item, both in the agenda and in the original org file.

`C-S-right`   org-agenda-todo-nextset
`C-S-left`   org-agenda-todo-previousset
Switch to the next/previous set of TODO keywords.

`C-k`   org-agenda-kill
Delete the current agenda item along with the entire subtree belonging to it in the original Org file. If the text to be deleted remotely is longer than one line,

the kill needs to be confirmed by the user. See variable `org-agenda-confirm-kill`.

`C-c C-w`   `org-agenda-refile`
Refile the entry at point.

`C-c C-x C-a` or short `a`   `org-agenda-archive-default-with-confirmation`
Archive the subtree corresponding to the entry at point using the default archiving command set in `org-archive-default-command`. When using the a key, confirmation will be required.

`C-c C-x a`   `org-agenda-toggle-archive-tag`
Toggle the ARCHIVE tag for the current headline.

`C-c C-x A`   `org-agenda-archive-to-archive-sibling`
Move the subtree corresponding to the current entry to its *archive sibling*.

`C-c C-x C-s` or short `$`   `org-agenda-archive`
Archive the subtree corresponding to the current headline. This means the entry will be moved to the configured archive location, most likely a different file.

`T`   `org-agenda-show-tags`
Show all tags associated with the current item. This is useful if you have turned off `org-agenda-show-inherited-tags`, but still want to see all tags of a headline occasionally.

`:`   `org-agenda-set-tags`
Set tags for the current headline. If there is an active region in the agenda, change a tag for all headings in the region.

`,`
Set the priority for the current item (`org-agenda-priority`). Org mode prompts for the priority character. If you reply with SPC, the priority cookie is removed from the entry.

`P`   `org-agenda-show-priority`
Display weighted priority of current item.

`+` or `S-up`   `org-agenda-priority-up`
Increase the priority of the current item. The priority is changed in the original buffer, but the agenda is not resorted. Use the `r` key for this.

`-` or `S-down`   `org-agenda-priority-down`
Decrease the priority of the current item.

`z` or `C-c C-z`   `org-agenda-add-note`
Add a note to the entry. This note will be recorded, and then filed to the same location where state change notes are put. Depending on `org-log-into-drawer`, this may be inside a drawer.

`C-c C-a`   `org-attach`
Dispatcher for all command related to attachments.

`C-c C-s`   `org-agenda-schedule`
Schedule this item. With prefix arg remove the scheduling timestamp

`C-c C-d`   `org-agenda-deadline`

    Set a deadline for this item. With prefix arg remove the deadline.

`S-right`   `org-agenda-do-date-later`

    Change the timestamp associated with the current line by one day into the future. If the date is in the past, the first call to this command will move it to today.

    With a numeric prefix argument, change it by that many days. For example, `3 6 5 S-right` will change it by a year. With a `C-u` prefix, change the time by one hour. If you immediately repeat the command, it will continue to change hours even without the prefix arg. With a double `C-u C-u` prefix, do the same for changing minutes.

    The stamp is changed in the original Org file, but the change is not directly reflected in the agenda buffer. Use `r` or `g` to update the buffer.

`S-left`   `org-agenda-do-date-earlier`

    Change the timestamp associated with the current line by one day into the past.

`>`   `org-agenda-date-prompt`

    Change the timestamp associated with the current line. The key > has been chosen, because it is the same as `S-.` on my keyboard.

`I`   `org-agenda-clock-in`

    Start the clock on the current item. If a clock is running already, it is stopped first.

`O`   `org-agenda-clock-out`

    Stop the previously started clock.

`X`   `org-agenda-clock-cancel`

    Cancel the currently running clock.

`J`   `org-agenda-clock-goto`

    Jump to the running clock in another window.

`k`   `org-agenda-capture`

    Like `org-capture`, but use the date at point as the default date for the capture template. See `org-capture-use-agenda-date` to make this the default behavior of `org-capture`.

Dragging agenda lines forward/backward

`M-<up>`   `org-agenda-drag-line-backward`

    Drag the line at point backward one line[12]. With a numeric prefix argument, drag backward by that many lines.

`M-<down>`   `org-agenda-drag-line-forward`

    Drag the line at point forward one line. With a numeric prefix argument, drag forward by that many lines.

---

[12] Moving agenda lines does not persist after an agenda refresh and does not modify the contributing `.org` files

Bulk remote editing selected entries

m   `org-agenda-bulk-mark`

     Mark the entry at point for bulk action. With numeric prefix argument, mark that many successive entries.

*   `org-agenda-bulk-mark-all`

     Mark all visible agenda entries for bulk action.

u   `org-agenda-bulk-unmark`

     Unmark entry at point for bulk action.

U   `org-agenda-bulk-remove-all-marks`

     Unmark all marked entries for bulk action.

M-m   `org-agenda-bulk-toggle`

     Toggle mark of the entry at point for bulk action.

M-*   `org-agenda-bulk-toggle-all`

     Toggle marks of all visible entries for bulk action.

%   `org-agenda-bulk-mark-regexp`

     Mark entries matching a regular expression for bulk action.

B   `org-agenda-bulk-action`

     Bulk action: act on all marked entries in the agenda. This will prompt for another key to select the action to be applied. The prefix arg to *B* will be passed through to the *s* and *d* commands, to bulk-remove these special timestamps. By default, marks are removed after the bulk. If you want them to persist, set `org-agenda-bulk-persistent-marks` to *t* or hit *p* at the prompt.

        *   Toggle persistent marks.

        \$ Archive all selected entries.

        A   Archive entries by moving them to their respective archive siblings.

        t   Change TODO state. This prompts for a single TODO keyword and changes the state of all selected entries, bypassing blocking and suppressing logging notes (but not timestamps).

        +   Add a tag to all selected entries.

        -       Remove a tag from all selected entries.

        s   Schedule all items to a new date. To shift existing schedule dates by a fixed number of days, use something starting with double plus at the prompt, for example '++8d' or '++2w'.

        d   Set deadline to a specific date.

        r   Prompt for a single refile target and move all entries. The entries will no longer be in the agenda; refresh (*g*) to bring them back.

        S   Reschedule randomly into the coming N days. N will be prompted for. With prefix arg (*C-u B S*), scatter only across weekdays.

f   Apply a function[13] to marked entries. For example, the function
               below sets the CATEGORY property of the entries to web.

```
(defun set-category ()
  (interactive "P")
  (let* ((marker (or (org-get-at-bol 'org-hd-marker)
                     (org-agenda-error)))
         (buffer (marker-buffer marker)))
    (with-current-buffer buffer
      (save-excursion
        (save-restriction
          (widen)
          (goto-char marker)
          (org-back-to-heading t)
          (org-set-property "CATEGORY" "web"))))))
```

Calendar commands

c   org-agenda-goto-calendar
               Open the Emacs calendar and move to the date at the agenda cursor.

c   org-calendar-goto-agenda
               When in the calendar, compute and show the Org mode agenda for the date at
               the cursor.

i   org-agenda-diary-entry
               Insert a new entry into the diary, using the date at the cursor and (for block
               entries) the date at the mark. This will add to the Emacs diary file[14], in a way
               similar to the i command in the calendar. The diary file will pop up in another
               window, where you can add the entry.

               If you configure org-agenda-diary-file to point to an Org mode file, Org
               will create entries (in Org mode syntax) in that file instead. Most entries will
               be stored in a date-based outline tree that will later make it easy to archive
               appointments from previous months/years. The tree will be built under an
               entry with a DATE_TREE property, or else with years as top-level entries. Emacs
               will prompt you for the entry text—if you specify it, the entry will be created
               in org-agenda-diary-file without further interaction. If you directly press
               RET at the prompt without typing text, the target file will be shown in another
               window for you to finish the entry there. See also the k r command.

M   org-agenda-phases-of-moon
               Show the phases of the moon for the three months around current date.

S   org-agenda-sunrise-sunset
               Show sunrise and sunset times. The geographical location must be set with
               calendar variables, see the documentation for the Emacs calendar.

C   org-agenda-convert-date
               Convert the date at cursor into many other cultural and historic calendars.

---

[13] You can also create persistent custom functions through org-agenda-bulk-custom-functions.

[14] This file is parsed for the agenda when org-agenda-include-diary is set.

H   `org-agenda-holidays`
    Show holidays for three months around the cursor date.

`M-x org-icalendar-combine-agenda-files RET`
    Export a single iCalendar file containing entries from all agenda files. This is a
    globally available command, and also available in the agenda menu.

Exporting to a file

`C-x C-w`   `org-agenda-write`
    Write the agenda view to a file. Depending on the extension of the selected
    file name, the view will be exported as HTML (`.html` or `.htm`), Postscript
    (`.ps`), PDF (`.pdf`), Org (`.org`) and plain text (any other extension). When
    exporting to Org, only the body of original headlines are exported, not subtrees
    or inherited tags. When called with a `C-u` prefix argument, immediately open
    the newly created file. Use the variable `org-agenda-exporter-settings` to
    set options for `ps-print` and for `htmlize` to be used during export.

Quit and Exit

q   `org-agenda-quit`
    Quit agenda, remove the agenda buffer.

x   `org-agenda-exit`
    Exit agenda, remove the agenda buffer and all buffers loaded by Emacs for the
    compilation of the agenda. Buffers created by the user to visit Org files will not
    be removed.

10.6 Custom agenda views

Custom agenda commands serve two purposes: to store and quickly access frequently used
TODO and tags searches, and to create special composite agenda buffers. Custom agenda
commands will be accessible through the dispatcher (see Section 10.2 [Agenda dispatcher],
page 99), just like the default commands.

10.6.1 Storing searches

The first application of custom searches is the definition of keyboard shortcuts for frequently
used searches, either creating an agenda buffer, or a sparse tree (the latter covering of course
only the current buffer).

   Custom commands are configured in the variable `org-agenda-custom-commands`. You
can customize this variable, for example by pressing `C-c a C`. You can also directly set it
with Emacs Lisp in `.emacs`. The following example contains all valid agenda views:

```
(setq org-agenda-custom-commands
      '(("x" agenda)
        ("y" agenda*)
        ("w" todo "WAITING")
        ("W" todo-tree "WAITING")
        ("u" tags "+boss-urgent")
        ("v" tags-todo "+boss-urgent")
        ("U" tags-tree "+boss-urgent")
        ("f" occur-tree "\\<FIXME\\>")
        ("h" . "HOME+Name tags searches") ; description for "h" prefix
        ("hl" tags "+home+Lisa")
        ("hp" tags "+home+Peter")
        ("hk" tags "+home+Kim")))
```

The initial string in each entry defines the keys you have to press after the dispatcher command `C-c a` in order to access the command. Usually this will be just a single character, but if you have many similar commands, you can also define two-letter combinations where the first character is the same in several combinations and serves as a prefix key[15]. The second parameter is the search type, followed by the string or regular expression to be used for the matching. The example above will therefore define:

`C-c a x`   as a global search for agenda entries planned[16] this week/day.

`C-c a y`   as a global search for agenda entries planned this week/day, but only those with an hour specification like `[h]h:mm`—think of them as appointments.

`C-c a w`   as a global search for TODO entries with ‘`WAITING`’ as the TODO keyword

`C-c a W`   as the same search, but only in the current buffer and displaying the results as a sparse tree

`C-c a u`   as a global tags search for headlines marked ‘`:boss:`’ but not ‘`:urgent:`’

`C-c a v`   as the same search as `C-c a u`, but limiting the search to headlines that are also TODO items

`C-c a U`   as the same search as `C-c a u`, but only in the current buffer and displaying the result as a sparse tree

`C-c a f`   to create a sparse tree (again: current buffer only) with all entries containing the word ‘`FIXME`’

`C-c a h`   as a prefix command for a HOME tags search where you have to press an additional key (`l`, `p` or `k`) to select a name (Lisa, Peter, or Kim) as additional tag to match.

Note that the `*-tree` agenda views need to be called from an Org buffer as they operate on the current buffer only.

---

[15] You can provide a description for a prefix key by inserting a cons cell with the prefix and the description.

[16] *Planned* means here that these entries have some planning information attached to them, like a timestamp, a scheduled or a deadline string. See `org-agenda-entry-types` on how to set what planning information will be taken into account.

10.6.2 Block agenda

Another possibility is the construction of agenda views that comprise the results of *several* commands, each of which creates a block in the agenda buffer. The available commands include `agenda` for the daily or weekly agenda (as created with *C-c* a a), `alltodo` for the global TODO list (as constructed with *C-c* a t), and the matching commands discussed above: `todo`, `tags`, and `tags-todo`. Here are two examples:

(setq org-agenda-custom-commands
     '(("h" "Agenda and Home-related tasks"
       ((agenda "")
        (tags-todo "home")
        (tags "garden")))
      ("o" "Agenda and Office-related tasks"
       ((agenda "")
        (tags-todo "work")
        (tags "office")))))

This will define *C-c* a h to create a multi-block view for stuff you need to attend to at home. The resulting agenda buffer will contain your agenda for the current week, all TODO items that carry the tag 'home', and also all lines tagged with 'garden'. Finally the command *C-c* a o provides a similar view for office tasks.

10.6.3 Setting options for custom commands

Org mode contains a number of variables regulating agenda construction and display. The global variables define the behavior for all agenda commands, including the custom commands. However, if you want to change some settings just for a single custom view, you can do so. Setting options requires inserting a list of variable names and values at the right spot in `org-agenda-custom-commands`. For example:

(setq org-agenda-custom-commands
     '(("w" todo "WAITING"
       ((org-agenda-sorting-strategy '(priority-down))
        (org-agenda-prefix-format " Mixed: ")))
      ("U" tags-tree "+boss-urgent"
       ((org-show-following-heading nil)
        (org-show-hierarchy-above nil)))
      ("N" search ""
       ((org-agenda-files '("~org/notes.org"))
        (org-agenda-text-search-extra-files nil)))))

Now the *C-c* a w command will sort the collected entries only by priority, and the prefix format is modified to just say ' Mixed: ' instead of giving the category of the entry. The sparse tags tree of *C-c* a U will now turn out ultra-compact, because neither the headline hierarchy above the match, nor the headline following the match will be shown. The command *C-c* a N will do a text search limited to only a single file.

For command sets creating a block agenda, `org-agenda-custom-commands` has two separate spots for setting options. You can add options that should be valid for just a single command in the set, and options that should be valid for all commands in the set. The former are just added to the command entry; the latter must come after the list of command entries. Going back to the block agenda example (see Section 10.6.2 [Block agenda], page 122), let's change the sorting strategy for the *C-c a h* commands to `priority-down`, but let's sort the results for GARDEN tags query in the opposite order, `priority-up`. This would look like this:

(setq org-agenda-custom-commands
    '(("h" "Agenda and Home-related tasks"
     ((agenda)
      (tags-todo "home")
      (tags "garden"
         ((org-agenda-sorting-strategy '(priority-up)))))
      ((org-agenda-sorting-strategy '(priority-down))))
     ("o" "Agenda and Office-related tasks"
     ((agenda)
      (tags-todo "work")
      (tags "office")))))

As you see, the values and parentheses setting is a little complex. When in doubt, use the customize interface to set this variable—it fully supports its structure. Just one caveat: when setting options in this interface, the *values* are just Lisp expressions. So if the value is a string, you need to add the double-quotes around the value yourself.

To control whether an agenda command should be accessible from a specific context, you can customize `org-agenda-custom-commands-contexts`. Let's say for example that you have an agenda command "o" displaying a view that you only need when reading emails. Then you would configure this option like this:

(setq org-agenda-custom-commands-contexts
    '(("o" (in-mode . "message-mode"))))

You can also tell that the command key "o" should refer to another command key "r". In that case, add this command key like this:

(setq org-agenda-custom-commands-contexts
    '(("o" "r" (in-mode . "message-mode"))))

See the docstring of the variable for more information.

10.7 Exporting agenda views

If you are away from your computer, it can be very useful to have a printed version of some agenda views to carry around. Org mode can export custom agenda views as plain text, HTML[17], Postscript, PDF[18], and iCalendar files. If you want to do this only occasionally, use the command

C-x C-w   `org-agenda-write`
        Write the agenda view to a file. Depending on the extension of the selected file
        name, the view will be exported as HTML (extension `.html` or `.htm`), Postscript
        (extension `.ps`), iCalendar (extension `.ics`), or plain text (any other extension).

---

[17] You need to install Hrvoje Niksic's `htmlize.el`.

[18] To create PDF output, the ghostscript `ps2pdf` utility must be installed on the system. Selecting a PDF file will also create the postscript file.

Use the variable `org-agenda-exporter-settings` to set options for `ps-print`
and for `htmlize` to be used during export, for example

(setq org-agenda-exporter-settings
      '((ps-number-of-columns 2)
        (ps-landscape-mode t)
        (org-agenda-add-entry-text-maxlines 5)
        (htmlize-output-type 'css)))

If you need to export certain agenda views frequently, you can associate any custom
agenda command with a list of output file names[19]. Here is an example that first defines
custom commands for the agenda and the global TODO list, together with a number of
files to which to export them. Then we define two block agenda commands and specify file
names for them as well. File names can be relative to the current working directory, or
absolute.

(setq org-agenda-custom-commands
    '(("X" agenda "" nil ("agenda.html" "agenda.ps"))
      ("Y" alltodo "" nil ("todo.html" "todo.txt" "todo.ps"))
      ("h" "Agenda and Home-related tasks"
       ((agenda "")
        (tags-todo "home")
        (tags "garden"))
       nil
       ("~/views/home.html"))
      ("o" "Agenda and Office-related tasks"
       ((agenda)
        (tags-todo "work")
        (tags "office"))
       nil
       ("~/views/office.ps" "~/calendars/office.ics"))))

The extension of the file name determines the type of export. If it is `.html`, Org mode
will use the `htmlize.el` package to convert the buffer to HTML and save it to this file
name. If the extension is `.ps`, `ps-print-buffer-with-faces` is used to produce Postscript
output. If the extension is `.ics`, iCalendar export is run export over all files that were used
to construct the agenda, and limit the export to entries listed in the agenda. Any other
extension produces a plain ASCII file.

The export files are *not* created when you use one of those commands interactively
because this might use too much overhead. Instead, there is a special command to produce
all specified files in one step:

`C-c a e`   `org-store-agenda-views`
    Export all agenda views that have export file names associated with them.

You can use the options section of the custom agenda commands to also set options for
the export commands. For example:

---

[19] If you want to store standard views like the weekly agenda or the global TODO list as well, you need to
define custom commands for them in order to be able to specify file names.

```
(setq org-agenda-custom-commands
   '(("X" agenda ""
      ((ps-number-of-columns 2)
       (ps-landscape-mode t)
       (org-agenda-prefix-format " [ ] ")
       (org-agenda-with-colors nil)
       (org-agenda-remove-tags t))
      ("theagenda.ps"))))
```

This command sets two options for the Postscript exporter, to make it print in two columns in landscape format—the resulting page can be cut in two and then used in a paper agenda. The remaining settings modify the agenda prefix to omit category and scheduling information, and instead include a checkbox to check off items. We also remove the tags to make the lines compact, and we don't want to use colors for the black-and-white printer. Settings specified in **org-agenda-exporter-settings** will also apply, but the settings in **org-agenda-custom-commands** take precedence.

From the command line you may also use

```
emacs -eval (org-batch-store-agenda-views) -kill
```

or, if you need to modify some parameters[20]

```
emacs -eval '(org-batch-store-agenda-views              \
              org-agenda-span (quote month)             \
              org-agenda-start-day "2007-11-01"         \
              org-agenda-include-diary nil              \
              org-agenda-files (quote ("~/org/project.org")))' \
        -kill
```

which will create the agenda views restricted to the file `~/org/project.org`, without diary entries and with a 30-day extent.

You can also extract agenda information in a way that allows further processing by other programs. See Section A.10 [Extracting agenda information], page 236, for more information.

10.8 Using column view in the agenda

Column view (see Section 7.5 [Column view], page 66) is normally used to view and edit properties embedded in the hierarchical structure of an Org file. It can be quite useful to use column view also from the agenda, where entries are collected by certain criteria.

`C-c C-x C-c`   org-agenda-columns
        Turn on column view in the agenda.

To understand how to use this properly, it is important to realize that the entries in the agenda are no longer in their proper outline environment. This causes the following issues:

1. Org needs to make a decision which COLUMNS format to use. Since the entries in the agenda are collected from different files, and different files may have different COLUMNS formats, this is a non-trivial problem. Org first checks if the variable **org-agenda-overriding-columns-format** is currently set, and if so, takes the format from there.

---

[20] Quoting depends on the system you use, please check the FAQ for examples.

Otherwise it takes the format associated with the first item in the agenda, or, if that item does not have a specific format (defined in a property, or in its file), it uses `org-columns-default-format`.

2. If any of the columns has a summary type defined (see Section 7.5.1.2 [Column attributes], page 66), turning on column view in the agenda will visit all relevant agenda files and make sure that the computations of this property are up to date. This is also true for the special `CLOCKSUM` property. Org will then sum the values displayed in the agenda. In the daily/weekly agenda, the sums will cover a single day; in all other views they cover the entire block. It is vital to realize that the agenda may show the same entry *twice* (for example as scheduled and as a deadline), and it may show two entries from the same hierarchy (for example a *parent* and its *child*). In these cases, the summation in the agenda will lead to incorrect results because some values will count double.

3. When the column view in the agenda shows the `CLOCKSUM`, that is always the entire clocked time for this item. So even in the daily/weekly agenda, the clocksum listed in column view may originate from times outside the current view. This has the advantage that you can compare these values with a column listing the planned total effort for a task—one of the major applications for column view in the agenda. If you want information about clocked time in the displayed period use clock table mode (press `R` in the agenda).

4. When the column view in the agenda shows the `CLOCKSUM_T`, that is always today's clocked time for this item. So even in the weekly agenda, the clocksum listed in column view only originates from today. This lets you compare the time you spent on a task for today, with the time already spent (via `CLOCKSUM`) and with the planned total effort for it.

11 Markup for rich export

When exporting Org mode documents, the exporter tries to reflect the structure of the document as accurately as possible in the back-end. Since export targets like HTML and LaTeX allow much richer formatting, Org mode has rules on how to prepare text for rich export. This section summarizes the markup rules used in an Org mode buffer.

11.1 Structural markup elements

Document title

The title of the exported document is taken from the special line

```
#+TITLE: This is the title of the document
```

If this line does not exist, the title will be the name of the file associated with the buffer, without extension, or the buffer name.

If you are exporting only a subtree, its heading will become the title of the document. If the subtree has a property EXPORT_TITLE, that will take precedence.

Headings and sections

The outline structure of the document as described in Chapter 2 [Document structure], page 6, forms the basis for defining sections of the exported document. However, since the outline structure is also used for (for example) lists of tasks, only the first three outline levels will be used as headings. Deeper levels will become itemized lists. You can change the location of this switch globally by setting the variable `org-export-headline-levels`, or on a per-file basis with a line

```
#+OPTIONS: H:4
```

Table of contents

The table of contents is normally inserted directly before the first headline of the file. The depth of the table is by default the same as the number of headline levels, but you can choose a smaller number, or turn off the table of contents entirely, by configuring the variable `org-export-with-toc`, or on a per-file basis with a line like

```
#+OPTIONS: toc:2          (only to two levels in TOC)
#+OPTIONS: toc:nil        (no default TOC at all)
```

If you would like to move the table of contents to a different location, you should turn off the default table using `org-export-with-toc` or #+OPTIONS and insert #+TOC: `headlines N` at the desired location(s).

```
#+OPTIONS: toc:nil        (no default TOC)
...
#+TOC: headlines 2        (insert TOC here, with two headline levels)
```

Multiple #+TOC: `headline` lines are allowed. The same TOC keyword can also generate a list of all tables (resp. all listings) with a caption in the buffer.

```
#+TOC: listings           (build a list of listings)
#+TOC: tables             (build a list of tables)
```

The headline's title usually determines its corresponding entry in a table of contents. However, it is possible to specify an alternative title by setting `ALT_TITLE` property accordingly. It will then be used when building the table.

Lists

Plain lists as described in Section 2.7 [Plain lists], page 12, are translated to the back-end's syntax for such lists. Most back-ends support unordered, ordered, and description lists.

Paragraphs, line breaks, and quoting

Paragraphs are separated by at least one empty line. If you need to enforce a line break within a paragraph, use '\\' at the end of a line.

To keep the line breaks in a region, but otherwise use normal formatting, you can use this construct, which can also be used to format poetry.

```
#+BEGIN_VERSE
 Great clouds overhead
 Tiny black birds rise and fall
 Snow covers Emacs

     -- AlexSchroeder
#+END_VERSE
```

When quoting a passage from another document, it is customary to format this as a paragraph that is indented on both the left and the right margin. You can include quotations in Org mode documents like this:

```
#+BEGIN_QUOTE
Everything should be made as simple as possible,
but not any simpler -- Albert Einstein
#+END_QUOTE
```

If you would like to center some text, do it like this:

```
#+BEGIN_CENTER
Everything should be made as simple as possible, \\
but not any simpler
#+END_CENTER
```

Footnote markup

Footnotes defined in the way described in Section 2.10 [Footnotes], page 16, will be exported by all back-ends. Org allows multiple references to the same note, and multiple footnotes side by side.

Emphasis and monospace

You can make words *bold*, /italic/, _underlined_, =verbatim= and ~code~, and, if you must, '+strike-through+'. Text in the code and verbatim string is not processed for Org mode specific syntax, it is exported verbatim.

To turn off fontification for marked up text, you can set `org-fontify-emphasized-text` to `nil`. To narrow down the list of available markup syntax, you can customize `org-emphasis-alist`. To fine tune what characters are allowed before and after the markup characters, you can tweak `org-emphasis-regexp-components`. Beware that changing one of the above variables will no take effect until you reload Org, for which you may need to restart Emacs.

Horizontal rules

A line consisting of only dashes, and at least 5 of them, will be exported as a horizontal line.

Comment lines

Lines starting with zero or more whitespace characters followed by one '#' and a whitespace are treated as comments and, as such, are not exported.

Likewise, regions surrounded by '#+BEGIN_COMMENT' ... '#+END_COMMENT' are not exported.

Finally, a 'COMMENT' keyword at the beginning of an entry, but after any other keyword or priority cookie, comments out the entire subtree. In this case, the subtree is not exported and no code block within it is executed either. The command below helps changing the comment status of a headline.

C-c ;   Toggle the 'COMMENT' keyword at the beginning of an entry.

11.2 Images and Tables

Both the native Org mode tables (see Chapter 3 [Tables], page 19) and tables formatted with the `table.el` package will be exported properly. For Org mode tables, the lines before the first horizontal separator line will become table header lines. You can use the following lines somewhere before the table to assign a caption and a label for cross references, and in the text you can refer to the object with `[[tab:basic-data]]` (see Section 4.2 [Internal links], page 37):

```
#+CAPTION: This is the caption for the next table (or link)
#+NAME:   tab:basic-data
  | ... | ...|
  |-----|----|
```

Optionally, the caption can take the form:

```
#+CAPTION[Caption for list of tables]: Caption for table.
```

Some back-ends allow you to directly include images into the exported document. Org does this, if a link to an image files does not have a description part, for example `[[./img/a.jpg]]`. If you wish to define a caption for the image and maybe a label for internal cross references, make sure that the link is on a line by itself and precede it with #+CAPTION and #+NAME as follows:

```
#+CAPTION: This is the caption for the next figure link (or table)
#+NAME:   fig:SED-HR4049
[[./img/a.jpg]]
```

Such images can be displayed within the buffer. See Section 4.4 [Handling links], page 40.

Even though images and tables are prominent examples of captioned structures, the same caption mechanism can apply to many others (e.g., LaTeX equations, source code blocks). Depending on the export back-end, those may or may not be handled.

11.3 Literal examples

You can include literal examples that should not be subjected to markup. Such examples will be typeset in monospace, so this is well suited for source code and similar examples.

```
#+BEGIN_EXAMPLE
Some example from a text file.
#+END_EXAMPLE
```

Note that such blocks may be *indented* in order to align nicely with indented text and in particular with plain list structure (see Section 2.7 [Plain lists], page 12). For simplicity when using small examples, you can also start the example lines with a colon followed by a space. There may also be additional whitespace before the colon:

```
Here is an example
   : Some example from a text file.
```

If the example is source code from a programming language, or any other text that can be marked up by font-lock in Emacs, you can ask for the example to look like the fontified Emacs buffer[1]. This is done with the 'src' block, where you also need to specify the name of the major mode that should be used to fontify the example[2], see Section 15.2 [Easy templates], page 212 for shortcuts to easily insert code blocks.

```
#+BEGIN_SRC emacs-lisp
  (defun org-xor (a b)
    "Exclusive or."
    (if a (not b) b))
#+END_SRC
```

Both in `example` and in `src` snippets, you can add a `-n` switch to the end of the BEGIN line, to get the lines of the example numbered. If you use a `+n` switch, the numbering from the previous numbered snippet will be continued in the current one. In literal examples, Org will interpret strings like '(ref:name)' as labels, and use them as targets for special hyperlinks like [[(name)]] (i.e., the reference name enclosed in single parenthesis). In HTML, hovering the mouse over such a link will remote-highlight the corresponding code line, which is kind of cool.

You can also add a `-r` switch which *removes* the labels from the source code[3]. With the `-n` switch, links to these references will be labeled by the line numbers from the code listing, otherwise links will use the labels with no parentheses. Here is an example:

```
#+BEGIN_SRC emacs-lisp -n -r
(save-excursion                      (ref:sc)
   (goto-char (point-min)))          (ref:jump)
#+END_SRC
In line [[(sc)]] we remember the current position.  [[(jump)][Line (jump)]]
jumps to point-min.
```

---

[1] This works automatically for the HTML back-end (it requires version 1.34 of the `htmlize.el` package, which is distributed with Org). Fontified code chunks in LaTeX can be achieved using either the listings or the minted package. Refer to `org-latex-listings` documentation for details.

[2] Code in 'src' blocks may also be evaluated either interactively or on export. See see Chapter 14 [Working with source code], page 184 for more information on evaluating code blocks.

[3] Adding `-k` to `-n -r` will *keep* the labels in the source code while using line numbers for the links, which might be useful to explain those in an Org mode example code.

Finally, you can use `-i` to preserve the indentation of a specific code block (see Section 14.2 [Editing source code], page 185).

If the syntax for the label format conflicts with the language syntax, use a `-l` switch to change the format, for example '`#+BEGIN_SRC pascal -n -r -l "((%s))"`'. See also the variable `org-coderef-label-format`.

HTML export also allows examples to be published as text areas (see Section 12.6.9 [Text areas in HTML export], page 149).

Because the `#+BEGIN_...` and `#+END_...` patterns need to be added so often, shortcuts are provided using the Easy templates facility (see Section 15.2 [Easy templates], page 212).

`C-c '`   Edit the source code example at point in its native mode. This works by switching to a temporary buffer with the source code. You need to exit by pressing `C-c '` again[4]. The edited version will then replace the old version in the Org buffer. Fixed-width regions (where each line starts with a colon followed by a space) will be edited using `artist-mode`[5] to allow creating ASCII drawings easily. Using this command in an empty line will create a new fixed-width region.

`C-c l`   Calling `org-store-link` while editing a source code example in a temporary buffer created with `C-c '` will prompt for a label. Make sure that it is unique in the current buffer, and insert it with the proper formatting like '`(ref:label)`' at the end of the current line. Then the label is stored as a link '`(label)`', for retrieval with `C-c C-l`.

11.4 Include files

During export, you can include the content of another file. For example, to include your `.emacs` file, you could use:

```
#+INCLUDE: "~/.emacs" src emacs-lisp
```

The first parameter names the the file to include. The optional second and third parameter specify the markup (i.e., '`example`' or '`src`'), and, if the markup is '`src`', the language for formatting the contents.

If markup is requested, the included content will be placed within an appropriate block[6]. No changes to the included content are made and it is the responsibility of the user to ensure that the result is valid Org syntax. For markup '`example`' and '`src`', which is requesting a literal example, the content will be code-escaped before inclusion.

If no markup is requested, the text will be assumed to be in Org mode format and will be processed normally. However, footnote labels (see Section 2.10 [Footnotes], page 16) in the file will be made local to that file. Contents of the included file will belong to the same structure (headline, item) containing the `INCLUDE` keyword. In particular, headlines within the file will become children of the current section. That behavior can be changed

---

[4] Upon exit, lines starting with '`*`', '`,*`', '`#+`' and '`,#+`' will get a comma prepended, to keep them from being interpreted by Org as outline nodes or special syntax. These commas will be stripped for editing with `C-c '`, and also for export.

[5] You may select a different-mode with the variable `org-edit-fixed-width-region-mode`.

[6] While you can request paragraphs ('`verse`', '`quote`', '`center`'), but this places severe restrictions on the type of content that is permissible

by providing an additional keyword parameter, `:minlevel`. In that case, all headlines in the included file will be shifted so the one with the lowest level reaches that specified level. For example, to make a file become a sibling of the current top-level headline, use

```
#+INCLUDE: "~/my-book/chapter2.org" :minlevel 1
```

You can also include a portion of a file by specifying a lines range using the `:lines` keyword parameter. The line at the upper end of the range will not be included. The start and/or the end of the range may be omitted to use the obvious defaults.

```
#+INCLUDE: "~/.emacs" :lines "5-10"    Include lines 5 to 10, 10 excluded
#+INCLUDE: "~/.emacs" :lines "-10"     Include lines 1 to 10, 10 excluded
#+INCLUDE: "~/.emacs" :lines "10-"     Include lines from 10 to EOF
```

`C-c '`   Visit the include file at point.

11.5 Index entries

You can specify entries that will be used for generating an index during publishing. This is done by lines starting with `#+INDEX`. An entry the contains an exclamation mark will create a sub item. See Section 13.1.8 [Generating an index], page 181 for more information.

```
* Curriculum Vitae
#+INDEX: CV
#+INDEX: Application!CV
```

11.6 Macro replacement

You can define text snippets with

```
#+MACRO: name    replacement text $1, $2 are arguments
```

which can be referenced `{{{name(arg1, arg2)}}}`[7].

These references, called macros, can be inserted anywhere Org markup is recognized: paragraphs, headlines, verse blocks, tables cells and lists. They cannot be used within ordinary keywords (starting with #+) but are allowed in `#+CAPTION`, `#+TITLE`, `#+AUTHOR` and `#+EMAIL`.

In addition to user-defined macros, a set of already defined macros can be used: `{{{title}}}`, `{{{author}}}`, etc., will reference information set by the `#+TITLE:`, `#+AUTHOR:`, and similar lines. Also, `{{{time(FORMAT)}}}` and `{{{modification-time(FORMAT)}}}` refer to current date time and to the modification time of the file being exported, respectively. *FORMAT* should be a format string understood by `format-time-string`.

The surrounding brackets can be made invisible by setting `org-hide-macro-markers` to t.

Macro expansion takes place during the very beginning of the export process.

---

[7] Since commas separate arguments, commas within arguments have to be escaped with a backslash character. Conversely, backslash characters before a comma, and only them, need to be escaped with another backslash character.

11.7 Embedded LaTeX

Plain ASCII is normally sufficient for almost all note taking. Exceptions include scientific notes, which often require mathematical symbols and the occasional formula. LaTeX[8] is widely used to typeset scientific documents. Org mode supports embedding LaTeX code into its files, because many academics are used to writing and reading LaTeX source code, and because it can be readily processed to produce pretty output for a number of export back-ends.

11.7.1 Special symbols

You can use LaTeX-like syntax to insert special symbols like '`\alpha`' to indicate the Greek letter, or '`\to`' to indicate an arrow. Completion for these symbols is available, just type '`\`' and maybe a few letters, and press *M-TAB* to see possible completions. Unlike LaTeX code, Org mode allows these symbols to be present without surrounding math delimiters, for example:

```
Angles are written as Greek letters \alpha, \beta and \gamma.
```

During export, these symbols will be transformed into the native format of the exporter back-end. Strings like `\alpha` will be exported as `&alpha;` in the HTML output, and as `$\alpha$` in the LaTeX output. Similarly, `\nbsp` will become ` ` in HTML and `~` in LaTeX. If you need such a symbol inside a word, terminate it like this: '`\Aacute{}stor`'.

A large number of entities is provided, with names taken from both HTML and LaTeX; see the variable **org-entities** for the complete list. '`\-`' is treated as a shy hyphen, and '`--`', '`---`', and '`...`' are all converted into special commands creating hyphens of different lengths or a compact set of dots.

If you would like to see entities displayed as UTF-8 characters, use the following command[9]:

*C-c C-x *   Toggle display of entities as UTF-8 characters. This does not change the buffer content which remains plain ASCII, but it overlays the UTF-8 character for display purposes only.

11.7.2 Subscripts and superscripts

Just like in LaTeX, '`^`' and '`_`' are used to indicate super- and subscripts. Again, these can be used without embedding them in math-mode delimiters. To increase the readability of ASCII text, it is not necessary (but OK) to surround multi-character sub- and superscripts with curly braces. For example

```
The mass of the sun is M_sun = 1.989 x 10^30 kg.  The radius of
the sun is R_{sun} = 6.96 x 10^8 m.
```

If you write a text where the underscore is often used in a different context, Org's convention to always interpret these as subscripts can get in your way. Configure the variable **org-use-sub-superscripts** to change this convention. For example, when setting this variable to {}, '`a_b`' will not be interpreted as a subscript, but '`a_{b}`' will.

---

[8] LaTeX is a macro system based on Donald E. Knuth's TeX system. Many of the features described here as "LaTeX" are really from TeX, but for simplicity I am blurring this distinction.

[9] You can turn this on by default by setting the variable **org-pretty-entities**, or on a per-file base with the #+STARTUP option **entitiespretty**.

`C-c C-x \`   In addition to showing entities as UTF-8 characters, this command will also
format sub- and superscripts in a WYSIWYM way.

11.7.3 LaTeX fragments

Going beyond symbols and sub- and superscripts, a full formula language is needed. Org
mode can contain LaTeX math fragments, and it supports ways to process these for several
export back-ends. When exporting to LaTeX, the code is obviously left as it is. When exporting to HTML, Org can invoke the MathJax library (see Section 12.6.8 [Math formatting in
HTML export], page 148) to process and display the math[10]. It can also process the mathematical expressions into images that can be displayed in a browser (see see Section 11.7.4
[Previewing LaTeX fragments], page 134).

LaTeX fragments don't need any special marking at all. The following snippets will be
identified as LaTeX source code:

- Environments of any kind[11]. The only requirement is that the `\begin` and `\end` statements appear on a new line, at the beginning of the line or after whitespaces only.
- Text within the usual LaTeX math delimiters. To avoid conflicts with currency specifications, single '`$`' characters are only recognized as math delimiters if the enclosed
  text contains at most two line breaks, is directly attached to the '`$`' characters with
  no whitespace in between, and if the closing '`$`' is followed by whitespace, punctuation
  or a dash. For the other delimiters, there is no such restriction, so when in doubt, use
  '`\(...\)`' as inline math delimiters.

For example:

```
\begin{equation}
x=\sqrt{b}
\end{equation}

If $a^2=b$ and \( b=2 \), then the solution must be
either $$ a=+\sqrt{2} $$ or \[ a=-\sqrt{2} \].
```

LaTeX processing can be configured with the variable `org-export-with-latex`. The
default setting is `t` which means `MathJax` for HTML, and no processing for ASCII and
LaTeX back-ends. You can also set this variable on a per-file basis using one of these lines:

```
#+OPTIONS: tex:t          Do the right thing automatically (MathJax)
#+OPTIONS: tex:nil        Do not process LaTeX fragments at all
#+OPTIONS: tex:verbatim   Verbatim export, for jsMath or so
```

11.7.4 Previewing LaTeX fragments

If you have a working LaTeX installation and either **dvipng** or **convert** installed[12], LaTeX
fragments can be processed to produce images of the typeset expressions to be used for

---

[10] If you plan to use this regularly or on pages with significant page views, you should install `MathJax` on
your own server in order to limit the load of our server.

[11] When `MathJax` is used, only the environments recognized by `MathJax` will be processed. When `dvipng`
program or `imagemagick` suite is used to create images, any LaTeX environment will be handled.

[12] These are respectively available at http://sourceforge.net/projects/dvipng/
and from the `imagemagick` suite. Choose the converter by setting the variable
`org-latex-create-formula-image-program` accordingly.

inclusion while exporting to HTML (see see Section 11.7.3 [LaTeX fragments], page 134), or for inline previewing within Org mode.

You can customize the variables `org-format-latex-options` and `org-format-latex-header` to influence some aspects of the preview. In particular, the `:scale` (and for HTML export, `:html-scale`) property of the former can be used to adjust the size of the preview images.

`C-c C-x C-l`
>Produce a preview image of the LaTeX fragment at point and overlay it over the source code. If there is no fragment at point, process all fragments in the current entry (between two headlines). When called with a prefix argument, process the entire subtree. When called with two prefix arguments, or when the cursor is before the first headline, process the entire buffer.

`C-c C-c`   Remove the overlay preview images.

You can turn on the previewing of all LaTeX fragments in a file with

>`#+STARTUP: latexpreview`

To disable it, simply use

>`#+STARTUP: nolatexpreview`

11.7.5 Using CDLaTeX to enter math

CDLaTeX mode is a minor mode that is normally used in combination with a major LaTeX mode like AUCTeX in order to speed-up insertion of environments and math templates. Inside Org mode, you can make use of some of the features of CDLaTeX mode. You need to install `cdlatex.el` and `texmathp.el` (the latter comes also with AUCTeX) from `http://www.astro.uva.nl/~dominik/Tools/cdlatex`. Don't use CDLaTeX mode itself under Org mode, but use the light version `org-cdlatex-mode` that comes as part of Org mode. Turn it on for the current buffer with *M-x org-cdlatex-mode RET*, or for all Org files with

(add-hook 'org-mode-hook 'turn-on-org-cdlatex)

When this mode is enabled, the following features are present (for more details see the documentation of CDLaTeX mode):

- Environment templates can be inserted with `C-c {`.
- The `TAB` key will do template expansion if the cursor is inside a LaTeX fragment[13]. For example, `TAB` will expand `fr` to `\frac{}{}` and position the cursor correctly inside the first brace. Another `TAB` will get you into the second brace. Even outside fragments, `TAB` will expand environment abbreviations at the beginning of a line. For example, if you write 'equ' at the beginning of a line and press `TAB`, this abbreviation will be expanded to an `equation` environment. To get a list of all abbreviations, type *M-x cdlatex-command-help RET*.
- Pressing _ and ^ inside a LaTeX fragment will insert these characters together with a pair of braces. If you use `TAB` to move out of the braces, and if the braces surround only a single character or macro, they are removed again (depending on the variable `cdlatex-simplify-sub-super-scripts`).

---

[13] Org mode has a method to test if the cursor is inside such a fragment, see the documentation of the function `org-inside-LaTeX-fragment-p`.

- Pressing the backquote ' followed by a character inserts math macros, also outside LaTeX fragments. If you wait more than 1.5 seconds after the backquote, a help window will pop up.

- Pressing the single-quote ' followed by another character modifies the symbol before point with an accent or a font. If you wait more than 1.5 seconds after the single-quote, a help window will pop up. Character modification will work only inside LaTeX fragments; outside the quote is normal.

11.8 Special blocks

Org syntax includes pre-defined blocks (see [Paragraphs], page 128 and Section 11.3 [Literal examples], page 130). It is also possible to create blocks containing raw code targeted at a specific back-end (e.g., '#+BEGIN_LATEX').

Any other block is a *special block*.

For example, '#+BEGIN_ABSTRACT' and '#+BEGIN_VIDEO' are special blocks. The first one is useful when exporting to LaTeX, the second one when exporting to HTML5.

Each export back-end decides if they should be exported, and how. When the block is ignored, its contents are still exported, as if the opening and closing block lines were not there. For example, when exporting a '#+BEGIN_TEST' block, HTML back-end wraps its contents within a '<div name="test">' tag.

Refer to back-end specific documentation for more information.

12 Exporting

The Org mode export facilities can be used to export Org documents or parts of Org documents to a variety of other formats. In addition, these facilities can be used with `orgtbl-mode` and/or `orgstruct-mode` in foreign buffers so you can author tables and lists in Org syntax and convert them in place to the target language.

ASCII export produces a readable and simple version of an Org file for printing and sharing notes. HTML export allows you to easily publish notes on the web, or to build full-fledged websites. LaTeX export lets you use Org mode and its structured editing functions to create arbitrarily complex LaTeX files for any kind of document. OpenDocument Text (ODT) export allows seamless collaboration across organizational boundaries. Markdown export lets you seamlessly collaborate with other developers. Finally, iCal export can extract entries with deadlines or appointments to produce a file in the iCalendar format.

12.1 The export dispatcher

The main entry point for export related tasks is the dispatcher, a hierarchical menu from which it is possible to select an export format and toggle export options[1] from which it is possible to select an export format and to toggle export options.

`C-c C-e`   org-export-dispatch
> Dispatch for export and publishing commands. When called with a `C-u` prefix argument, repeat the last export command on the current buffer while preserving toggled options. If the current buffer hasn't changed and subtree export was activated, the command will affect that same subtree.

Normally the entire buffer is exported, but if there is an active region only that part of the buffer will be exported.

Several export options (see Section 12.3 [Export settings], page 138) can be toggled from the export dispatcher with the following key combinations:

`C-a`   Toggle asynchronous export. Asynchronous export uses an external Emacs process that is configured with a specified initialization file.

> While exporting asynchronously, the output is not displayed, but stored in a place called "the export stack". This stack can be displayed by calling the dispatcher with a double `C-u` prefix argument, or with & key from the dispatcher menu.

> To make this behavior the default, customize the variable `org-export-in-background`.

`C-b`   Toggle body-only export. Its effect depends on the back-end used. Typically, if the back-end has a header section (like `<head>`...`</head>` in the HTML back-end), a body-only export will not include this header.

`C-s`   Toggle subtree export. The top heading becomes the document title.

> You can change the default state of this option by setting `org-export-initial-scope`.

---

[1] It is also possible to use a less intrusive interface by setting `org-export-dispatch-use-expert-ui` to a non-`nil` value. In that case, only a prompt is visible from the minibuffer. From there one can still switch back to regular menu by pressing ?.

`C-v`   Toggle visible-only export. Only export the text that is currently visible, i.e.
                not hidden by outline visibility in the buffer.

12.2 Export back-ends

An export back-end is a library that translates Org syntax into a foreign format. An export
format is not available until the proper back-end has been loaded.

By default, the following four back-ends are loaded: `ascii`, `html`, `icalendar` and `latex`.
It is possible to add more (or remove some) by customizing `org-export-backends`.

Built-in back-ends include:

- ascii (ASCII format)
- beamer (LaTeX Beamer format)
- html (HTML format)
- icalendar (iCalendar format)
- latex (LaTeX format)
- man (Man page format)
- md (Markdown format)
- odt (OpenDocument Text format)
- org (Org format)
- texinfo (Texinfo format)

Other back-ends might be found in the **contrib/** directory (see Section 1.2 [Installation],
page 2).

12.3 Export settings

Export options can be set: globally with variables; for an individual file by making variables
buffer-local with in-buffer settings (see Section 15.6 [In-buffer settings], page 214), by setting
individual keywords, or by specifying them in a compact form with the `#+OPTIONS` keyword;
or for a tree by setting properties (see Chapter 7 [Properties and columns], page 62). Options
set at a specific level override options set at a more general level.

In-buffer settings may appear anywhere in the file, either directly or indirectly through
a file included using '`#+SETUPFILE: filename`' syntax. Option keyword sets tailored to
a particular back-end can be inserted from the export dispatcher (see Section 12.1 [The
export dispatcher], page 137) using the `Insert template` command by pressing `#`. To
insert keywords individually, a good way to make sure the keyword is correct is to type `#+`
and then to use `M-<TAB>` for completion.

The export keywords available for every back-end, and their equivalent global variables,
include:

'`AUTHOR`'   The document author (`user-full-name`).

'`CREATOR`'   Entity responsible for output generation (`org-export-creator-string`).

'`DATE`'   A date or a time-stamp[2].

---

[2] The variable `org-export-date-timestamp-format` defines how this time-stamp will be exported.

'DESCRIPTION'
> The document description. Back-ends handle it as they see fit (e.g., for the XHTML meta tag), if at all. You can use several such keywords for long descriptions.

'EMAIL'   The email address (`user-mail-address`).

'KEYWORDS'
> The keywords defining the contents of the document. Back-ends handle it as they see fit (e.g., for the XHTML meta tag), if at all. You can use several such keywords if the list is long.

'LANGUAGE'
> The language used for translating some strings (`org-export-default-language`). E.g., '#+LANGUAGE: fr' will tell Org to translate *File* (english) into *Fichier* (french) in the clocktable.

'SELECT_TAGS'
> The tags that select a tree for export (`org-export-select-tags`). The default value is `:export:`. Within a subtree tagged with `:export:`, you can still exclude entries with `:noexport:` (see below). When headlines are selectively exported with `:export:` anywhere in a file, text before the first headline is ignored.

'EXCLUDE_TAGS'
> The tags that exclude a tree from export (`org-export-exclude-tags`). The default value is `:noexport:`. Entries with the `:noexport:` tag will be unconditionally excluded from the export, even if they have an `:export:` tag. Code blocks contained in excluded subtrees will still be executed during export even though the subtree is not exported.

'TITLE'   The title to be shown (otherwise derived from buffer's name). You can use several such keywords for long titles.

The `#+OPTIONS` keyword is a compact[3] form that recognizes the following arguments:

'`:`   Toggle smart quotes (`org-export-with-smart-quotes`).

`*:`   Toggle emphasized text (`org-export-with-emphasize`).

`-:`   Toggle conversion of special strings (`org-export-with-special-strings`).

`::`   Toggle fixed-width sections (`org-export-with-fixed-width`).

`<:`   Toggle inclusion of any time/date active/inactive stamps (`org-export-with-timestamps`).

`:`   Toggle line-break-preservation (`org-export-preserve-breaks`).

`^:`   Toggle TeX-like syntax for sub- and superscripts. If you write "`^:{}`", '`a_{b}`' will be interpreted, but the simple '`a_b`' will be left as it is (`org-export-with-sub-superscripts`).

`arch:`   Configure export of archived trees. Can be set to `headline` to only process the headline, skipping its contents (`org-export-with-archived-trees`).

---

[3] If you want to configure many options this way, you can use several `#+OPTIONS` lines.

`author:` Toggle inclusion of author name into exported file (`org-export-with-author`).

`c:` Toggle inclusion of CLOCK keywords (`org-export-with-clocks`).

`creator:` Configure inclusion of creator info into exported file. It may be set to `comment` (`org-export-with-creator`).

`d:` Toggle inclusion of drawers, or list drawers to include (`org-export-with-drawers`).

`e:` Toggle inclusion of entities (`org-export-with-entities`).

`email:` Toggle inclusion of the author's e-mail into exported file (`org-export-with-email`).

`f:` Toggle the inclusion of footnotes (`org-export-with-footnotes`).

`H:` Set the number of headline levels for export (`org-export-headline-levels`). Below that level, headlines are treated differently. In most back-ends, they become list items.

`inline:` Toggle inclusion of inlinetasks (`org-export-with-inlinetasks`).

`num:` Toggle section-numbers (`org-export-with-section-numbers`). It can also be set to a number 'n', so only headlines at that level or above will be numbered.

`p:` Toggle export of planning information (`org-export-with-planning`). "Planning information" is the line containing the SCHEDULED:, the DEADLINE: or the CLOSED: cookies or a combination of them.

`pri:` Toggle inclusion of priority cookies (`org-export-with-priority`).

`prop:` Toggle inclusion of property drawers, or list properties to include (`org-export-with-properties`).

`stat:` Toggle inclusion of statistics cookies (`org-export-with-statistics-cookies`).

`tags:` Toggle inclusion of tags, may also be `not-in-toc` (`org-export-with-tags`).

`tasks:` Toggle inclusion of tasks (TODO items), can be `nil` to remove all tasks, `todo` to remove DONE tasks, or a list of keywords to keep (`org-export-with-tasks`).

`tex:` Configure export of LaTeX fragments and environments. It may be set to `verbatim` (`org-export-with-latex`).

`timestamp:`
Toggle inclusion of the creation time into exported file (`org-export-timestamp-file`).

`toc:` Toggle inclusion of the table of contents, or set the level limit (`org-export-with-toc`).

`todo:` Toggle inclusion of TODO keywords into exported text (`org-export-with-todo-keywords`).

`|:` Toggle inclusion of tables (`org-export-with-tables`).

When exporting only a subtree, each of the previous keywords[4] can be overridden locally by special node properties. These begin with 'EXPORT_', followed by the name of the keyword they supplant. For example, 'DATE' and 'OPTIONS' keywords become, respectively, 'EXPORT_DATE' and 'EXPORT_OPTIONS' properties. Subtree export also supports the self-explicit 'EXPORT_FILE_NAME' property[5].

If `org-export-allow-bind-keywords` is non-nil, Emacs variables can become buffer-local during export by using the BIND keyword. Its syntax is '#+BIND: variable value'. This is particularly useful for in-buffer settings that cannot be changed using specific keywords.

12.4 ASCII/Latin-1/UTF-8 export

ASCII export produces a simple and very readable version of an Org mode file, containing only plain ASCII. Latin-1 and UTF-8 export augment the file with special characters and symbols available in these encodings.

Upon exporting, text is filled and justified, when appropriate, according the text width set in `org-ascii-text-width`.

Links are exported in a footnote-like style, with the descriptive part in the text and the link in a note before the next heading. See the variable `org-ascii-links-to-notes` for details and other options.

ASCII export commands

`C-c C-e t a/l/u`   org-ascii-export-to-ascii
> Export as an ASCII file. For an Org file, `myfile.org`, the ASCII file will be `myfile.txt`. The file will be overwritten without warning. When the original file is `myfile.txt`, the resulting file becomes `myfile.txt.txt` in order to prevent data loss.

`C-c C-e t A/L/U`   org-ascii-export-as-ascii
> Export to a temporary buffer. Do not create a file.

Header and sectioning structure

In the exported version, the first three outline levels become headlines, defining a general document structure. Additional levels are exported as lists. The transition can also occur at a different level (see Section 12.3 [Export settings], page 138).

Quoting ASCII text

You can insert text that will only appear when using ASCII back-end with the following constructs:

    Text @@ascii:and additional text@@ within a paragraph.

    #+ASCII: Some text

---

[4] With the exception of 'SETUPFILE'.

[5] There is no buffer-wide equivalent for this property. The file name in this case is derived from the file associated to the buffer, if possible, or asked to the user otherwise.

```
#+BEGIN_ASCII
All lines in this block will appear only when using this back-end.
#+END_ASCII
```

ASCII specific attributes

ASCII back-end only understands one attribute, `:width`, which specifies the length, in characters, of a given horizontal rule. It must be specified using an `ATTR_ASCII` line, directly preceding the rule.

```
#+ATTR_ASCII: :width 10
-----
```

ASCII special blocks

In addition to `#+BEGIN_CENTER` blocks (see [Paragraphs], page 128), it is possible to justify contents to the left or the right of the page with the following dedicated blocks.

```
#+BEGIN_JUSTIFYLEFT
It's just a jump to the left...
#+END_JUSTIFYLEFT

#+BEGIN_JUSTIFYRIGHT
...and then a step to the right.
#+END_JUSTIFYRIGHT
```

12.5 Beamer export

The LaTeX class *Beamer* allows production of high quality presentations using LaTeX and pdf processing. Org mode has special support for turning an Org mode file or tree into a Beamer presentation.

Beamer export commands

C-c C-e l b   org-beamer-export-to-latex

> Export as a LaTeX file. For an Org file `myfile.org`, the LaTeX file will be `myfile.tex`. The file will be overwritten without warning.

C-c C-e l B   org-beamer-export-as-latex

> Export to a temporary buffer. Do not create a file.

C-c C-e l P   org-beamer-export-to-pdf

> Export as LaTeX and then process to PDF.

C-c C-e l O

> Export as LaTeX and then process to PDF, then open the resulting PDF file.

Sectioning, Frames and Blocks

Any tree with not-too-deep level nesting should in principle be exportable as a Beamer presentation. Headlines fall into three categories: sectioning elements, frames and blocks.

− Headlines become frames when their level is equal to **org-beamer-frame-level** or H value in an **OPTIONS** line (see Section 12.3 [Export settings], page 138).

Though, if a headline in the current tree has a `BEAMER_ENV` property set to either to `frame` or `fullframe`, its level overrides the variable. A `fullframe` is a frame with an empty (ignored) title.

— All frame's children become `block` environments. Special block types can be enforced by setting headline's `BEAMER_ENV` property[6] to an appropriate value (see `org-beamer-environments-default` for supported values and `org-beamer-environments-extra` for adding more).

— As a special case, if the `BEAMER_ENV` property is set to either `appendix`, `note`, `noteNH` or `againframe`, the headline will become, respectively, an appendix, a note (within frame or between frame, depending on its level), a note with its title ignored or an `\againframe` command. In the latter case, a `BEAMER_REF` property is mandatory in order to refer to the frame being resumed, and contents are ignored.

Also, a headline with an `ignoreheading` environment will have its contents only inserted in the output. This special value is useful to have data between frames, or to properly close a `column` environment.

Headlines also support `BEAMER_ACT` and `BEAMER_OPT` properties. The former is translated as an overlay/action specification, or a default overlay specification when enclosed within square brackets. The latter specifies options[7] for the current frame or block. The export back-end will automatically wrap properties within angular or square brackets when appropriate.

Moreover, headlines handle the `BEAMER_COL` property. Its value should be a decimal number representing the width of the column as a fraction of the total text width. If the headline has no specific environment, its title will be ignored and its contents will fill the column created. Otherwise, the block will fill the whole column and the title will be preserved. Two contiguous headlines with a non-`nil` `BEAMER_COL` value share the same `columns` LaTeX environment. It will end before the next headline without such a property. This environment is generated automatically. Although, it can also be explicitly created, with a special `columns` value for `BEAMER_ENV` property (if it needs to be set up with some specific options, for example).

Beamer specific syntax

Beamer back-end is an extension of LaTeX back-end. As such, all LaTeX specific syntax (e.g., '#+LATEX:' or '#+ATTR_LATEX:') is recognized. See Section 12.7 [LaTeX and PDF export], page 151 for more information.

Beamer export introduces a number of keywords to insert code in the document's header. Four control appearance of the presentation: #+BEAMER_THEME, #+BEAMER_COLOR_THEME, #+BEAMER_FONT_THEME, #+BEAMER_INNER_THEME and #+BEAMER_OUTER_THEME. All of them accept optional arguments within square brackets. The last one, #+BEAMER_HEADER, is more generic and allows you to append any line of code in the header.

```
#+BEAMER_THEME: Rochester [height=20pt]
#+BEAMER_COLOR_THEME: spruce
```

---

[6] If this property is set, the entry will also get a `:B_environment:` tag to make this visible. This tag has no semantic meaning, it is only a visual aid.

[7] The `fragile` option is added automatically if it contains code that requires a verbatim environment, though.

Table of contents generated from `toc:t` OPTION keyword are wrapped within a `frame` environment. Those generated from a TOC keyword (see [Table of contents], page 127) are not. In that case, it is also possible to specify options, enclosed within square brackets.

```
#+TOC: headlines [currentsection]
```

Beamer specific code can be inserted with the following constructs:

```
#+BEAMER: \pause


#+BEGIN_BEAMER
All lines in this block will appear only when using this back-end.
#+END_BEAMER


Text @@beamer:some code@@ within a paragraph.
```

In particular, this last example can be used to add overlay specifications to objects whose type is among `bold`, `item`, `link`, `radio-target` and `target`, when the value is enclosed within angular brackets and put at the beginning the object.

```
A *@@beamer:<2->@@useful* feature
```

Eventually, every plain list has support for `:environment`, `:overlay` and `:options` attributes through `ATTR_BEAMER` affiliated keyword. The first one allows the use of a different environment, the second sets overlay specifications and the last one inserts optional arguments in current list environment.

```
#+ATTR_BEAMER: :overlay +-
- item 1
- item 2
```

Editing support

You can turn on a special minor mode `org-beamer-mode` for faster editing with:

```
#+STARTUP: beamer
```

`C-c C-b`   `org-beamer-select-environment`
    In `org-beamer-mode`, this key offers fast selection of a Beamer environment or the `BEAMER_COL` property.

An example

Here is a simple example Org document that is intended for Beamer export.

```
#+TITLE: Example Presentation
#+AUTHOR: Carsten Dominik
#+OPTIONS: H:2 toc:t num:t
#+LATEX_CLASS: beamer
#+LATEX_CLASS_OPTIONS: [presentation]
#+BEAMER_THEME: Madrid
#+COLUMNS: %45ITEM %10BEAMER_ENV(Env) %10BEAMER_ACT(Act) %4BEAMER_COL(Col) %8BEAMER_OPT(Opt)


* This is the first structural section


** Frame 1
*** Thanks to Eric Fraga                                     :B_block:
    :PROPERTIES:
    :BEAMER_COL: 0.48
```

```
         :BEAMER_ENV: block
         :END:
         for the first viable Beamer setup in Org
*** Thanks to everyone else                                          :B_block:
         :PROPERTIES:
         :BEAMER_COL: 0.48
         :BEAMER_ACT: <2->
         :BEAMER_ENV: block
         :END:
         for contributing to the discussion
**** This will be formatted as a beamer note                         :B_note:
          :PROPERTIES:
          :BEAMER_env: note
          :END:
** Frame 2 (where we will not use columns)
*** Request
         Please test this stuff!
```

12.6 HTML export

Org mode contains an HTML (XHTML 1.0 strict) exporter with extensive HTML formatting, in ways similar to John Gruber's *markdown* language, but with additional support for tables.

12.6.1 HTML export commands

C-c C-e h h   org-html-export-to-html
> Export as an HTML file. For an Org file `myfile.org`, the HTML file will be `myfile.html`. The file will be overwritten without warning. *C-c C-e h o* Export as an HTML file and immediately open it with a browser.

C-c C-e h H   org-html-export-as-html
> Export to a temporary buffer. Do not create a file.

12.6.2 HTML doctypes

Org can export to various (X)HTML flavors.

Setting the variable `org-html-doctype` allows you to export to different (X)HTML variants. The exported HTML will be adjusted according to the syntax requirements of that variant. You can either set this variable to a doctype string directly, in which case the exporter will try to adjust the syntax automatically, or you can use a ready-made doctype. The ready-made options are:

- "html4-strict"
- "html4-transitional"
- "html4-frameset"
- "xhtml-strict"
- "xhtml-transitional"
- "xhtml-frameset"
- "xhtml-11"
- "html5"
- "xhtml5"

See the variable `org-html-doctype-alist` for details. The default is "xhtml-strict".

Fancy HTML5 export

HTML5 introduces several new element types. By default, Org will not make use of these element types, but you can set `org-html-html5-fancy` to t (or set `html5-fancy` item in an `OPTIONS` line), to enable a few new block-level elements. These are created using arbitrary #+BEGIN and #+END blocks. For instance:

```
#+BEGIN_ASIDE
Lorem ipsum
#+END_ASIDE
```

Will export to:

```
<aside>
  <p>Lorem ipsum</p>
</aside>
```

While this:

```
#+ATTR_HTML: :controls controls :width 350
#+BEGIN_VIDEO
#+HTML: <source src="movie.mp4" type="video/mp4">
#+HTML: <source src="movie.ogg" type="video/ogg">
Your browser does not support the video tag.
#+END_VIDEO
```

Becomes:

```
<video controls="controls" width="350">
  <source src="movie.mp4" type="video/mp4">
  <source src="movie.ogg" type="video/ogg">
  <p>Your browser does not support the video tag.</p>
</video>
```

Special blocks that do not correspond to HTML5 elements (see `org-html-html5-elements`) will revert to the usual behavior, i.e., `#+BEGIN_LEDERHOSEN` will still export to '`<div class="lederhosen">`'.

Headlines cannot appear within special blocks. To wrap a headline and its contents in e.g., '`<section>`' or '`<article>`' tags, set the `HTML_CONTAINER` property on the headline itself.

12.6.3 HTML preamble and postamble

The HTML exporter lets you define a preamble and a postamble.

The default value for `org-html-preamble` is t, which means that the preamble is inserted depending on the relevant format string in `org-html-preamble-format`.

Setting `org-html-preamble` to a string will override the default format string. If you set it to a function, it will insert the output of the function, which must be a string. Setting to `nil` will not insert any preamble.

The default value for `org-html-postamble` is 'auto, which means that the HTML exporter will look for information about the author, the email, the creator and the date, and build the postamble from these values. Setting `org-html-postamble` to t will insert the postamble from the relevant format string found in `org-html-postamble-format`. Setting it to `nil` will not insert any postamble.

12.6.4 Quoting HTML tags

Plain '<' and '>' are always transformed to '<' and '>' in HTML export. If you want to include raw HTML code, which should only appear in HTML export, mark it with '@@html:' as in '@@html:@@bold text@@html:@@'. For more extensive HTML that should be copied verbatim to the exported file use either

```
#+HTML: Literal HTML code for export
```

or

```
#+BEGIN_HTML
All lines between these markers are exported literally
#+END_HTML
```

12.6.5 Links in HTML export

Internal links (see Section 4.2 [Internal links], page 37) will continue to work in HTML. This includes automatic links created by radio targets (see Section 4.2.1 [Radio targets], page 38). Links to external files will still work if the target file is on the same *relative* path as the published Org file. Links to other `.org` files will be translated into HTML links under the assumption that an HTML version also exists of the linked file, at the same relative path. 'id:' links can then be used to jump to specific entries across files. For information related to linking files while publishing them to a publishing directory see Section 13.1.6 [Publishing links], page 180.

If you want to specify attributes for links, you can do so using a special `#+ATTR_HTML` line to define attributes that will be added to the `<a>` or `<img>` tags. Here is an example that sets `title` and `style` attributes for a link:

```
#+ATTR_HTML: :title The Org mode homepage :style color:red;
[[http://orgmode.org]]
```

12.6.6 Tables in HTML export

Org mode tables are exported to HTML using the table attributes defined in `org-html-table-default-attributes`. The default setting makes tables without cell borders and frame. If you would like to change this for individual tables, place something like the following before the table:

```
#+CAPTION: This is a table with lines around and between cells
#+ATTR_HTML: :border 2 :rules all :frame border
```

You can also group columns in the HTML output (see Section 3.3 [Column groups], page 23).

Below is a list of options for customizing tables HTML export.

`org-html-table-align-individual-fields`
> Non-nil means attach style attributes for alignment to each table field.

`org-html-table-caption-above`
> When non-nil, place caption string at the beginning of the table.

`org-html-table-data-tags`
> The opening and ending tags for table data fields.

`org-html-table-default-attributes`
> Default attributes and values which will be used in table tags.

`org-html-table-header-tags`
> The opening and ending tags for table header fields.

`org-html-table-row-tags`
> The opening and ending tags for table rows.

`org-html-table-use-header-tags-for-first-column`
> Non-nil means format column one in tables with header tags.

12.6.7 Images in HTML export

HTML export can inline images given as links in the Org file, and it can make an image the clickable part of a link. By default[8], images are inlined if a link does not have a description. So '`[[file:myimg.jpg]]`' will be inlined, while '`[[file:myimg.jpg][the image]]`' will just produce a link '`the image`' that points to the image. If the description part itself is a `file:` link or a `http:` URL pointing to an image, this image will be inlined and activated so that clicking on the image will activate the link. For example, to include a thumbnail that will link to a high resolution version of the image, you could use:

```
[[file:highres.jpg][file:thumb.jpg]]
```

If you need to add attributes to an inlined image, use a `#+ATTR_HTML`. In the example below we specify the `alt` and `title` attributes to support text viewers and accessibility, and align it to the right.

```
#+CAPTION: A black cat stalking a spider
#+ATTR_HTML: :alt cat/spider image :title Action! :align right
[[./img/a.jpg]]
```

You could use `http` addresses just as well.

12.6.8 Math formatting in HTML export

LaTeX math snippets (see Section 11.7.3 [LaTeX fragments], page 134) can be displayed in two different ways on HTML pages. The default is to use the MathJax system which should work out of the box with Org mode installation because `http://orgmode.org` serves **MathJax** for Org mode users for small applications and for testing purposes. **If you plan to use this regularly or on pages with significant page views, you should install[9] MathJax on your own server in order to limit the load of our server.** To configure MathJax, use the variable `org-html-mathjax-options` or insert something like the following into the buffer:

```
#+HTML_MATHJAX: align:"left" mathml:t path:"/MathJax/MathJax.js"
```

See the docstring of the variable `org-html-mathjax-options` for the meaning of the parameters in this line.

---

[8] But see the variable `org-html-inline-images`.

[9] Installation instructions can be found on the MathJax website, see `http://www.mathjax.org/resources/docs/?installation.html`.

If you prefer, you can also request that LaTeX fragments are processed into small images that will be inserted into the browser page. Before the availability of MathJax, this was the default method for Org files. This method requires that the `dvipng` program or `imagemagick` suite is available on your system. You can still get this processing with

```
#+OPTIONS: tex:dvipng
```

or:

```
#+OPTIONS: tex:imagemagick
```

12.6.9 Text areas in HTML export

An alternative way to publish literal code examples in HTML is to use text areas, where the example can even be edited before pasting it into an application. It is triggered by `:textarea` attribute at an `example` or `src` block.

You may also use `:height` and `:width` attributes to specify the height and width of the text area, which default to the number of lines in the example, and 80, respectively. For example

```
#+ATTR_HTML: :textarea t :width 40
#+BEGIN_EXAMPLE
  (defun org-xor (a b)
    "Exclusive or."
    (if a (not b) b))
#+END_EXAMPLE
```

12.6.10 CSS support

You can modify the CSS style definitions for the exported file. The HTML exporter assigns the following special CSS classes[10] to appropriate parts of the document—your style specifications may change these, in addition to any of the standard classes like for headlines, tables, etc.

`p.author`	author information, including email
`p.date`	publishing date
`p.creator`	creator info, about org mode version
`.title`	document title
`.todo`	TODO keywords, all not-done states
`.done`	the DONE keywords, all states that count as done
`.WAITING`	each TODO keyword also uses a class named after itself
`.timestamp`	timestamp
`.timestamp-kwd`	keyword associated with a timestamp, like SCHEDULED
`.timestamp-wrapper`	span around keyword plus timestamp
`.tag`	tag in a headline
`._HOME`	each tag uses itself as a class, "@" replaced by "_"
`.target`	target for links
`.linenr`	the line number in a code example
`.code-highlighted`	for highlighting referenced code lines
`div.outline-N`	div for outline level N (headline plus text))

---

[10] If the classes on TODO keywords and tags lead to conflicts, use the variables `org-html-todo-kwd-class-prefix` and `org-html-tag-class-prefix` to make them unique.

`div.outline-text-N`	extra div for text at outline level N
`.section-number-N`	section number in headlines, different for each level
`.figure-number`	label like "Figure 1:"
`.table-number`	label like "Table 1:"
`.listing-number`	label like "Listing 1:"
`div.figure`	how to format an inlined image
`pre.src`	formatted source code
`pre.example`	normal example
`p.verse`	verse paragraph
`div.footnotes`	footnote section headline
`p.footnote`	footnote definition paragraph, containing a footnote
`.footref`	a footnote reference number (always a <sup>)
`.footnum`	footnote number in footnote definition (always <sup>)

Each exported file contains a compact default style that defines these classes in a basic way[11]. You may overwrite these settings, or add to them by using the variables **org-html-head** and **org-html-head-extra**. You can override the global values of these variables for each file by using these keywords:

\#+HTML_HEAD: <link rel="stylesheet" type="text/css" href="style1.css" />
\#+HTML_HEAD_EXTRA: <link rel="alternate stylesheet" type="text/css" href="style2.css" />

For longer style definitions, you can use several such lines. You could also directly write a **<style> </style>** section in this way, without referring to an external file.

In order to add styles to a subtree, use the `:HTML_CONTAINER_CLASS:` property to assign a class to the tree. In order to specify CSS styles for a particular headline, you can use the id specified in a `:CUSTOM_ID:` property.

12.6.11 JavaScript supported display of web pages

Sebastian Rose has written a JavaScript program especially designed to enhance the web viewing experience of HTML files created with Org. This program allows you to view large files in two different ways. The first one is an *Info*-like mode where each section is displayed separately and navigation can be done with the *n* and *p* keys (and some other keys as well, press *?* for an overview of the available keys). The second view type is a *folding* view much like Org provides inside Emacs. The script is available at http://orgmode.org/ org-info.js and you can find the documentation for it at http://orgmode.org/worg/ code/org-info-js/. We host the script at our site, but if you use it a lot, you might not want to be dependent on http://orgmode.org and prefer to install a local copy on your own web server.

All it then takes to use this program is adding a single line to the Org file:

\#+INFOJS_OPT: view:info toc:nil

If this line is found, the HTML header will automatically contain the code needed to invoke the script. Using the line above, you can set the following viewing options:

path: The path to the script. The default is to grab the script from

---

[11] This style is defined in the constant `org-html-style-default`, which you should not modify. To turn inclusion of these defaults off, customize `org-html-head-include-default-style` or set `html-style` to `nil` in an `OPTIONS` line.

	`http://orgmode.org/org-info.js`, but you might want to have a local copy and use a path like '`../scripts/org-info.js`'.
`view:`	Initial view when the website is first shown. Possible values are:

`info`	Info-like interface with one section per page.
`overview`	Folding interface, initially showing only top-level.
`content`	Folding interface, starting with all headlines visible.
`showall`	Folding interface, all headlines and text visible.

`sdepth:`	Maximum headline level that will still become an independent section for info and folding modes. The default is taken from `org-export-headline-levels` (= the H switch in `#+OPTIONS`). If this is smaller than in `org-export-headline-levels`, each info/folding section can still contain child headlines.
`toc:`	Should the table of contents *initially* be visible? Even when `nil`, you can always get to the "toc" with *i*.
`tdepth:`	The depth of the table of contents. The defaults are taken from the variables `org-export-headline-levels` and `org-export-with-toc`.
`ftoc:`	Does the CSS of the page specify a fixed position for the "toc"? If yes, the toc will never be displayed as a section.
`ltoc:`	Should there be short contents (children) in each section? Make this `above` if the section should be above initial text.
`mouse:`	Headings are highlighted when the mouse is over them. Should be '`underline`' (default) or a background color like '`#cccccc`'.
`buttons:`	Should view-toggle buttons be everywhere? When `nil` (the default), only one such button will be present.

You can choose default values for these options by customizing the variable `org-html-infojs-options`. If you always want to apply the script to your pages, configure the variable `org-html-use-infojs`.

12.7 LaTeX and PDF export

LaTeX export can produce an arbitrarily complex LaTeX document of any standard or custom document class. With further processing[12], which the LaTeX exporter is able to control, this back-end is able to produce PDF output. Because the LaTeX exporter can be configured to use the `hyperref` package, the default setup produces fully-linked PDF output.

As in LaTeX, blank lines are meaningful for this back-end: a paragraph will not be started if two contiguous syntactical elements are not separated by an empty line.

This back-end also offers enhanced support for footnotes. Thus, it handles nested footnotes, footnotes in tables and footnotes in a list item's description.

---

[12] The default LaTeX output is designed for processing with `pdftex` or LaTeX. It includes packages that are not compatible with `xetex` and possibly `luatex`. The LaTeX exporter can be configured to support alternative TeX engines, see the options `org-latex-default-packages-alist` and `org-latex-packages-alist`.

12.7.1 LaTeX export commands

`C-c C-e l l`   `org-latex-export-to-latex`
> Export as a LaTeX file. For an Org file `myfile.org`, the LaTeX file will be `myfile.tex`. The file will be overwritten without warning.

`C-c C-e l L`   `org-latex-export-as-latex`
> Export to a temporary buffer. Do not create a file.

`C-c C-e l p`   `org-latex-export-to-pdf`
> Export as LaTeX and then process to PDF.

`C-c C-e l o`
> Export as LaTeX and then process to PDF, then open the resulting PDF file.

12.7.2 Header and sectioning structure

By default, the first three outline levels become headlines, defining a general document structure. Additional levels are exported as `itemize` or `enumerate` lists. The transition can also occur at a different level (see Section 12.3 [Export settings], page 138).

By default, the LaTeX output uses the class `article`.

You can change this globally by setting a different value for `org-latex-default-class` or locally by adding an option like `#+LATEX_CLASS: myclass` in your file, or with a `EXPORT_LATEX_CLASS` property that applies when exporting a region containing only this (sub)tree. The class must be listed in `org-latex-classes`. This variable defines a header template for each class[13], and allows you to define the sectioning structure for each class. You can also define your own classes there.

The `LATEX_CLASS_OPTIONS` keyword or `EXPORT_LATEX_CLASS_OPTIONS` property can specify the options for the `\documentclass` macro. These options have to be provided, as expected by LaTeX, within square brackets.

You can also use the `LATEX_HEADER` and `LATEX_HEADER_EXTRA`[14] keywords in order to add lines to the header. See the docstring of `org-latex-classes` for more information.

An example is shown below.

```
#+LATEX_CLASS: article
#+LATEX_CLASS_OPTIONS: [a4paper]
#+LATEX_HEADER: \usepackage{xyz}


* Headline 1
  some text
```

12.7.3 Quoting LaTeX code

Embedded LaTeX as described in Section 11.7 [Embedded LaTeX], page 133, will be correctly inserted into the LaTeX file. Furthermore, you can add special code that should only be present in LaTeX export with the following constructs:

---

[13] Into which the values of `org-latex-default-packages-alist` and `org-latex-packages-alist` are spliced.

[14] Unlike `LATEX_HEADER`, contents from `LATEX_HEADER_EXTRA` keywords will not be loaded when previewing LaTeX snippets (see Section 11.7.4 [Previewing LaTeX fragments], page 134).

```
Code within @@latex:some code@@ a paragraph.

#+LATEX: Literal LaTeX code for export

#+BEGIN_LATEX
All lines between these markers are exported literally
#+END_LATEX
```

12.7.4 LaTeX specific attributes

LaTeX understands attributes specified in an `ATTR_LATEX` line. They affect tables, images, plain lists, special blocks and source blocks.

Tables in LaTeX export

For LaTeX export of a table, you can specify a label and a caption (see Section 11.2 [Images and tables], page 129). You can also use attributes to control table layout and contents. Valid LaTeX attributes include:

`:mode`   Nature of table's contents. It can be set to `table`, `math`, `inline-math` or `verbatim`. In particular, when in `math` or `inline-math` mode, every cell is exported as-is, horizontal rules are ignored and the table will be wrapped in a math environment. Also, contiguous tables sharing the same math mode will be wrapped within the same environment. Default mode is determined in `org-latex-default-table-mode`.

`:environment`

      Environment used for the table. It can be set to any LaTeX table environment, like `tabularx`[15], `longtable`, `array`, `tabu`[16], `bmatrix`... It defaults to `org-latex-default-table-environment` value.

`:caption`   `#+CAPTION` keyword is the simplest way to set a caption for a table (see Section 11.2 [Images and tables], page 129). If you need more advanced commands for that task, you can use `:caption` attribute instead. Its value should be raw LaTeX code. It has precedence over `#+CAPTION`.

`:float`
`:placement`

      The `:float` specifies the float environment for the table. Possible values are `sideways`[17], `multicolumn`, `t` and `nil`. When unspecified, a table with a caption will have a `table` environment. Moreover, the `:placement` attribute can specify the positioning of the float. Note: `:placement` is ignored for `:float sideways` tables.

`:align`
`:font`
`:width`   Set, respectively, the alignment string of the table, its font size and its width. They only apply on regular tables.

---

[15] Requires adding the `tabularx` package to `org-latex-packages-alist`.

[16] Requires adding the `tabu` package to `org-latex-packages-alist`.

[17] Formerly, the value was `sidewaystable`. This is deprecated since Org 8.3.

:spread   Boolean specific to the `tabu` and `longtabu` environments, and only takes effect when used in conjunction with the `:width` attribute. When `:spread` is non-`nil`, the table will be spread or shrunk by the value of `:width`.

:booktabs
:center
:rmlines   They toggle, respectively, `booktabs` usage (assuming the package is properly loaded), table centering and removal of every horizontal rule but the first one (in a "table.el" table only). In particular, `org-latex-tables-booktabs` (respectively `org-latex-tables-centered`) activates the first (respectively second) attribute globally.

:math-prefix
:math-suffix
:math-arguments   A string that will be inserted, respectively, before the table within the math environment, after the table within the math environment, and between the macro name and the contents of the table. The `:math-arguments` attribute is used for matrix macros that require more than one argument (e.g., `qbordermatrix`).

Thus, attributes can be used in a wide array of situations, like writing a table that will span over multiple pages, or a matrix product:

```
#+ATTR_LATEX: :environment longtable :align l|lp{3cm}r|l
| ..... | ..... |
| ..... | ..... |
```

```
#+ATTR_LATEX: :mode math :environment bmatrix :math-suffix \times
| a | b |
| c | d |
#+ATTR_LATEX: :mode math :environment bmatrix
| 1 | 2 |
| 3 | 4 |
```

In the example below, LaTeX command \bicaption{HeadingA}{HeadingB} will set the caption.

```
#+ATTR_LATEX: :caption \bicaption{HeadingA}{HeadingB}
| ..... | ..... |
| ..... | ..... |
```

Images in LaTeX export

Images that are linked to without a description part in the link, like '`[[file:img.jpg]]`' or '`[[./img.jpg]]`' will be inserted into the PDF output file resulting from LaTeX processing. Org will use an `\includegraphics` macro to insert the image[18].

You can specify specify image width or height with, respectively, `:width` and `:height` attributes. It is also possible to add any other option with the `:options` attribute, as shown in the following example:

---

[18] In the case of TikZ (http://sourceforge.net/projects/pgf/) images, it will become an `\input` macro wrapped within a `tikzpicture` environment.

```
#+ATTR_LATEX: :width 5cm :options angle=90
[[./img/sed-hr4049.pdf]]
```

If you need a specific command for the caption, use `:caption` attribute. It will override standard `#+CAPTION` value, if any.

```
#+ATTR_LATEX: :caption \bicaption{HeadingA}{HeadingB}
[[./img/sed-hr4049.pdf]]
```

If you have specified a caption as described in Section 11.2 [Images and tables], page 129, the picture will be wrapped into a `figure` environment and thus become a floating element. You can also ask Org to export an image as a float without specifying caption by setting the `:float` attribute. You may also set it to:

— `t`: if you want to use the standard 'figure' environment. It is used by default if you provide a caption to the image.

— `multicolumn`: if you wish to include an image which spans multiple columns in a page. This will export the image wrapped in a `figure*` environment.

— `wrap`: if you would like to let text flow around the image. It will make the figure occupy the left half of the page.

— `sideways`: if you would like the image to appear alone on a separate page rotated ninety degrees using the `sidewaysfigure` environment. Setting this `:float` option will ignore the `:placement` setting.

— `nil`: if you need to avoid any floating environment, even when a caption is provided.

To modify the placement option of any floating environment, set the `placement` attribute.

```
#+ATTR_LATEX: :float wrap :width 0.38\textwidth :placement {r}{0.4\textwidth}
[[./img/hst.png]]
```

If the `:comment-include` attribute is set to a non-nil value, the LaTeX `\includegraphics` macro will be commented out.

Plain lists in LaTeX export

Plain lists accept two optional attributes: `:environment` and `:options`. The first one allows the use of a non-standard environment (e.g., 'inparaenum'). The second one specifies additional arguments for that environment.

```
#+ATTR_LATEX: :environment compactitem :options [$\circ$]
- you need ``paralist'' package to reproduce this example.
```

Source blocks in LaTeX export

In addition to syntax defined in Section 11.3 [Literal examples], page 130, names and captions (see Section 11.2 [Images and tables], page 129), source blocks also accept two additional attributes: `:float` and `:options`.

You may set the former to

— `t`: if you want to make the source block a float. It is the default value when a caption is provided.

— `multicolumn`: if you wish to include a source block which spans multiple columns in a page.

— `nil`: if you need to avoid any floating environment, even when a caption is provided. It is useful for source code that may not fit in a single page.

```
#+ATTR_LATEX: :float nil
#+BEGIN_SRC emacs-lisp
Code that may not fit in a single page.
#+END_SRC
```

The latter allows to specify options relative to the package used to highlight code in the output (e.g., `listings`). This is the local counterpart to `org-latex-listings-options` and `org-latex-minted-options` variables, which see.

```
#+ATTR_LATEX: :options commentstyle=\bfseries
#+BEGIN_SRC emacs-lisp
  (defun Fib (n)                            ; Count rabbits.
    (if (< n 2) n (+ (Fib (- n 1)) (Fib (- n 2)))))
#+END_SRC
```

Special blocks in LaTeX export

In LaTeX back-end, special blocks become environments of the same name. Value of `:options` attribute will be appended as-is to that environment's opening string. For example:

```
#+BEGIN_ABSTRACT
We demonstrate how to solve the Syracuse problem.
#+END_ABSTRACT

#+ATTR_LATEX: :options [Proof of important theorem]
#+BEGIN_PROOF
...
Therefore, any even number greater than 2 is the sum of two primes.
#+END_PROOF
```

becomes

```
\begin{abstract}
We demonstrate how to solve the Syracuse problem.
\end{abstract}

\begin{proof}[Proof of important theorem]
...
Therefore, any even number greater than 2 is the sum of two primes.
\end{proof}
```

If you need to insert a specific caption command, use `:caption` attribute. It will override standard `#+CAPTION` value, if any. For example:

```
#+ATTR_LATEX: :caption \MyCaption{HeadingA}
#+BEGIN_PROOF
...
#+END_PROOF
```

Horizontal rules

Width and thickness of a given horizontal rule can be controlled with, respectively, `:width` and `:thickness` attributes:

```
#+ATTR_LATEX: :width .6\textwidth :thickness 0.8pt
-----
```

12.8 Markdown export

`md` export back-end generates Markdown syntax[19] for an Org mode buffer.

It is built over HTML back-end: any construct not supported by Markdown syntax (e.g., tables) will be controlled and translated by `html` back-end (see Section 12.6 [HTML export], page 145).

Markdown export commands

C-c C-e m m   org-md-export-to-markdown

      Export as a text file written in Markdown syntax. For an Org file, `myfile.org`, the resulting file will be `myfile.md`. The file will be overwritten without warning.

C-c C-e m M   org-md-export-as-markdown

      Export to a temporary buffer. Do not create a file.

C-c C-e m o

      Export as a text file with Markdown syntax, then open it.

Header and sectioning structure

Markdown export can generate both `atx` and `setext` types for headlines, according to `org-md-headline-style`. The former introduces a hard limit of two levels, whereas the latter pushes it to six. Headlines below that limit are exported as lists. You can also set a soft limit before that one (see Section 12.3 [Export settings], page 138).

12.9 OpenDocument text export

Org mode[20] supports export to OpenDocument Text (ODT) format. Documents created by this exporter use the *OpenDocument-v1.2 specification*[21] and are compatible with LibreOffice 3.4.

12.9.1 Pre-requisites for ODT export

The ODT exporter relies on the `zip` program to create the final output. Check the availability of this program before proceeding further.

12.9.2 ODT export commands

---

[19] Vanilla flavor, as defined at `http://daringfireball.net/projects/markdown/`.

[20] Versions 7.8 or later

[21] Open Document Format for Office Applications (OpenDocument) Version 1.2

Exporting to ODT

`C-c C-e o o`   `org-odt-export-to-odt`
> Export as OpenDocument Text file.
>
> If `org-odt-preferred-output-format` is specified, automatically convert the exported file to that format. See [Automatically exporting to other formats], page 158.
>
> For an Org file `myfile.org`, the ODT file will be `myfile.odt`. The file will be overwritten without warning. If there is an active region,[22] only the region will be exported. If the selected region is a single tree,[23] the tree head will become the document title. If the tree head entry has, or inherits, an `EXPORT_FILE_NAME` property, that name will be used for the export.
>
> `C-c C-e o O` Export as an OpenDocument Text file and open the resulting file.
>
> If `org-odt-preferred-output-format` is specified, open the converted file instead. See [Automatically exporting to other formats], page 158.

12.9.3 Extending ODT export

The ODT exporter can interface with a variety of document converters and supports popular converters out of the box. As a result, you can use it to export to formats like 'doc' or convert a document from one format (say 'csv') to another format (say 'ods' or 'xls').

If you have a working installation of LibreOffice, a document converter is pre-configured for you and you can use it right away. If you would like to use `unoconv` as your preferred converter, customize the variable `org-odt-convert-process` to point to `unoconv`. You can also use your own favorite converter or tweak the default settings of the `LibreOffice` and 'unoconv' converters. See [Configuring a document converter], page 163.

Automatically exporting to other formats

Very often, you will find yourself exporting to ODT format, only to immediately save the exported document to other formats like 'doc', 'docx', 'rtf', 'pdf' etc. In such cases, you can specify your preferred output format by customizing the variable `org-odt-preferred-output-format`. This way, the export commands (see [Exporting to ODT], page 158) can be extended to export to a format that is of immediate interest to you.

Converting between document formats

There are many document converters in the wild which support conversion to and from various file formats, including, but not limited to the ODT format. LibreOffice converter, mentioned above, is one such converter. Once a converter is configured, you can interact with it using the following command.

`M-x org-odt-convert RET`
> Convert an existing document from one format to another. With a prefix argument, also open the newly produced file.

---

[22] This requires `transient-mark-mode` to be turned on

[23] To select the current subtree, use `C-c @`

12.9.4 Applying custom styles

The ODT exporter ships with a set of OpenDocument styles (see [Working with Open-Document style files], page 164) that ensure a well-formatted output. These factory styles, however, may not cater to your specific tastes. To customize the output, you can either modify the above styles files directly, or generate the required styles using an application like LibreOffice. The latter method is suitable for expert and non-expert users alike, and is described here.

Applying custom styles: the easy way

1. Create a sample `example.org` file with the below settings and export it to ODT format.

   `#+OPTIONS: H:10 num:t`

2. Open the above `example.odt` using LibreOffice. Use the `Stylist` to locate the target styles—these typically have the 'Org' prefix—and modify those to your taste. Save the modified file either as an OpenDocument Text (`.odt`) or OpenDocument Template (`.ott`) file.

3. Customize the variable `org-odt-styles-file` and point it to the newly created file. For additional configuration options see [Overriding factory styles], page 164.

   If you would like to choose a style on a per-file basis, you can use the `#+ODT_STYLES_FILE` option. A typical setting will look like

   `#+ODT_STYLES_FILE: "/path/to/example.ott"`

   or

   `#+ODT_STYLES_FILE: ("/path/to/file.ott" ("styles.xml" "image/hdr.png"))`

Using third-party styles and templates

You can use third-party styles and templates for customizing your output. This will produce the desired output only if the template provides all style names that the 'ODT' exporter relies on. Unless this condition is met, the output is going to be less than satisfactory. So it is highly recommended that you only work with templates that are directly derived from the factory settings.

12.9.5 Links in ODT export

ODT exporter creates native cross-references for internal links. It creates Internet-style links for all other links.

A link with no description and destined to a regular (un-itemized) outline heading is replaced with a cross-reference and section number of the heading.

A '`\ref{label}`'-style reference to an image, table etc. is replaced with a cross-reference and sequence number of the labeled entity. See Section 12.9.9 [Labels and captions in ODT export], page 163.

12.9.6 Tables in ODT export

Export of native Org mode tables (see Chapter 3 [Tables], page 19) and simple `table.el` tables is supported. However, export of complex `table.el` tables—tables that have column or row spans—is not supported. Such tables are stripped from the exported document.

By default, a table is exported with top and bottom frames and with rules separating row and column groups (see Section 3.3 [Column groups], page 23). Furthermore, all tables are typeset to occupy the same width. If the table specifies alignment and relative width for its columns (see Section 3.2 [Column width and alignment], page 22) then these are honored on export.[24]

You can control the width of the table by specifying `:rel-width` property using an `#+ATTR_ODT` line.

For example, consider the following table which makes use of all the rules mentioned above.

```
#+ATTR_ODT: :rel-width 50
| Area/Month    |  Jan |  Feb |  Mar |  Sum |
|---------------+------+------+------+------|
| /             |  <   |      |      |  <   |
| <l13>         | <r5> | <r5> | <r5> | <r6> |
| North America |    1 |   21 |  926 |  948 |
| Middle East   |    6 |   75 |  844 |  925 |
| Asia Pacific  |    9 |   27 |  790 |  826 |
|---------------+------+------+------+------|
| Sum           |   16 |  123 | 2560 | 2699 |
```

On export, the table will occupy 50% of text area. The columns will be sized (roughly) in the ratio of 13:5:5:5:6. The first column will be left-aligned and rest of the columns will be right-aligned. There will be vertical rules after separating the header and last columns from other columns. There will be horizontal rules separating the header and last rows from other rows.

If you are not satisfied with the above formatting options, you can create custom table styles and associate them with a table using the `#+ATTR_ODT` line. See [Customizing tables in ODT export], page 166.

12.9.7 Images in ODT export

Embedding images

You can embed images within the exported document by providing a link to the desired image file with no link description. For example, to embed 'img.png' do either of the following:

```
[[file:img.png]]
```

```
[[./img.png]]
```

Embedding clickable images

You can create clickable images by providing a link whose description is a link to an image file. For example, to embed a image `org-mode-unicorn.png` which when clicked jumps to `http://Orgmode.org` website, do the following

```
[[http://orgmode.org][./org-mode-unicorn.png]]
```

---

[24] The column widths are interpreted as weighted ratios with the default weight being 1

Sizing and scaling of embedded images

You can control the size and scale of the embedded images using the `#+ATTR_ODT` attribute.

The exporter specifies the desired size of the image in the final document in units of centimeters. In order to scale the embedded images, the exporter queries for pixel dimensions of the images using one of a) ImageMagick's `identify` program or b) Emacs 'create-image' and 'image-size' APIs[25]. The pixel dimensions are subsequently converted in to units of centimeters using `org-odt-pixels-per-inch`. The default value of this variable is set to `display-pixels-per-inch`. You can tweak this variable to achieve the best results.

The examples below illustrate the various possibilities.

Explicitly size the image
> To embed `img.png` as a 10 cm x 10 cm image, do the following:
>
> ```
> #+ATTR_ODT: :width 10 :height 10
> [[./img.png]]
> ```

Scale the image
> To embed `img.png` at half its size, do the following:
>
> ```
> #+ATTR_ODT: :scale 0.5
> [[./img.png]]
> ```

Scale the image to a specific width
> To embed `img.png` with a width of 10 cm while retaining the original height:width ratio, do the following:
>
> ```
> #+ATTR_ODT: :width 10
> [[./img.png]]
> ```

Scale the image to a specific height
> To embed `img.png` with a height of 10 cm while retaining the original height:width ratio, do the following
>
> ```
> #+ATTR_ODT: :height 10
> [[./img.png]]
> ```

Anchoring of images

You can control the manner in which an image is anchored by setting the `:anchor` property of it's `#+ATTR_ODT` line. You can specify one of the following three values for the `:anchor` property: '`"as-char"`', '`"paragraph"`' and '`"page"`'.

To create an image that is anchored to a page, do the following:

```
#+ATTR_ODT: :anchor "page"
[[./img.png]]
```

12.9.8 Math formatting in ODT export

The ODT exporter has special support for handling math.

---

[25] Use of `ImageMagick` is only desirable. However, if you routinely produce documents that have large images or you export your Org files that has images using a Emacs batch script, then the use of `ImageMagick` is mandatory.

Working with LaTeX math snippets

LaTeX math snippets (see Section 11.7.3 [LaTeX fragments], page 134) can be embedded in the ODT document in one of the following ways:

1. MathML

   This option is activated on a per-file basis with

   ```
   #+OPTIONS: LaTeX:t
   ```

   With this option, LaTeX fragments are first converted into MathML fragments using an external LaTeX-to-MathML converter program. The resulting MathML fragments are then embedded as an OpenDocument Formula in the exported document.

   You can specify the LaTeX-to-MathML converter by customizing the variables `org-latex-to-mathml-convert-command` and `org-latex-to-mathml-jar-file`.

   If you prefer to use `MathToWeb`[26] as your converter, you can configure the above variables as shown below.

   ```
   (setq org-latex-to-mathml-convert-command
       "java -jar %j -unicode -force -df %o %I"
       org-latex-to-mathml-jar-file
       "/path/to/mathtoweb.jar")
   ```

   You can use the following commands to quickly verify the reliability of the LaTeX-to-MathML converter.

   M-x org-odt-export-as-odf RET

   > Convert a LaTeX math snippet to an OpenDocument formula (`.odf`) file.

   M-x org-odt-export-as-odf-and-open RET

   > Convert a LaTeX math snippet to an OpenDocument formula (`.odf`) file and open the formula file with the system-registered application.

2. PNG images

   This option is activated on a per-file basis with

   ```
   #+OPTIONS: tex:dvipng
   ```

   or:

   ```
   #+OPTIONS: tex:imagemagick
   ```

   With this option, LaTeX fragments are processed into PNG images and the resulting images are embedded in the exported document. This method requires that the `dvipng` program or `imagemagick` suite be available on your system.

Working with MathML or OpenDocument formula files

For various reasons, you may find embedding LaTeX math snippets in an ODT document less than reliable. In that case, you can embed a math equation by linking to its MathML (`.mml`) source or its OpenDocument formula (`.odf`) file as shown below:

```
[[./equation.mml]]
```

or

```
[[./equation.odf]]
```

---

[26] See MathToWeb

12.9.9 Labels and captions in ODT export

You can label and caption various category of objects—an inline image, a table, a LaTeX fragment or a Math formula—using #+LABEL and #+CAPTION lines. See Section 11.2 [Images and tables], page 129. ODT exporter enumerates each labeled or captioned object of a given category separately. As a result, each such object is assigned a sequence number based on order of it's appearance in the Org file.

In the exported document, a user-provided caption is augmented with the category and sequence number. Consider the following inline image in an Org file.

```
#+CAPTION: Bell curve
#+LABEL:   fig:SED-HR4049
[[./img/a.png]]
```

It could be rendered as shown below in the exported document.

```
Figure 2: Bell curve
```

You can modify the category component of the caption by customizing the option `org-odt-category-map-alist`. For example, to tag all embedded images with the string 'Illustration' (instead of the default '`Figure`') use the following setting:

(setq org-odt-category-map-alist
    (("__Figure__" "Illustration" "value" "Figure" org-odt–enumerable-image-p)))

With this, previous image will be captioned as below in the exported document.

```
Illustration 2: Bell curve
```

12.9.10 Literal examples in ODT export

Export of literal examples (see Section 11.3 [Literal examples], page 130) with full fontification is supported. Internally, the exporter relies on `htmlfontify.el` to generate all style definitions needed for a fancy listing.[27] The auto-generated styles have '`OrgSrc`' as prefix and inherit their color from the faces used by Emacs `font-lock` library for the source language.

If you prefer to use your own custom styles for fontification, you can do so by customizing the option `org-odt-create-custom-styles-for-srcblocks`.

You can turn off fontification of literal examples by customizing the option `org-odt-fontify-srcblocks`.

12.9.11 Advanced topics in ODT export

If you rely heavily on ODT export, you may want to exploit the full set of features that the exporter offers. This section describes features that would be of interest to power users.

Configuring a document converter

The ODT exporter can work with popular converters with little or no extra configuration from your side. See Section 12.9.3 [Extending ODT export], page 158. If you are using a converter that is not supported by default or if you would like to tweak the default converter settings, proceed as below.

---

[27] Your `htmlfontify.el` library must at least be at Emacs 24.1 levels for fontification to be turned on.

1. Register the converter

   Name your converter and add it to the list of known converters by customizing the
   option `org-odt-convert-processes`. Also specify how the converter can be invoked
   via command-line to effect the conversion.

2. Configure its capabilities

   Specify the set of formats the converter can handle by customizing the variable
   `org-odt-convert-capabilities`. Use the default value for this variable as a guide
   for configuring your converter. As suggested by the default setting, you can specify
   the full set of formats supported by the converter and not limit yourself to specifying
   formats that are related to just the OpenDocument Text format.

3. Choose the converter

   Select the newly added converter as the preferred one by customizing the option
   `org-odt-convert-process`.

Working with OpenDocument style files

This section explores the internals of the ODT exporter and the means by which it produces
styled documents. Read this section if you are interested in exploring the automatic and
custom OpenDocument styles used by the exporter.

a) Factory styles

The ODT exporter relies on two files for generating its output. These files are bundled with
the distribution under the directory pointed to by the variable `org-odt-styles-dir`. The
two files are:

- `OrgOdtStyles.xml`

  This file contributes to the `styles.xml` file of the final 'ODT' document. This file gets
  modified for the following purposes:

  1. To control outline numbering based on user settings.
  2. To add styles generated by `htmlfontify.el` for fontification of code blocks.

- `OrgOdtContentTemplate.xml`

  This file contributes to the `content.xml` file of the final 'ODT' document. The contents
  of the Org outline are inserted between the '`<office:text>`'...'`</office:text>`' elements of this file.

  Apart from serving as a template file for the final `content.xml`, the file serves the
  following purposes:

  1. It contains automatic styles for formatting of tables which are referenced by the
     exporter.
  2. It contains '`<text:sequence-decl>`'...'`</text:sequence-decl>`' elements that
     control how various entities—tables, images, equations, etc.—are numbered.

b) Overriding factory styles

The following two variables control the location from which the ODT exporter picks up the
custom styles and content template files. You can customize these variables to override the
factory styles used by the exporter.

- `org-odt-styles-file`

  Use this variable to specify the `styles.xml` that will be used in the final output. You can specify one of the following values:

  1. A `styles.xml` file

     Use this file instead of the default `styles.xml`

  2. A `.odt` or `.ott` file

     Use the `styles.xml` contained in the specified OpenDocument Text or Template file

  3. A `.odt` or `.ott` file and a subset of files contained within them

     Use the `styles.xml` contained in the specified OpenDocument Text or Template file. Additionally extract the specified member files and embed those within the final 'ODT' document.

     Use this option if the `styles.xml` file references additional files like header and footer images.

  4. `nil`

     Use the default `styles.xml`

- `org-odt-content-template-file`

  Use this variable to specify the blank `content.xml` that will be used in the final output.

Creating one-off styles

There are times when you would want one-off formatting in the exported document. You can achieve this by embedding raw OpenDocument XML in the Org file. The use of this feature is better illustrated with couple of examples.

1. Embedding ODT tags as part of regular text

   You can inline OpenDocument syntax by enclosing it within '`@@odt:...@@`' markup. For example, to highlight a region of text do the following:

   ```
   @@odt:<text:span text:style-name="Highlight">This is a highlighted
   text</text:span>@@.  But this is a regular text.
   ```

   Hint: To see the above example in action, edit your `styles.xml` (see [Factory styles], page 164) and add a custom '`Highlight`' style as shown below.

   ```
   <style:style style:name="Highlight" style:family="text">
     <style:text-properties fo:background-color="#ff0000"/>
   </style:style>
   ```

2. Embedding a one-line OpenDocument XML

   You can add a simple OpenDocument one-liner using the `#+ODT:` directive. For example, to force a page break do the following:

   ```
   #+ODT: <text:p text:style-name="PageBreak"/>
   ```

   Hint: To see the above example in action, edit your `styles.xml` (see [Factory styles], page 164) and add a custom '`PageBreak`' style as shown below.

   ```
   <style:style style:name="PageBreak" style:family="paragraph"
                style:parent-style-name="Text_20_body">
     <style:paragraph-properties fo:break-before="page"/>
   </style:style>
   ```

3. Embedding a block of OpenDocument XML

You can add a large block of OpenDocument XML using the `#+BEGIN_ODT...#+END_ODT` construct.

For example, to create a one-off paragraph that uses bold text, do the following:

```
#+BEGIN_ODT
<text:p text:style-name="Text_20_body_20_bold">
This paragraph is specially formatted and uses bold text.
</text:p>
#+END_ODT
```

Customizing tables in ODT export

You can override the default formatting of the table by specifying a custom table style with the `#+ATTR_ODT` line. For a discussion on default formatting of tables see Section 12.9.6 [Tables in ODT export], page 159.

This feature closely mimics the way table templates are defined in the OpenDocument-v1.2 specification.[28]

To have a quick preview of this feature, install the below setting and export the table that follows:

```
(setq org-odt-table-styles
    (append org-odt-table-styles
        '(("TableWithHeaderRowAndColumn" "Custom"
           ((use-first-row-styles . t)
            (use-first-column-styles . t)))
          ("TableWithFirstRowandLastRow" "Custom"
           ((use-first-row-styles . t)
            (use-last-row-styles . t))))))

#+ATTR_ODT: :style "TableWithHeaderRowAndColumn"
| Name  | Phone | Age |
| Peter | 1234  | 17  |
| Anna  | 4321  | 25  |
```

In the above example, you used a template named 'Custom' and installed two table styles with the names 'TableWithHeaderRowAndColumn' and 'TableWithFirstRowandLastRow'. (**Important:** The OpenDocument styles needed for producing the above template have been pre-defined for you. These styles are available under the section marked 'Custom Table Template' in `OrgOdtContentTemplate.xml` (see [Factory styles], page 164). If you need additional templates you have to define these styles yourselves.

To use this feature proceed as follows:

1. Create a table template[29]

   A table template is nothing but a set of 'table-cell' and 'paragraph' styles for each of the following table cell categories:

   − Body

---

[28] OpenDocument-v1.2 Specification

[29] See the `<table:table-template>` element of the OpenDocument-v1.2 specification

- First column
- Last column
- First row
- Last row
- Even row
- Odd row
- Even column
- Odd Column

The names for the above styles must be chosen based on the name of the table template using a well-defined convention.

The naming convention is better illustrated with an example. For a table template with the name 'Custom', the needed style names are listed in the following table.

Table cell type	table-cell style	paragraph style
Body	'CustomTableCell'	'CustomTableParagraph'
First column	'CustomFirstColumnTableCell'	'CustomFirstColumnTableParagraph'
Last column	'CustomLastColumnTableCell'	'CustomLastColumnTableParagraph'
First row	'CustomFirstRowTableCell'	'CustomFirstRowTableParagraph'
Last row	'CustomLastRowTableCell'	'CustomLastRowTableParagraph'
Even row	'CustomEvenRowTableCell'	'CustomEvenRowTableParagraph'
Odd row	'CustomOddRowTableCell'	'CustomOddRowTableParagraph'
Even column	'CustomEvenColumnTableCell'	'CustomEvenColumnTableParagraph'
Odd column	'CustomOddColumnTableCell'	'CustomOddColumnTableParagraph'

To create a table template with the name 'Custom', define the above styles in the `<office:automatic-styles>`...`</office:automatic-styles>` element of the content template file (see [Factory styles], page 164).

2. Define a table style[30]

   To define a table style, create an entry for the style in the variable `org-odt-table-styles` and specify the following:

   - the name of the table template created in step (1)
   - the set of cell styles in that template that are to be activated

   For example, the entry below defines two different table styles 'TableWithHeaderRowAndColumn' and 'TableWithFirstRowandLastRow' based on the same template 'Custom'. The styles achieve their intended effect by selectively activating the individual cell styles in that template.

   (setq org-odt-table-styles
       (append org-odt-table-styles

---

[30] See the attributes `table:template-name`, `table:use-first-row-styles`, `table:use-last-row-styles`, `table:use-first-column-styles`, `table:use-last-column-styles`, `table:use-banding-rows-styles`, and `table:use-banding-column-styles` of the `<table:table>` element in the OpenDocument-v1.2 specification

```
'(("TableWithHeaderRowAndColumn" "Custom"
  ((use-first-row-styles . t)
   (use-first-column-styles . t)))
 ("TableWithFirstRowandLastRow" "Custom"
  ((use-first-row-styles . t)
   (use-last-row-styles . t)))))))
```

3. Associate a table with the table style

   To do this, specify the table style created in step (2) as part of the `ATTR_ODT` line as shown below.

```
#+ATTR_ODT: :style "TableWithHeaderRowAndColumn"
| Name  | Phone | Age |
| Peter | 1234  | 17  |
| Anna  | 4321  | 25  |
```

Validating OpenDocument XML

Occasionally, you will discover that the document created by the ODT exporter cannot be opened by your favorite application. One of the common reasons for this is that the `.odt` file is corrupt. In such cases, you may want to validate the document against the OpenDocument RELAX NG Compact Syntax (RNC) schema.

For de-compressing the `.odt` file[31]: See Info file `emacs`, node `File Archives`. For general help with validation (and schema-sensitive editing) of XML files: See Info file `nxml-mode`, node `Introduction`.

If you have ready access to OpenDocument `.rnc` files and the needed schema-locating rules in a single folder, you can customize the variable `org-odt-schema-dir` to point to that directory. The ODT exporter will take care of updating the `rng-schema-locating-files` for you.

12.10 Org export

`org` export back-end creates a normalized version of the Org document in current buffer. In particular, it evaluates Babel code (see Section 14.5 [Evaluating code blocks], page 187) and removes other back-ends specific contents.

Org export commands

C-c C-e O o   org-org-export-to-org
> Export as an Org document. For an Org file, `myfile.org`, the resulting file will be `myfile.org.org`. The file will be overwritten without warning.

C-c C-e O O   org-org-export-as-org
> Export to a temporary buffer. Do not create a file.

C-c C-e O v
> Export to an Org file, then open it.

---

[31] `.odt` files are nothing but `zip` archives

12.11 iCalendar export

Some people use Org mode for keeping track of projects, but still prefer a standard calendar application for anniversaries and appointments. In this case it can be useful to show deadlines and other time-stamped items in Org files in the calendar application. Org mode can export calendar information in the standard iCalendar format. If you also want to have TODO entries included in the export, configure the variable `org-icalendar-include-todo`. Plain timestamps are exported as VEVENT, and TODO items as VTODO. It will also create events from deadlines that are in non-TODO items. Deadlines and scheduling dates in TODO items will be used to set the start and due dates for the TODO entry[32]. As categories, it will use the tags locally defined in the heading, and the file/tree category[33]. See the variable `org-icalendar-alarm-time` for a way to assign alarms to entries with a time.

The iCalendar standard requires each entry to have a globally unique identifier (UID). Org creates these identifiers during export. If you set the variable `org-icalendar-store-UID`, the UID will be stored in the `:ID:` property of the entry and re-used next time you report this entry. Since a single entry can give rise to multiple iCalendar entries (as a timestamp, a deadline, a scheduled item, and as a TODO item), Org adds prefixes to the UID, depending on what triggered the inclusion of the entry. In this way the UID remains unique, but a synchronization program can still figure out from which entry all the different instances originate.

C-c C-e c f   `org-icalendar-export-to-ics`
> Create iCalendar entries for the current buffer and store them in the same directory, using a file extension `.ics`.

C-c C-e c a   `org-icalendar-export-agenda-files`
> Like *C-c C-e c f*, but do this for all files in `org-agenda-files`. For each of these files, a separate iCalendar file will be written.

C-c C-e c c   `org-icalendar-combine-agenda-files`
> Create a single large iCalendar file from all files in `org-agenda-files` and write it to the file given by `org-icalendar-combined-agenda-file`.

The export will honor SUMMARY, DESCRIPTION and LOCATION[34] properties if the selected entries have them. If not, the summary will be derived from the headline, and the description from the body (limited to `org-icalendar-include-body` characters).

How this calendar is best read and updated, depends on the application you are using. The FAQ covers this issue.

12.12 Other built-in back-ends

On top of the aforementioned back-ends, Org comes with other built-in ones:

- `ox-man.el`: export to a man page.
- `ox-texinfo.el`: export to `Texinfo` format.

---

[32] See the variables `org-icalendar-use-deadline` and `org-icalendar-use-scheduled`.

[33] To add inherited tags or the TODO state, configure the variable `org-icalendar-categories`.

[34] The LOCATION property can be inherited from higher in the hierarchy if you configure `org-use-property-inheritance` accordingly.

To activate these export back-ends, customize `org-export-backends` or load them directly with e.g., (`require 'ox-texinfo`). This will add new keys in the export dispatcher (see Section 12.1 [The export dispatcher], page 137).

See the comment section of these files for more information on how to use them.

12.13 Export in foreign buffers

Most built-in back-ends come with a command to convert the selected region into a selected format and replace this region by the exported output. Here is a list of such conversion commands:

`org-html-convert-region-to-html`
> Convert the selected region into HTML.

`org-latex-convert-region-to-latex`
> Convert the selected region into LaTeX.

`org-texinfo-convert-region-to-texinfo`
> Convert the selected region into `Texinfo`.

`org-md-convert-region-to-md`
> Convert the selected region into `MarkDown`.

This is particularly useful for converting tables and lists in foreign buffers. E.g., in an HTML buffer, you can turn on `orgstruct-mode`, then use Org commands for editing a list, and finally select and convert the list with `M-x org-html-convert-region-to-html RET`.

12.14 Advanced configuration

Hooks

Two hooks are run during the first steps of the export process. The first one, `org-export-before-processing-hook` is called before expanding macros, Babel code and include keywords in the buffer. The second one, `org-export-before-parsing-hook`, as its name suggests, happens just before parsing the buffer. Their main use is for heavy duties, that is duties involving structural modifications of the document. For example, one may want to remove every headline in the buffer during export. The following code can achieve this:

```
(defun my-headline-removal (backend)
  "Remove all headlines in the current buffer.
BACKEND is the export back-end being used, as a symbol."
  (org-map-entries
   (lambda () (delete-region (point) (progn (forward-line) (point)))))))

(add-hook 'org-export-before-parsing-hook 'my-headline-removal)
```

Note that functions used in these hooks require a mandatory argument, a symbol representing the back-end used.

Filters

Filters are lists of functions applied on a specific part of the output from a given back-end. More explicitly, each time a back-end transforms an Org object or element into another language, all functions within a given filter type are called in turn on the string produced. The string returned by the last function will be the one used in the final output.

There are filter sets for each type of element or object, for plain text, for the parse tree, for the export options and for the final output. They are all named after the same scheme: `org-export-filter-TYPE-functions`, where `TYPE` is the type targeted by the filter. Valid types are:

bold	babel-call	center-block
clock	code	comment
comment-block	diary-sexp	drawer
dynamic-block	entity	example-block
export-block	export-snippet	final-output
fixed-width	footnote-definition	footnote-reference
headline	horizontal-rule	inline-babel-call
inline-src-block	inlinetask	italic
item	keyword	latex-environment
latex-fragment	line-break	link
node-property	options	paragraph
parse-tree	plain-list	plain-text
planning	property-drawer	quote-block
quote-section	radio-target	section
special-block	src-block	statistics-cookie
strike-through	subscript	superscript
table	table-cell	table-row
target	timestamp	underline
verbatim	verse-block	

For example, the following snippet allows me to use non-breaking spaces in the Org buffer and get them translated into LaTeX without using the `\nbsp` macro (where _ stands for the non-breaking space):

```
(defun my-latex-filter-nobreaks (text backend info)
  "Ensure \" \" are properly handled in LaTeX export."
  (when (org-export-derived-backend-p backend 'latex)
    (replace-regexp-in-string " " "~" text)))

(add-to-list 'org-export-filter-plain-text-functions
             'my-latex-filter-nobreaks)
```

Three arguments must be provided to a filter: the code being changed, the back-end used, and some information about the export process. You can safely ignore the third argument for most purposes. Note the use of `org-export-derived-backend-p`, which ensures that the filter will only be applied when using `latex` back-end or any other back-end derived from it (e.g., `beamer`).

Defining filters for individual files

You can customize the export for just a specific file by binding export filter variables using `#+BIND`. Here is an example where we introduce two filters, one to remove brackets from time stamps, and one to entirely remove any strike-through text. The functions doing the filtering are defined in an src block that allows the filter function definitions to exist in the file itself and ensures that the functions will be there when needed.

```
#+BIND: org-export-filter-timestamp-functions (tmp-f-timestamp)
#+BIND: org-export-filter-strike-through-functions (tmp-f-strike-through)
#+begin_src emacs-lisp :exports results :results none
  (defun tmp-f-timestamp (s backend info)
    (replace-regexp-in-string "&[lg]t;\\|[][]" "" s))
  (defun tmp-f-strike-through (s backend info) "")
#+end_src
```

Extending an existing back-end

This is obviously the most powerful customization, since the changes happen at the parser level. Indeed, some export back-ends are built as extensions of other ones (e.g. Markdown back-end an extension of HTML back-end).

Extending a back-end means that if an element type is not transcoded by the new back-end, it will be handled by the original one. Hence you can extend specific parts of a back-end without too much work.

As an example, imagine we want the `ascii` back-end to display the language used in a source block, when it is available, but only when some attribute is non-`nil`, like the following:

```
#+ATTR_ASCII: :language t
```

Because that back-end is lacking in that area, we are going to create a new back-end, `my-ascii` that will do the job.

```
(defun my-ascii-src-block (src-block contents info)
  "Transcode a SRC-BLOCK element from Org to ASCII.
CONTENTS is nil.  INFO is a plist used as a communication
channel."
  (if (not (org-export-read-attribute :attr_ascii src-block :language))
    (org-export-with-backend 'ascii src-block contents info)
  (concat
  (format ",-[ %s ]-\n%s`---"
          (org-element-property :language src-block)
          (replace-regexp-in-string
           "^" "| "
           (org-element-normalize-string
            (org-export-format-code-default src-block info)))))))

(org-export-define-derived-backend 'my-ascii 'ascii
  :translate-alist '((src-block . my-ascii-src-block)))
```

The `my-ascii-src-block` function looks at the attribute above the element. If it isn't true, it gives hand to the `ascii` back-end. Otherwise, it creates a box around the code, leaving room for the language. A new back-end is then created. It only changes its behavior when translating `src-block` type element. Now, all it takes to use the new back-end is calling the following from an Org buffer:

```
(org-export-to-buffer 'my-ascii "*Org MY-ASCII Export*")
```

It is obviously possible to write an interactive function for this, install it in the export dispatcher menu, and so on.

13 Publishing

Org includes a publishing management system that allows you to configure automatic HTML conversion of *projects* composed of interlinked org files. You can also configure Org to automatically upload your exported HTML pages and related attachments, such as images and source code files, to a web server.

You can also use Org to convert files into PDF, or even combine HTML and PDF conversion so that files are available in both formats on the server.

Publishing has been contributed to Org by David O'Toole.

13.1 Configuration

Publishing needs significant configuration to specify files, destination and many other properties of a project.

13.1.1 The variable `org-publish-project-alist`

Publishing is configured almost entirely through setting the value of one variable, called `org-publish-project-alist`. Each element of the list configures one project, and may be in one of the two following forms:

```
("project-name" :property value :property value ...)
```
    i.e., a well-formed property list with alternating keys and values

or

```
("project-name" :components ("project-name" "project-name" ...))
```

In both cases, projects are configured by specifying property values. A project defines the set of files that will be published, as well as the publishing configuration to use when publishing those files. When a project takes the second form listed above, the individual members of the `:components` property are taken to be sub-projects, which group together files requiring different publishing options. When you publish such a "meta-project", all the components will also be published, in the sequence given.

13.1.2 Sources and destinations for files

Most properties are optional, but some should always be set. In particular, Org needs to know where to look for source files, and where to put published files.

`:base-directory`	Directory containing publishing source files
`:publishing-directory`	Directory where output files will be published. You can directly publish to a web server using a file name syntax appropriate for the Emacs `tramp` package. Or you can publish to a local directory and use external tools to upload your website (see Section 13.2 [Uploading files], page 181).
`:preparation-function`	Function or list of functions to be called before starting the publishing process, for example, to run `make` for updating files to be published. The project property list is scoped into this call as the variable `project-plist`.

`:completion-function`	Function or list of functions called after finishing the publishing process, for example, to change permissions of the resulting files. The project property list is scoped into this call as the variable `project-plist`.

13.1.3 Selecting files

By default, all files with extension `.org` in the base directory are considered part of the project. This can be modified by setting the properties

`:base-extension`	Extension (without the dot!) of source files. This actually is a regular expression. Set this to the symbol `any` if you want to get all files in `:base-directory`, even without extension.
`:exclude`	Regular expression to match file names that should not be published, even though they have been selected on the basis of their extension.
`:include`	List of files to be included regardless of `:base-extension` and `:exclude`.
`:recursive`	non-`nil` means, check base-directory recursively for files to publish.

13.1.4 Publishing action

Publishing means that a file is copied to the destination directory and possibly transformed in the process. The default transformation is to export Org files as HTML files, and this is done by the function `org-html-publish-to-html`, which calls the HTML exporter (see Section 12.6 [HTML export], page 145). But you also can publish your content as PDF files using `org-latex-publish-to-pdf` or as `ascii`, `Texinfo`, etc., using the corresponding functions.

If you want to publish the Org file as an `.org` file but with the *archived, commented* and *tag-excluded* trees removed, use the function `org-org-publish-to-org`. This will produce `file.org` and put it in the publishing directory. If you want a htmlized version of this file, set the parameter `:htmlized-source` to `t`, it will produce `file.org.html` in the publishing directory[1].

Other files like images only need to be copied to the publishing destination. For this you can use `org-publish-attachment`. For non-org files, you always need to specify the publishing function:

`:publishing-function`	Function executing the publication of a file. This may also be a list of functions, which will all be called in turn.
`:htmlized-source`	non-`nil` means, publish htmlized source.

The function must accept three arguments: a property list containing at least a `:publishing-directory` property, the name of the file to be published and the path to

---

[1] If the publishing directory is the same than the source directory, `file.org` will be exported as `file.org.org`, so probably don't want to do this.

the publishing directory of the output file. It should take the specified file, make the necessary transformation (if any) and place the result into the destination folder.

13.1.5 Options for the exporters

The property list can be used to set export options during the publishing process. In most cases, these properties correspond to user variables in Org. While some properties are available for all export back-ends, most of them are back-end specific. The following sections list properties along with the variable they belong to. See the documentation string of these options for details.

When a property is given a value in `org-publish-project-alist`, its setting overrides the value of the corresponding user variable (if any) during publishing. Options set within a file (see Section 12.3 [Export settings], page 138), however, override everything.

Generic properties

`:archived-trees`	`org-export-with-archived-trees`
`:exclude-tags`	`org-export-exclude-tags`
`:headline-levels`	`org-export-headline-levels`
`:language`	`org-export-default-language`
`:preserve-breaks`	`org-export-preserve-breaks`
`:section-numbers`	`org-export-with-section-numbers`
`:select-tags`	`org-export-select-tags`
`:with-author`	`org-export-with-author`
`:with-creator`	`org-export-with-creator`
`:with-drawers`	`org-export-with-drawers`
`:with-email`	`org-export-with-email`
`:with-emphasize`	`org-export-with-emphasize`
`:with-fixed-width`	`org-export-with-fixed-width`
`:with-footnotes`	`org-export-with-footnotes`
`:with-latex`	`org-export-with-latex`
`:with-planning`	`org-export-with-planning`
`:with-priority`	`org-export-with-priority`
`:with-properties`	`org-export-with-properties`
`:with-special-strings`	`org-export-with-special-strings`
`:with-sub-superscript`	`org-export-with-sub-superscripts`
`:with-tables`	`org-export-with-tables`
`:with-tags`	`org-export-with-tags`
`:with-tasks`	`org-export-with-tasks`
`:with-timestamps`	`org-export-with-timestamps`
`:with-toc`	`org-export-with-toc`
`:with-todo-keywords`	`org-export-with-todo-keywords`

ASCII specific properties

`:ascii-bullets`	`org-ascii-bullets`
`:ascii-caption-above`	`org-ascii-caption-above`
`:ascii-charset`	`org-ascii-charset`
`:ascii-global-margin`	`org-ascii-global-margin`

```
:ascii-format-drawer-function         org-ascii-format-drawer-function
:ascii-format-inlinetask-function     org-ascii-format-inlinetask-function
:ascii-headline-spacing               org-ascii-headline-spacing
:ascii-indented-line-width            org-ascii-indented-line-width
:ascii-inlinetask-width               org-ascii-inlinetask-width
:ascii-inner-margin                   org-ascii-inner-margin
:ascii-links-to-notes                 org-ascii-links-to-notes
:ascii-paragraph-spacing              org-ascii-paragraph-spacing
:ascii-quote-margin                   org-ascii-quote-margin
:ascii-table-keep-all-vertical-lines  org-ascii-table-keep-all-vertical-lines
:ascii-table-use-ascii-art            org-ascii-table-use-ascii-art
:ascii-table-widen-columns            org-ascii-table-widen-columns
:ascii-text-width                     org-ascii-text-width
:ascii-underline                      org-ascii-underline
:ascii-verbatim-format                org-ascii-verbatim-format
```

Beamer specific properties

```
:beamer-theme                 org-beamer-theme
:beamer-column-view-format    org-beamer-column-view-format
:beamer-environments-extra    org-beamer-environments-extra
:beamer-frame-default-options org-beamer-frame-default-options
:beamer-outline-frame-options org-beamer-outline-frame-options
:beamer-outline-frame-title   org-beamer-outline-frame-title
```

HTML specific properties

```
:html-container                    org-html-container-element
:html-divs                         org-html-divs
:html-doctype                      org-html-doctype
:html-extension                    org-html-extension
:html-footnote-format              org-html-footnote-format
:html-footnote-separator           org-html-footnote-separator
:html-footnotes-section            org-html-footnotes-section
:html-format-drawer-function       org-html-format-drawer-function
:html-format-headline-function     org-html-format-headline-function
:html-format-inlinetask-function   org-html-format-inlinetask-function
:html-head-extra                   org-html-head-extra
:html-head-include-default-style   org-html-head-include-default-style
:html-head-include-scripts         org-html-head-include-scripts
:html-head                         org-html-head
:html-home/up-format               org-html-home/up-format
:html-html5-fancy                  org-html-html5-fancy
:html-indent                       org-html-indent
:html-infojs-options               org-html-infojs-options
:html-infojs-template              org-html-infojs-template
:html-inline-image-rules           org-html-inline-image-rules
:html-inline-images                org-html-inline-images
```

```
:html-link-home                          org-html-link-home
:html-link-org-files-as-html             org-html-link-org-files-as-html
:html-link-up                            org-html-link-up
:html-link-use-abs-url                   org-html-link-use-abs-url
:html-mathjax-options                    org-html-mathjax-options
:html-mathjax-template                   org-html-mathjax-template
:html-metadata-timestamp-format          org-html-metadata-timestamp-format
:html-postamble-format                   org-html-postamble-format
:html-postamble                          org-html-postamble
:html-preamble-format                    org-html-preamble-format
:html-preamble                           org-html-preamble
:html-table-attributes                   org-html-table-default-attributes
:html-table-caption-above                org-html-table-caption-above
:html-table-data-tags                    org-html-table-data-tags
:html-table-header-tags                  org-html-table-header-tags
:html-table-row-tags                     org-html-table-row-tags
:html-tag-class-prefix                   org-html-tag-class-prefix
:html-text-markup-alist                  org-html-text-markup-alist
:html-todo-kwd-class-prefix              org-html-todo-kwd-class-prefix
:html-toplevel-hlevel                    org-html-toplevel-hlevel
:html-use-infojs                         org-html-use-infojs
:html-use-unicode-chars                  org-html-use-unicode-chars
:html-validation-link                    org-html-validation-link
:html-xml-declaration                    org-html-xml-declaration
```

LaTeX specific properties

```
:latex-active-timestamp-format           org-latex-active-timestamp-format
:latex-classes                           org-latex-classes
:latex-class                             org-latex-default-class
:latex-default-figure-position           org-latex-default-figure-position
:latex-default-table-environment         org-latex-default-table-environment
:latex-default-table-mode                org-latex-default-table-mode
:latex-diary-timestamp-format            org-latex-diary-timestamp-format
:latex-footnote-separator                org-latex-footnote-separator
:latex-format-drawer-function            org-latex-format-drawer-function
:latex-format-headline-function          org-latex-format-headline-function
:latex-format-inlinetask-function        org-latex-format-inlinetask-function
:latex-hyperref-template                 org-latex-hyperref-template
:latex-image-default-height              org-latex-image-default-height
:latex-image-default-option              org-latex-image-default-option
:latex-image-default-width               org-latex-image-default-width
:latex-inactive-timestamp-format         org-latex-inactive-timestamp-format
:latex-inline-image-rules                org-latex-inline-image-rules
:latex-link-with-unknown-path-format     org-latex-link-with-unknown-path-format
:latex-listings-langs                    org-latex-listings-langs
:latex-listings-options                  org-latex-listings-options
```

```
:latex-listings                       org-latex-listings
:latex-minted-langs                   org-latex-minted-langs
:latex-minted-options                 org-latex-minted-options
:latex-table-caption-above            org-latex-table-caption-above
:latex-table-scientific-notation      org-latex-table-scientific-notation
:latex-tables-booktabs                org-latex-tables-booktabs
:latex-tables-centered                org-latex-tables-centered
:latex-text-markup-alist              org-latex-text-markup-alist
:latex-title-command                  org-latex-title-command
:latex-toc-command                    org-latex-toc-command
```

Markdown specific properties

```
:md-headline-style    org-md-headline-style
```

ODT specific properties

```
:odt-content-template-file            org-odt-content-template-file
:odt-display-outline-level            org-odt-display-outline-level
:odt-fontify-srcblocks                org-odt-fontify-srcblocks
:odt-format-drawer-function           org-odt-format-drawer-function
:odt-format-headline-function         org-odt-format-headline-function
:odt-format-inlinetask-function       org-odt-format-inlinetask-function
:odt-inline-formula-rules             org-odt-inline-formula-rules
:odt-inline-image-rules               org-odt-inline-image-rules
:odt-pixels-per-inch                  org-odt-pixels-per-inch
:odt-styles-file                      org-odt-styles-file
:odt-table-styles                     org-odt-table-styles
:odt-use-date-fields                  org-odt-use-date-fields
```

Texinfo specific properties

```
:texinfo-active-timestamp-format      org-texinfo-active-timestamp-format
:texinfo-classes                      org-texinfo-classes
:texinfo-class                        org-texinfo-default-class
:texinfo-def-table-markup             org-texinfo-def-table-markup
:texinfo-diary-timestamp-format       org-texinfo-diary-timestamp-format
:texinfo-filename                     org-texinfo-filename
:texinfo-format-drawer-function       org-texinfo-format-drawer-function
:texinfo-format-headline-function     org-texinfo-format-headline-function
:texinfo-format-inlinetask-function   org-texinfo-format-inlinetask-function
:texinfo-inactive-timestamp-format    org-texinfo-inactive-timestamp-format
:texinfo-link-with-unknown-path-format  org-texinfo-link-with-unknown-path-format
:texinfo-node-description-column      org-texinfo-node-description-column
:texinfo-table-scientific-notation    org-texinfo-table-scientific-notation
:texinfo-tables-verbatim              org-texinfo-tables-verbatim
:texinfo-text-markup-alist            org-texinfo-text-markup-alist
```

13.1.6 Links between published files

To create a link from one Org file to another, you would use something like '`[[file:foo.org][The foo]]`' or simply '`file:foo.org.`' (see Chapter 4 [Hyperlinks], page 37). When published, this link becomes a link to `foo.html`. You can thus interlink the pages of your "org web" project and the links will work as expected when you publish them to HTML. If you also publish the Org source file and want to link to it, use an `http:` link instead of a `file:` link, because `file:` links are converted to link to the corresponding `html` file.

You may also link to related files, such as images. Provided you are careful with relative file names, and provided you have also configured Org to upload the related files, these links will work too. See Section 13.3.2 [Complex example], page 182, for an example of this usage.

13.1.7 Generating a sitemap

The following properties may be used to control publishing of a map of files for a given project.

`:auto-sitemap`	When non-`nil`, publish a sitemap during `org-publish-current-project` or `org-publish-all`.
`:sitemap-filename`	Filename for output of sitemap. Defaults to `sitemap.org` (which becomes `sitemap.html`).
`:sitemap-title`	Title of sitemap page. Defaults to name of file.
`:sitemap-function`	Plug-in function to use for generation of the sitemap. Defaults to `org-publish-org-sitemap`, which generates a plain list of links to all files in the project.
`:sitemap-sort-folders`	Where folders should appear in the sitemap. Set this to `first` (default) or `last` to display folders first or last, respectively. Any other value will mix files and folders.
`:sitemap-sort-files`	How the files are sorted in the site map. Set this to `alphabetically` (default), `chronologically` or `anti-chronologically`. `chronologically` sorts the files with older date first while `anti-chronologically` sorts the files with newer date first. `alphabetically` sorts the files alphabetically. The date of a file is retrieved with `org-publish-find-date`.
`:sitemap-ignore-case`	Should sorting be case-sensitive? Default `nil`.

`:sitemap-file-entry-format`	With this option one can tell how a sitemap's entry is formatted in the sitemap. This is a format string with some escape sequences: `%t` stands for the title of the file, `%a` stands for the author of the file and `%d` stands for the date of the file. The date is retrieved with the `org-publish-find-date` function and formatted with `org-publish-sitemap-date-format`. Default `%t`.
`:sitemap-date-format`	Format string for the `format-time-string` function that tells how a sitemap entry's date is to be formatted. This property bypasses `org-publish-sitemap-date-format` which defaults to `%Y-%m-%d`.
`:sitemap-sans-extension`	When non-`nil`, remove filenames' extensions from the generated sitemap. Useful to have cool URIs (see `http://www.w3.org/Provider/Style/URI`). Defaults to `nil`.

13.1.8 Generating an index

Org mode can generate an index across the files of a publishing project.

`:makeindex`	When non-`nil`, generate in index in the file `theindex.org` and publish it as `theindex.html`.

The file will be created when first publishing a project with the `:makeindex` set. The file only contains a statement `#+INCLUDE: "theindex.inc"`. You can then build around this include statement by adding a title, style information, etc.

13.2 Uploading files

For those people already utilizing third party sync tools such as `rsync` or `unison`, it might be preferable not to use the built in *remote* publishing facilities of Org mode which rely heavily on Tramp. Tramp, while very useful and powerful, tends not to be so efficient for multiple file transfer and has been known to cause problems under heavy usage.

Specialized synchronization utilities offer several advantages. In addition to timestamp comparison, they also do content and permissions/attribute checks. For this reason you might prefer to publish your web to a local directory (possibly even *in place* with your Org files) and then use `unison` or `rsync` to do the synchronization with the remote host.

Since Unison (for example) can be configured as to which files to transfer to a certain remote destination, it can greatly simplify the project publishing definition. Simply keep all files in the correct location, process your Org files with `org-publish` and let the synchronization tool do the rest. You do not need, in this scenario, to include attachments such as `jpg`, `css` or `gif` files in the project definition since the 3rd party tool syncs them.

Publishing to a local directory is also much faster than to a remote one, so that you can afford more easily to republish entire projects. If you set `org-publish-use-timestamps-flag` to `nil`, you gain the main benefit of re-including any changed external files such as source example files you might include with `#+INCLUDE:`. The timestamp mechanism in Org is not smart enough to detect if included files have been modified.

13.3 Sample configuration

Below we provide two example configurations. The first one is a simple project publishing only a set of Org files. The second example is more complex, with a multi-component project.

13.3.1 Example: simple publishing configuration

This example publishes a set of Org files to the `public_html` directory on the local machine.

```
(setq org-publish-project-alist
      '(("org"
        :base-directory "~/org/"
        :publishing-directory "~/public_html"
        :section-numbers nil
        :with-toc nil
        :html-head "<link rel=\"stylesheet\"
                href=\"../other/mystyle.css\"
                type=\"text/css\"/>")))
```

13.3.2 Example: complex publishing configuration

This more complicated example publishes an entire website, including Org files converted to HTML, image files, Emacs Lisp source code, and style sheets. The publishing directory is remote and private files are excluded.

To ensure that links are preserved, care should be taken to replicate your directory structure on the web server, and to use relative file paths. For example, if your Org files are kept in `~/org` and your publishable images in `~/images`, you would link to an image with

```
file:../images/myimage.png
```

On the web server, the relative path to the image should be the same. You can accomplish this by setting up an "images" folder in the right place on the web server, and publishing images to it.

```
(setq org-publish-project-alist
      '(("orgfiles"
        :base-directory "~/org/"
        :base-extension "org"
        :publishing-directory "/ssh:user@host:~/html/notebook/"
        :publishing-function org-html-publish-to-html
        :exclude "PrivatePage.org"   ;; regexp
        :headline-levels 3
        :section-numbers nil
        :with-toc nil
        :html-head "<link rel=\"stylesheet\"
                href=\"../other/mystyle.css\" type=\"text/css\"/>"
        :html-preamble t)

       ("images"
        :base-directory "~/images/"
        :base-extension "jpg\\|gif\\|png"
```

```
:publishing-directory "/ssh:user@host:~/html/images/"
:publishing-function org-publish-attachment)

("other"
 :base-directory "~/other/"
 :base-extension "css\\|el"
 :publishing-directory "/ssh:user@host:~/html/other/"
 :publishing-function org-publish-attachment)
("website" :components ("orgfiles" "images" "other"))))
```

13.4 Triggering publication

Once properly configured, Org can publish with the following commands:

C-c C-e P x   org-publish

> Prompt for a specific project and publish all files that belong to it.

C-c C-e P p   org-publish-current-project

> Publish the project containing the current file.

C-c C-e P f   org-publish-current-file

> Publish only the current file.

C-c C-e P a   org-publish-all

> Publish every project.

Org uses timestamps to track when a file has changed. The above functions normally only publish changed files. You can override this and force publishing of all files by giving a prefix argument to any of the commands above, or by customizing the variable `org-publish-use-timestamps-flag`. This may be necessary in particular if files include other files via `#+SETUPFILE:` or `#+INCLUDE:`.

14 Working with source code

Source code can be included in Org mode documents using a 'src' block, e.g.:

```
#+BEGIN_SRC emacs-lisp
  (defun org-xor (a b)
    "Exclusive or."
    (if a (not b) b))
#+END_SRC
```

Org mode provides a number of features for working with live source code, including editing of code blocks in their native major-mode, evaluation of code blocks, converting code blocks into source files (known as *tangling* in literate programming), and exporting code blocks and their results in several formats. This functionality was contributed by Eric Schulte and Dan Davison, and was originally named Org-babel.

The following sections describe Org mode's code block handling facilities.

14.1 Structure of code blocks

Live code blocks can be specified with a 'src' block or inline.[1] The structure of a 'src' block is

```
#+NAME: <name>
#+BEGIN_SRC <language> <switches> <header arguments>
  <body>
#+END_SRC
```

The #+NAME: line is optional, and can be used to name the code block. Live code blocks require that a language be specified on the #+BEGIN_SRC line. Switches and header arguments are optional.

Live code blocks can also be specified inline using

```
src_<language>{<body>}
```

or

```
src_<language>[<header arguments>]{<body>}
```

<#+NAME: name>

This line associates a name with the code block. This is similar to the #+NAME: Name lines that can be used to name tables in Org mode files. Referencing the name of a code block makes it possible to evaluate the block from other places in the file, from other files, or from Org mode table formulas (see Section 3.5 [The spreadsheet], page 24). Names are assumed to be unique and the behavior of Org mode when two or more blocks share the same name is undefined.

<language>

The language of the code in the block (see Section 14.7 [Languages], page 189).

<switches>

Optional switches control code block export (see the discussion of switches in Section 11.3 [Literal examples], page 130)

---

[1] Note that 'src' blocks may be inserted using Org mode's Section 15.2 [Easy templates], page 212 system

`<header arguments>`
> Optional header arguments control many aspects of evaluation, export and tangling of code blocks (see Section 14.8 [Header arguments], page 190). Header arguments can also be set on a per-buffer or per-subtree basis using properties.

`source code, header arguments`
`<body>`   Source code in the specified language.

14.2 Editing source code

Use *C-c '* to edit the current code block. This brings up a language major-mode edit buffer containing the body of the code block. Manually saving this buffer with `C-x C-s` will write the contents back to the Org buffer. You can also set `org-edit-src-auto-save-idle-delay` to save the base buffer after some idle delay, or `org-edit-src-turn-on-auto-save` to auto-save this buffer into a separate file using `auto-save-mode`. Use *C-c '* again to exit.

The `org-src-mode` minor mode will be active in the edit buffer. The following variables can be used to configure the behavior of the edit buffer. See also the customization group `org-edit-structure` for further configuration options.

`org-src-lang-modes`
> If an Emacs major-mode named `<lang>-mode` exists, where `<lang>` is the language named in the header line of the code block, then the edit buffer will be placed in that major-mode. This variable can be used to map arbitrary language names to existing major modes.

`org-src-window-setup`
> Controls the way Emacs windows are rearranged when the edit buffer is created.

`org-src-preserve-indentation`
> By default, the value is `nil`, which means that when code blocks are evaluated during export or tangled, they are re-inserted into the code block, which may replace sequences of spaces with tab characters. When non-nil, whitespace in code blocks will be preserved during export or tangling, exactly as it appears. This variable is especially useful for tangling languages such as Python, in which whitespace indentation in the output is critical.

`org-src-ask-before-returning-to-edit-buffer`
> By default, Org will ask before returning to an open edit buffer. Set this variable to `nil` to switch without asking.

To turn on native code fontification in the *Org* buffer, configure the variable `org-src-fontify-natively`.

14.3 Exporting code blocks

It is possible to export the *code* of code blocks, the *results* of code block evaluation, *both* the code and the results of code block evaluation, or *none*. For most languages, the default exports code. However, for some languages (e.g., `ditaa`) the default exports the results of code block evaluation. For information on exporting code block bodies, see Section 11.3 [Literal examples], page 130.

The `:exports` header argument can be used to specify export behavior (note that these arguments are only relevant for code blocks, not inline code):

Header arguments:

`:exports code`

> The default in most languages. The body of the code block is exported, as described in Section 11.3 [Literal examples], page 130.

`:exports results`

> The code block will be evaluated each time to buffer is exported, and the results will be placed in the Org mode buffer for export, either updating previous results of the code block located anywhere in the buffer or, if no previous results exist, placing the results immediately after the code block. The body of the code block will not be exported.

`:exports both`

> Both the code block and its results will be exported.

`:exports none`

> Neither the code block nor its results will be exported.

It is possible to inhibit the evaluation of code blocks during export. Setting the `org-export-babel-evaluate` variable to `nil` will ensure that no code blocks are evaluated as part of the export process. This can be useful in situations where potentially untrusted Org mode files are exported in an automated fashion, for example when Org mode is used as the markup language for a wiki. It is also possible to set this variable to `inline-only`. In that case, only inline code blocks will be evaluated, in order to insert their results. Non-inline code blocks are assumed to have their results already inserted in the buffer by manual evaluation. This setting is useful to avoid expensive recalculations during export, not to provide security.

Code blocks in commented subtrees (see [Comment lines], page 129) are never evaluated on export. However, code blocks in subtrees excluded from export (see Section 12.3 [Export settings], page 138) may be evaluated on export.

14.4 Extracting source code

Creating pure source code files by extracting code from source blocks is referred to as "tangling"—a term adopted from the literate programming community. During "tangling" of code blocks their bodies are expanded using `org-babel-expand-src-block` which can expand both variable and "noweb" style references (see Section 14.10 [Noweb reference syntax], page 210).

Header arguments

`:tangle no`

> The default. The code block is not included in the tangled output.

`:tangle yes`

> Include the code block in the tangled output. The output file name is the name of the org file with the extension '`.org`' replaced by the extension for the block language.

`:tangle filename`

> Include the code block in the tangled output to file '`filename`'.

Functions

`org-babel-tangle`

> Tangle the current file. Bound to *C-c C-v t*.
>
> With prefix argument only tangle the current code block.

`org-babel-tangle-file`

> Choose a file to tangle. Bound to *C-c C-v f*.

Hooks

`org-babel-post-tangle-hook`

> This hook is run from within code files tangled by `org-babel-tangle`. Example applications could include post-processing, compilation or evaluation of tangled code files.

Jumping between code and Org

When tangling code from an Org-mode buffer to a source code file, you'll frequently find yourself viewing the file of tangled source code (e.g., many debuggers point to lines of the source code file). It is useful to be able to navigate from the tangled source to the Org-mode buffer from which the code originated.

The `org-babel-tangle-jump-to-org` function provides this jumping from code to Org-mode functionality. Two header arguments are required for jumping to work, first the **padline** (Section 14.8.2.12 [padline], page 201) option must be set to true (the default setting), second the **comments** (Section 14.8.2.11 [comments], page 201) header argument must be set to **links**, which will insert comments into the source code buffer which point back to the original Org-mode file.

14.5 Evaluating code blocks

Code blocks can be evaluated[2] and the results of evaluation optionally placed in the Org mode buffer. The results of evaluation are placed following a line that begins by default with `#+RESULTS` and optionally a cache identifier and/or the name of the evaluated code block. The default value of `#+RESULTS` can be changed with the customizable variable `org-babel-results-keyword`.

By default, the evaluation facility is only enabled for Lisp code blocks specified as `emacs-lisp`. However, source code blocks in many languages can be evaluated within Org mode (see Section 14.7 [Languages], page 189 for a list of supported languages and Section 14.1 [Structure of code blocks], page 184 for information on the syntax used to define a code block).

There are a number of ways to evaluate code blocks. The simplest is to press *C-c C-c* or *C-c C-v e* with the point on a code block[3]. This will call the `org-babel-execute-src-block` function to evaluate the block and insert its results into the Org mode buffer.

---

[2] Whenever code is evaluated there is a potential for that code to do harm. Org mode provides safeguards to ensure that code is only evaluated after explicit confirmation from the user. For information on these safeguards (and on how to disable them) see Section 15.4 [Code evaluation security], page 213.

[3] The option `org-babel-no-eval-on-ctrl-c-ctrl-c` can be used to remove code evaluation from the *C-c C-c* key binding.

It is also possible to evaluate named code blocks from anywhere in an Org mode buffer or an Org mode table. These named code blocks can be located in the current Org mode buffer or in the "Library of Babel" (see Section 14.6 [Library of Babel], page 188). Named code blocks can be evaluated with a separate #+CALL: line or inline within a block of text. In both cases the result is wrapped according to the value of *org-babel-inline-result-wrap*, which by default is "=%s=" for markup that produces verbatim text.

The syntax of the #+CALL: line is

```
#+CALL: <name>(<arguments>)
#+CALL: <name>[<inside header arguments>](<arguments>) <end header arguments>
```

The syntax for inline evaluation of named code blocks is

```
... call_<name>(<arguments>) ...
... call_<name>[<inside header arguments>](<arguments>)[<end header arguments>] ...
```

<name>   The name of the code block to be evaluated (see Section 14.1 [Structure of code blocks], page 184).

<arguments>

Arguments specified in this section will be passed to the code block. These arguments use standard function call syntax, rather than header argument syntax. For example, a #+CALL: line that passes the number four to a code block named **double**, which declares the header argument :var n=2, would be written as #+CALL: double(n=4).

<inside header arguments>

Inside header arguments are passed through and applied to the named code block. These arguments use header argument syntax rather than standard function call syntax. Inside header arguments affect how the code block is evaluated. For example, [:results output] will collect the results of everything printed to STDOUT during execution of the code block.

<end header arguments>

End header arguments are applied to the calling instance and do not affect evaluation of the named code block. They affect how the results are incorporated into the Org mode buffer and how the call line is exported. For example, :results html will insert the results of the call line evaluation in the Org buffer, wrapped in a BEGIN_HTML: block.

For more examples of passing header arguments to #+CALL: lines see [Header arguments in function calls], page 192.

14.6 Library of Babel

The "Library of Babel" consists of code blocks that can be called from any Org mode file. Code blocks defined in the "Library of Babel" can be called remotely as if they were in the current Org mode buffer (see Section 14.5 [Evaluating code blocks], page 187 for information on the syntax of remote code block evaluation).

The central repository of code blocks in the "Library of Babel" is housed in an Org mode file located in the 'contrib' directory of Org mode.

Users can add code blocks they believe to be generally useful to their "Library of Babel." The code blocks can be stored in any Org mode file and then loaded into the library with `org-babel-lob-ingest`.

Code blocks located in any Org mode file can be loaded into the "Library of Babel" with the `org-babel-lob-ingest` function, bound to *C-c C-v i*.

14.7 Languages

Code blocks in the following languages are supported.

Language	Identifier	Language	Identifier
Asymptote	asymptote	Awk	awk
Emacs Calc	calc	C	C
C++	C++	Clojure	clojure
CSS	css	ditaa	ditaa
Graphviz	dot	Emacs Lisp	emacs-lisp
gnuplot	gnuplot	Haskell	haskell
Java	java		
Javascript	js	LaTeX	latex
Ledger	ledger	Lisp	lisp
Lilypond	lilypond	MATLAB	matlab
Mscgen	mscgen	Objective Caml	ocaml
Octave	octave	Org mode	org
Oz	oz	Perl	perl
Plantuml	plantuml	Python	python
R	R	Ruby	ruby
Sass	sass	Scheme	scheme
GNU Screen	screen	shell	sh
SQL	sql	SQLite	sqlite

Language-specific documentation is available for some languages. If available, it can be found at `http://orgmode.org/worg/org-contrib/babel/languages.html`.

The option `org-babel-load-languages` controls which languages are enabled for evaluation (by default only `emacs-lisp` is enabled). This variable can be set using the customization interface or by adding code like the following to your emacs configuration.

> The following disables `emacs-lisp` evaluation and enables evaluation of `R` code blocks.

```
(org-babel-do-load-languages
 'org-babel-load-languages
 '((emacs-lisp . nil)
   (R . t)))
```

It is also possible to enable support for a language by loading the related elisp file with `require`.

> The following adds support for evaluating `clojure` code blocks.

```
(require 'ob-clojure)
```

14.8 Header arguments

Code block functionality can be configured with header arguments. This section provides an overview of the use of header arguments, and then describes each header argument in detail.

14.8.1 Using header arguments

The values of header arguments can be set in several way. When the header arguments in each layer have been determined, they are combined in order from the first, least specific (having the lowest priority) up to the last, most specific (having the highest priority). A header argument with a higher priority replaces the same header argument specified at lower priority.

System-wide header arguments

System-wide values of header arguments can be specified by adapting the `org-babel-default-header-args` variable:

```
:session    => "none"
:results    => "replace"
:exports    => "code"
:cache      => "no"
:noweb      => "no"
```

For example, the following example could be used to set the default value of `:noweb` header arguments to `yes`. This would have the effect of expanding `:noweb` references by default when evaluating source code blocks.

```
(setq org-babel-default-header-args
    (cons '(:noweb . "yes")
        (assq-delete-all :noweb org-babel-default-header-args)))
```

Language-specific header arguments

Each language can define its own set of default header arguments in variable `org-babel-default-header-args:<lang>`, where `<lang>` is the name of the language. See the language-specific documentation available online at `http://orgmode.org/worg/org-contrib/babel`.

Header arguments in Org mode properties

Buffer-wide header arguments may be specified as properties through the use of `#+PROPERTY:` lines placed anywhere in an Org mode file (see Section 7.1 [Property syntax], page 62).

For example the following would set `session` to `*R*` (only for R code blocks), and `results` to `silent` for every code block in the buffer, ensuring that all execution took place in the same session, and no results would be inserted into the buffer.

```
#+PROPERTY: header-args:R  :session *R*
#+PROPERTY: header-args    :results silent
```

Header arguments read from Org mode properties can also be set on a per-subtree basis using property drawers (see Section 7.1 [Property syntax], page 62). When properties are used to set default header arguments, they are always looked up with inheritance, regardless of the value of `org-use-property-inheritance`. Properties are evaluated as seen by the outermost call or source block.[4]

In the following example the value of the `:cache` header argument will default to `yes` in all code blocks in the subtree rooted at the following heading:

```
* outline header
  :PROPERTIES:
  :header-args:    :cache yes
  :END:
```

Properties defined in this way override the properties set in `org-babel-default-header-args` and are applied for all activated languages. It is convenient to use the `org-set-property` function bound to *C-c C-x p* to set properties in Org mode documents.

Language-specific header arguments in Org mode properties

Language-specific header arguments are also read from properties `header-args:<lang>` where `<lang>` is the name of the language targeted. As an example

```
* Heading
  :PROPERTIES:
  :header-args:clojure:    :session *clojure-1*
  :header-args:R:          :session *R*
  :END:
** Subheading
  :PROPERTIES:
  :header-args:clojure:    :session *clojure-2*
  :END:
```

would independently set a default session header argument for R and clojure for calls and source blocks under subtree "Heading" and change to a different clojure setting for evaluations under subtree "Subheading", while the R session is inherited from "Heading" and therefore unchanged.

Code block specific header arguments

The most common way to assign values to header arguments is at the code block level. This can be done by listing a sequence of header arguments and their values as part of the `#+BEGIN_SRC` line. Properties set in this way override both the values of `org-babel-default-header-args` and header arguments specified as properties. In the following example, the `:results` header argument is set to `silent`, meaning the results of execution will not be inserted in the buffer, and the `:exports` header argument is set to `code`, meaning only the body of the code block will be preserved on export to HTML or LaTeX.

```
#+NAME: factorial
#+BEGIN_SRC haskell :results silent :exports code :var n=0
fac 0 = 1
```

---

[4] The deprecated syntax for default header argument properties, using the name of the header argument as a property name directly, evaluates the property as seen by the corresponding source block definition. This behavior has been kept for backwards compatibility.

```
        fac n = n * fac (n-1)
        #+END_SRC
```

Similarly, it is possible to set header arguments for inline code blocks

```
        src_haskell[:exports both]{fac 5}
```

Code block header arguments can span multiple lines using `#+HEADER:` or `#+HEADERS:` lines preceding a code block or nested between the `#+NAME:` line and the `#+BEGIN_SRC` line of a named code block.

Multi-line header arguments on an un-named code block:

```
        #+HEADERS: :var data1=1
        #+BEGIN_SRC emacs-lisp :var data2=2
          (message "data1:%S, data2:%S" data1 data2)
        #+END_SRC

        #+RESULTS:
        : data1:1, data2:2
```

Multi-line header arguments on a named code block:

```
        #+NAME: named-block
        #+HEADER: :var data=2
        #+BEGIN_SRC emacs-lisp
          (message "data:%S" data)
        #+END_SRC

        #+RESULTS: named-block
        : data:2
```

Header arguments in function calls

At the most specific level, header arguments for "Library of Babel" or `#+CALL:` lines can be set as shown in the two examples below. For more information on the structure of `#+CALL:` lines see Section 14.5 [Evaluating code blocks], page 187.

The following will apply the `:exports results` header argument to the evaluation of the `#+CALL:` line.

```
        #+CALL: factorial(n=5) :exports results
```

The following will apply the `:session special` header argument to the evaluation of the `factorial` code block.

```
        #+CALL: factorial[:session special](n=5)
```

14.8.2 Specific header arguments

Header arguments consist of an initial colon followed by the name of the argument in lowercase letters. The following header arguments are defined:

Additional header arguments are defined on a language-specific basis, see Section 14.7 [Languages], page 189.

14.8.2.1 :var

The :var header argument is used to pass arguments to code blocks. The specifics of how arguments are included in a code block vary by language; these are addressed in the language-specific documentation. However, the syntax used to specify arguments is the same across all languages. In every case, variables require a default value when they are declared.

The values passed to arguments can either be literal values, references, or Emacs Lisp code (see Section 14.8.2.1 [var], page 193). References include anything in the Org mode file that takes a #+NAME: or #+RESULTS: line: tables, lists, #+BEGIN_EXAMPLE blocks, other code blocks and the results of other code blocks.

Note: When a reference is made to another code block, the referenced block will be evaluated unless it has current cached results (see Section 14.8.2.18 [cache], page 203).

Argument values can be indexed in a manner similar to arrays (see Section 14.8.2.1 [var], page 193).

The following syntax is used to pass arguments to code blocks using the :var header argument.

    :var name=assign

The argument, **assign**, can either be a literal value, such as a string '"**string**"' or a number '9', or a reference to a table, a list, a literal example, another code block (with or without arguments), or the results of evaluating another code block.

Here are examples of passing values by reference:

table   an Org mode table named with either a #+NAME: line

```
#+NAME: example-table
| 1 |
| 2 |
| 3 |
| 4 |

#+NAME: table-length
#+BEGIN_SRC emacs-lisp :var table=example-table
(length table)
#+END_SRC

#+RESULTS: table-length
: 4
```

list   a simple list named with a #+NAME: line (note that nesting is not carried through to the source code block)

```
#+NAME: example-list
  - simple
    - not
    - nested
  - list

#+BEGIN_SRC emacs-lisp :var x=example-list
```

```
    (print x)
#+END_SRC

#+RESULTS:
| simple | list |
```

code block without arguments

a code block name (from the example above), as assigned by `#+NAME:`, optionally followed by parentheses

```
#+BEGIN_SRC emacs-lisp :var length=table-length()
(* 2 length)
#+END_SRC

#+RESULTS:
: 8
```

code block with arguments

a code block name, as assigned by `#+NAME:`, followed by parentheses and optional arguments passed within the parentheses following the code block name using standard function call syntax

```
#+NAME: double
#+BEGIN_SRC emacs-lisp :var input=8
(* 2 input)
#+END_SRC

#+RESULTS: double
: 16

#+NAME: squared
#+BEGIN_SRC emacs-lisp :var input=double(input=1)
(* input input)
#+END_SRC

#+RESULTS: squared
: 4
```

literal example

a literal example block named with a `#+NAME:` line

```
#+NAME: literal-example
#+BEGIN_EXAMPLE
A literal example
on two lines
#+END_EXAMPLE

#+NAME: read-literal-example
#+BEGIN_SRC emacs-lisp :var x=literal-example
  (concatenate 'string x " for you.")
#+END_SRC
```

```
#+RESULTS: read-literal-example
: A literal example
: on two lines for you.
```

Indexable variable values

It is possible to reference portions of variable values by "indexing" into the variables. Indexes are 0 based with negative values counting back from the end. If an index is separated by ,s then each subsequent section will index into the next deepest nesting or dimension of the value. Note that this indexing occurs *before* other table related header arguments like :hlines, :colnames and :rownames are applied. The following example assigns the last cell of the first row the table example-table to the variable data:

```
#+NAME: example-table
| 1 | a |
| 2 | b |
| 3 | c |
| 4 | d |

#+BEGIN_SRC emacs-lisp :var data=example-table[0,-1]
  data
#+END_SRC

#+RESULTS:
: a
```

Ranges of variable values can be referenced using two integers separated by a :, in which case the entire inclusive range is referenced. For example the following assigns the middle three rows of example-table to data.

```
#+NAME: example-table
| 1 | a |
| 2 | b |
| 3 | c |
| 4 | d |
| 5 | 3 |

#+BEGIN_SRC emacs-lisp :var data=example-table[1:3]
  data
#+END_SRC

#+RESULTS:
| 2 | b |
| 3 | c |
| 4 | d |
```

Additionally, an empty index, or the single character *, are both interpreted to mean the entire range and as such are equivalent to 0:-1, as shown in the following example in which the entire first column is referenced.

```
#+NAME: example-table
| 1 | a |
| 2 | b |
| 3 | c |
| 4 | d |

#+BEGIN_SRC emacs-lisp :var data=example-table[,0]
  data
#+END_SRC

#+RESULTS:
| 1 | 2 | 3 | 4 |
```

It is possible to index into the results of code blocks as well as tables. Any number of dimensions can be indexed. Dimensions are separated from one another by commas, as shown in the following example.

```
#+NAME: 3D
#+BEGIN_SRC emacs-lisp
  '(((1  2  3)  (4  5  6)  (7  8  9))
    ((10 11 12) (13 14 15) (16 17 18))
    ((19 20 21) (22 23 24) (25 26 27)))
#+END_SRC

#+BEGIN_SRC emacs-lisp :var data=3D[1,,1]
  data
#+END_SRC

#+RESULTS:
| 11 | 14 | 17 |
```

Emacs Lisp evaluation of variables

Emacs lisp code can be used to initialize variable values. When a variable value starts with (, [, ' or ' it will be evaluated as Emacs Lisp and the result of the evaluation will be assigned as the variable value. The following example demonstrates use of this evaluation to reliably pass the file-name of the Org mode buffer to a code block—note that evaluation of header arguments is guaranteed to take place in the original Org mode file, while there is no such guarantee for evaluation of the code block body.

```
#+BEGIN_SRC sh :var filename=(buffer-file-name) :exports both
  wc -w $filename
#+END_SRC
```

Note that values read from tables and lists will not be evaluated as Emacs Lisp, as shown in the following example.

```
#+NAME: table
| (a b c) |

#+HEADERS: :var data=table[0,0]
#+BEGIN_SRC perl
```

```
    $data
#+END_SRC

#+RESULTS:
: (a b c)
```

14.8.2.2 :results

There are four classes of `:results` header argument. Only one option per class may be supplied per code block.

- **collection** header arguments specify how the results should be collected from the code block
- **type** header arguments specify what type of result the code block will return—which has implications for how they will be processed before insertion into the Org mode buffer
- **format** header arguments specify what type of result the code block will return—which has implications for how they will be inserted into the Org mode buffer
- **handling** header arguments specify how the results of evaluating the code block should be handled.

Collection

The following options are mutually exclusive, and specify how the results should be collected from the code block.

- `value` This is the default. The result is the value of the last statement in the code block. This header argument places the evaluation in functional mode. Note that in some languages, e.g., Python, use of this result type requires that a **return** statement be included in the body of the source code block. E.g., `:results value`.
- `output` The result is the collection of everything printed to STDOUT during the execution of the code block. This header argument places the evaluation in scripting mode. E.g., `:results output`.

Type

The following options are mutually exclusive and specify what type of results the code block will return. By default, results are inserted as either a table or scalar depending on their value.

- `table`, `vector` The results should be interpreted as an Org mode table. If a single value is returned, it will be converted into a table with one row and one column. E.g., `:results value table`.
- `list` The results should be interpreted as an Org mode list. If a single scalar value is returned it will be converted into a list with only one element.
- `scalar`, `verbatim` The results should be interpreted literally—they will not be converted into a table. The results will be inserted into the Org mode buffer as quoted text. E.g., `:results value verbatim`.
- `file` The results will be interpreted as the path to a file, and will be inserted into the Org mode buffer as a file link. E.g., `:results value file`.

Format

The following options are mutually exclusive and specify what type of results the code block will return. By default, results are inserted according to the type as specified above.

- `raw` The results are interpreted as raw Org mode code and are inserted directly into the buffer. If the results look like a table they will be aligned as such by Org mode. E.g., `:results value raw`.

- `org` The results are will be enclosed in a `BEGIN_SRC org` block. They are not comma-escaped by default but they will be if you hit *TAB* in the block and/or if you export the file. E.g., `:results value org`.

- `html` Results are assumed to be HTML and will be enclosed in a `BEGIN_HTML` block. E.g., `:results value html`.

- `latex` Results assumed to be LaTeX and are enclosed in a `BEGIN_LaTeX` block. E.g., `:results value latex`.

- `code` Result are assumed to be parsable code and are enclosed in a code block. E.g., `:results value code`.

- `pp` The result is converted to pretty-printed code and is enclosed in a code block. This option currently supports Emacs Lisp, Python, and Ruby. E.g., `:results value pp`.

- `drawer` The result is wrapped in a RESULTS drawer. This can be useful for inserting `raw` or `org` syntax results in such a way that their extent is known and they can be automatically removed or replaced.

Handling

The following results options indicate what happens with the results once they are collected.

- `silent` The results will be echoed in the minibuffer but will not be inserted into the Org mode buffer. E.g., `:results output silent`.

- `replace` The default value. Any existing results will be removed, and the new results will be inserted into the Org mode buffer in their place. E.g., `:results output replace`.

- `append` If there are pre-existing results of the code block then the new results will be appended to the existing results. Otherwise the new results will be inserted as with `replace`.

- `prepend` If there are pre-existing results of the code block then the new results will be prepended to the existing results. Otherwise the new results will be inserted as with `replace`.

14.8.2.3 `:file`

The header argument `:file` is used to specify an external file in which to save code block results. After code block evaluation an Org mode style `[[file:]]` link (see Section 4.1 [Link format], page 37) to the file will be inserted into the Org mode buffer. Some languages including R, gnuplot, dot, and ditaa provide special handling of the `:file` header argument automatically wrapping the code block body in the boilerplate code required to save output to the specified file. This is often useful for saving graphical output of a code block to the specified file.

The argument to `:file` should be either a string specifying the path to a file, or a list of two strings in which case the first element of the list should be the path to a file and the second a description for the link.

14.8.2.4 `:file-desc`

The value of the `:file-desc` header argument is used to provide a description for file code block results which are inserted as Org mode links (see Section 4.1 [Link format], page 37). If the `:file-desc` header argument is given with no value the link path will be placed in both the "link" and the "description" portion of the Org mode link.

14.8.2.5 `:file-ext`

The value of the `:file-ext` header argument is used to provide an extension to write the file output to. It is combined with the `#+NAME:` of the source block and the value of the Section 14.8.2.6 [output-dir], page 199 header argument to generate a complete file name.

This header arg will be overridden by `:file`, and thus has no effect when the latter is specified.

14.8.2.6 `:output-dir`

The value of the `:output-dir` header argument is used to provide a directory to write the file output to. It may specify an absolute directory (beginning with /) or a relative directory (without /). It can be combined with the `#+NAME:` of the source block and the value of the Section 14.8.2.5 [file-ext], page 199 header argument to generate a complete file name, or used along with a Section 14.8.2.3 [file], page 198 header arg.

14.8.2.7 `:dir` and remote execution

While the `:file` header argument can be used to specify the path to the output file, `:dir` specifies the default directory during code block execution. If it is absent, then the directory associated with the current buffer is used. In other words, supplying `:dir path` temporarily has the same effect as changing the current directory with *M-x cd path RET*, and then not supplying `:dir`. Under the surface, `:dir` simply sets the value of the Emacs variable `default-directory`.

When using `:dir`, you should supply a relative path for file output (e.g., `:file myfile.jpg` or `:file results/myfile.jpg`) in which case that path will be interpreted relative to the default directory.

In other words, if you want your plot to go into a folder called `Work` in your home directory, you could use

```
#+BEGIN_SRC R :file myplot.png :dir ~/Work
matplot(matrix(rnorm(100), 10), type="l")
#+END_SRC
```

Remote execution

A directory on a remote machine can be specified using tramp file syntax, in which case the code will be evaluated on the remote machine. An example is

```
#+BEGIN_SRC R :file plot.png :dir /dand@yakuba.princeton.edu:
plot(1:10, main=system("hostname", intern=TRUE))
```

```
#+END_SRC
```

Text results will be returned to the local Org mode buffer as usual, and file output will be created on the remote machine with relative paths interpreted relative to the remote directory. An Org mode link to the remote file will be created.

So, in the above example a plot will be created on the remote machine, and a link of the following form will be inserted in the org buffer:

```
[[file:/scp:dand@yakuba.princeton.edu:/home/dand/plot.png][plot.png]]
```

Most of this functionality follows immediately from the fact that `:dir` sets the value of the Emacs variable `default-directory`, thanks to tramp. Those using XEmacs, or GNU Emacs prior to version 23 may need to install tramp separately in order for these features to work correctly.

Further points

- If `:dir` is used in conjunction with `:session`, although it will determine the starting directory for a new session as expected, no attempt is currently made to alter the directory associated with an existing session.

- `:dir` should typically not be used to create files during export with `:exports results` or `:exports both`. The reason is that, in order to retain portability of exported material between machines, during export links inserted into the buffer will *not* be expanded against **default directory**. Therefore, if **default-directory** is altered using `:dir`, it is probable that the file will be created in a location to which the link does not point.

14.8.2.8 `:exports`

The `:exports` header argument specifies what should be included in HTML or LaTeX exports of the Org mode file. Note that the `:exports` option is only relevant for code blocks, not inline code.

- `code` The default. The body of code is included into the exported file. E.g., `:exports code`.

- `results` The result of evaluating the code is included in the exported file. E.g., `:exports results`.

- `both` Both the code and results are included in the exported file. E.g., `:exports both`.

- `none` Nothing is included in the exported file. E.g., `:exports none`.

14.8.2.9 `:tangle`

The `:tangle` header argument specifies whether or not the code block should be included in tangled extraction of source code files.

- `tangle` The code block is exported to a source code file named after the full path (including the directory) and file name (w/o extension) of the Org mode file. E.g., `:tangle yes`.

- `no` The default. The code block is not exported to a source code file. E.g., `:tangle no`.

- `other` Any other string passed to the `:tangle` header argument is interpreted as a path (directory and file name relative to the directory of the Org mode file) to which the block will be exported. E.g., `:tangle path`.

14.8.2.10 :mkdirp

The :mkdirp header argument can be used to create parent directories of tangled files when missing. This can be set to **yes** to enable directory creation or to **no** to inhibit directory creation.

14.8.2.11 :comments

By default code blocks are tangled to source-code files without any insertion of comments beyond those which may already exist in the body of the code block. The :comments header argument can be set as follows to control the insertion of extra comments into the tangled code file.

- **no** The default. No extra comments are inserted during tangling.
- **link** The code block is wrapped in comments which contain pointers back to the original Org file from which the code was tangled.
- **yes** A synonym for "link" to maintain backwards compatibility.
- **org** Include text from the Org mode file as a comment. The text is picked from the leading context of the tangled code and is limited by the nearest headline or source block as the case may be.
- **both** Turns on both the "link" and "org" comment options.
- **noweb** Turns on the "link" comment option, and additionally wraps expanded noweb references in the code block body in link comments.

14.8.2.12 :padline

Control in insertion of padding lines around code block bodies in tangled code files. The default value is **yes** which results in insertion of newlines before and after each tangled code block. The following arguments are accepted.

- **yes** Insert newlines before and after each code block body in tangled code files.
- **no** Do not insert any newline padding in tangled output.

14.8.2.13 :no-expand

By default, code blocks are expanded with **org-babel-expand-src-block** during tangling. This has the effect of assigning values to variables specified with :var (see Section 14.8.2.1 [var], page 193), and of replacing "noweb" references (see Section 14.10 [Noweb reference syntax], page 210) with their targets. The :no-expand header argument can be used to turn off this behavior. Note: The :no-expand header argument has no impact on export, i.e. code blocks will irrespective of this header argument expanded for execution.

14.8.2.14 :session

The :session header argument starts a session for an interpreted language where state is preserved.

By default, a session is not started.

A string passed to the :session header argument will give the session a name. This makes it possible to run concurrent sessions for each interpreted language.

14.8.2.15 :noweb

The :noweb header argument controls expansion of "noweb" syntax references (see Section 14.10 [Noweb reference syntax], page 210) when the code block is evaluated, tangled, or exported. The :noweb header argument can have one of the five values: no, yes, tangle, or no-export strip-export.

- **no** The default. "Noweb" syntax references in the body of the code block will not be expanded before the code block is evaluated, tangled or exported.
- **yes** "Noweb" syntax references in the body of the code block will be expanded before the code block is evaluated, tangled or exported.
- **tangle** "Noweb" syntax references in the body of the code block will be expanded before the code block is tangled. However, "noweb" syntax references will not be expanded when the code block is evaluated or exported.
- **no-export** "Noweb" syntax references in the body of the code block will be expanded before the block is evaluated or tangled. However, "noweb" syntax references will not be expanded when the code block is exported.
- **strip-export** "Noweb" syntax references in the body of the code block will be expanded before the block is evaluated or tangled. However, "noweb" syntax references will be removed when the code block is exported.
- **eval** "Noweb" syntax references in the body of the code block will only be expanded before the block is evaluated.

Noweb prefix lines

Noweb insertions are now placed behind the line prefix of the <<reference>>. This behavior is illustrated in the following example. Because the <<example>> noweb reference appears behind the SQL comment syntax, each line of the expanded noweb reference will be commented.

This code block:

```
-- <<example>>
```

expands to:

```
-- this is the
-- multi-line body of example
```

Note that noweb replacement text that does not contain any newlines will not be affected by this change, so it is still possible to use inline noweb references.

14.8.2.16 :noweb-ref

When expanding "noweb" style references, the bodies of all code block with *either* a block name matching the reference name *or* a :noweb-ref header argument matching the reference name will be concatenated together to form the replacement text.

By setting this header argument at the subtree or file level, simple code block concatenation may be achieved. For example, when tangling the following Org mode file, the bodies of code blocks will be concatenated into the resulting pure code file[5].

---

[5] (The example needs property inheritance to be turned on for the **noweb-ref** property, see Section 7.4 [Property inheritance], page 65).

```
#+BEGIN_SRC sh :tangle yes :noweb yes :shebang #!/bin/sh
  <<fullest-disk>>
#+END_SRC
* the mount point of the fullest disk
  :PROPERTIES:
  :noweb-ref: fullest-disk
  :END:

** query all mounted disks
#+BEGIN_SRC sh
  df \
#+END_SRC

** strip the header row
#+BEGIN_SRC sh
  |sed '1d' \
#+END_SRC

** sort by the percent full
#+BEGIN_SRC sh
  |awk '{print $5 " " $6}'|sort -n |tail -1 \
#+END_SRC

** extract the mount point
#+BEGIN_SRC sh
  |awk '{print $2}'
#+END_SRC
```

The :noweb-sep (see Section 14.8.2.17 [noweb-sep], page 203) header argument holds the string used to separate accumulate noweb references like those above. By default a newline is used.

14.8.2.17 :noweb-sep

The :noweb-sep header argument holds the string used to separate accumulate noweb references (see Section 14.8.2.16 [noweb-ref], page 202). By default a newline is used.

14.8.2.18 :cache

The :cache header argument controls the use of in-buffer caching of the results of evaluating code blocks. It can be used to avoid re-evaluating unchanged code blocks. Note that the :cache header argument will not attempt to cache results when the :session header argument is used, because the results of the code block execution may be stored in the session outside of the Org mode buffer. The :cache header argument can have one of two values: yes or no.

- no The default. No caching takes place, and the code block will be evaluated every time it is called.

- yes Every time the code block is run a SHA1 hash of the code and arguments passed to the block will be generated. This hash is packed into the #+RESULTS: line and will be checked on subsequent executions of the code block. If the code block has not changed since the last time it was evaluated, it will not be re-evaluated.

Code block caches notice if the value of a variable argument to the code block has changed. If this is the case, the cache is invalidated and the code block is re-run. In the following example, `caller` will not be re-run unless the results of `random` have changed since it was last run.

```
#+NAME: random
#+BEGIN_SRC R :cache yes
runif(1)
#+END_SRC

#+RESULTS[a2a72cd647ad44515fab62e144796432793d68e1]: random
0.4659510825295

#+NAME: caller
#+BEGIN_SRC emacs-lisp :var x=random :cache yes
x
#+END_SRC

#+RESULTS[bec9c8724e397d5df3b696502df3ed7892fc4f5f]: caller
0.254227238707244
```

14.8.2.19 `:sep`

The `:sep` header argument can be used to control the delimiter used when writing tabular results out to files external to Org mode. This is used either when opening tabular results of a code block by calling the `org-open-at-point` function bound to *C-c C-o* on the code block, or when writing code block results to an external file (see Section 14.8.2.3 [file], page 198) header argument.

By default, when `:sep` is not specified output tables are tab delimited.

14.8.2.20 `:hlines`

Tables are frequently represented with one or more horizontal lines, or hlines. The `:hlines` argument to a code block accepts the values **yes** or **no**, with a default value of **no**.

- **no** Strips horizontal lines from the input table. In most languages this is the desired effect because an `hline` symbol is interpreted as an unbound variable and raises an error. Setting `:hlines` **no** or relying on the default value yields the following results.

```
#+NAME: many-cols
| a | b | c |
|---+---+---|
| d | e | f |
|---+---+---|
| g | h | i |

#+NAME: echo-table
#+BEGIN_SRC python :var tab=many-cols
```

```
      return tab
#+END_SRC

#+RESULTS: echo-table
| a | b | c |
| d | e | f |
| g | h | i |
```

- yes Leaves hlines in the table. Setting :hlines yes has this effect.

```
#+NAME: many-cols
| a | b | c |
|---+---+---|
| d | e | f |
|---+---+---|
| g | h | i |

#+NAME: echo-table
#+BEGIN_SRC python :var tab=many-cols :hlines yes
  return tab
#+END_SRC

#+RESULTS: echo-table
| a | b | c |
|---+---+---|
| d | e | f |
|---+---+---|
| g | h | i |
```

14.8.2.21 :colnames

The :colnames header argument accepts the values yes, no, or nil for unassigned. The default value is nil. Note that the behavior of the :colnames header argument may differ across languages.

- nil If an input table looks like it has column names (because its second row is an hline), then the column names will be removed from the table before processing, then reapplied to the results.

```
#+NAME: less-cols
| a |
|---|
| b |
| c |

#+NAME: echo-table-again
#+BEGIN_SRC python :var tab=less-cols
  return [[val + '*' for val in row] for row in tab]
#+END_SRC

#+RESULTS: echo-table-again
```

```
| a  |
|----|
| b* |
| c* |
```

Please note that column names are not removed before the table is indexed using variable indexing See Section 14.8.2.1 [var], page 193.

- **no** No column name pre-processing takes place

- **yes** Column names are removed and reapplied as with **nil** even if the table does not "look like" it has column names (i.e., the second row is not an hline)

14.8.2.22 :rownames

The :rownames header argument can take on the values **yes** or **no**, with a default value of **no**. Note that Emacs Lisp code blocks ignore the :rownames header argument entirely given the ease with which tables with row names may be handled directly in Emacs Lisp.

- **no** No row name pre-processing will take place.

- **yes** The first column of the table is removed from the table before processing, and is then reapplied to the results.

  ```
  #+NAME: with-rownames
  | one | 1 | 2 | 3 | 4 |  5 |
  | two | 6 | 7 | 8 | 9 | 10 |

  #+NAME: echo-table-once-again
  #+BEGIN_SRC python :var tab=with-rownames :rownames yes
    return [[val + 10 for val in row] for row in tab]
  #+END_SRC

  #+RESULTS: echo-table-once-again
  | one | 11 | 12 | 13 | 14 | 15 |
  | two | 16 | 17 | 18 | 19 | 20 |
  ```

Please note that row names are not removed before the table is indexed using variable indexing See Section 14.8.2.1 [var], page 193.

14.8.2.23 :shebang

Setting the :shebang header argument to a string value (e.g., :shebang "#!/bin/bash") causes the string to be inserted as the first line of any tangled file holding the code block, and the file permissions of the tangled file are set to make it executable.

14.8.2.24 :tangle-mode

The **tangle-mode** header argument controls the permission set on tangled files. The value of this header argument will be passed to **set-file-modes**. For example, to set a tangled file as read only use :tangle-mode (identity #o444), or to set a tangled file as executable use :tangle-mode (identity #o755). Blocks with **shebang** (Section 14.8.2.23 [shebang], page 206) header arguments will automatically be made executable unless the **tangle-mode** header argument is also used. The behavior is undefined if multiple code blocks with different values for the **tangle-mode** header argument are tangled to the same file.

14.8.2.25 :eval

The :eval header argument can be used to limit the evaluation of specific code blocks. The :eval header argument can be useful for protecting against the evaluation of dangerous code blocks or to ensure that evaluation will require a query regardless of the value of the org-confirm-babel-evaluate variable. The possible values of :eval and their effects are shown below.

never or no
> The code block will not be evaluated under any circumstances.

query   Evaluation of the code block will require a query.

never-export or no-export
> The code block will not be evaluated during export but may still be called interactively.

query-export
> Evaluation of the code block during export will require a query.

If this header argument is not set then evaluation is determined by the value of the org-confirm-babel-evaluate variable see Section 15.4 [Code evaluation security], page 213.

14.8.2.26 :wrap

The :wrap header argument is used to mark the results of source block evaluation. The header argument can be passed a string that will be appended to #+BEGIN_ and #+END_, which will then be used to wrap the results. If not string is specified then the results will be wrapped in a #+BEGIN/END_RESULTS block.

14.8.2.27 :post

The :post header argument is used to post-process the results of a code block execution. When a post argument is given, the results of the code block will temporarily be bound to the *this* variable. This variable may then be included in header argument forms such as those used in Section 14.8.2.1 [var], page 193 header argument specifications allowing passing of results to other code blocks, or direct execution via Emacs Lisp.

The following example illustrates the usage of the :post header argument.

```
#+name: attr_wrap
#+begin_src sh :var data="" :var width="\\textwidth" :results output
  echo "#+ATTR_LATEX :width $width"
  echo "$data"
#+end_src

#+header: :file /tmp/it.png
#+begin_src dot :post attr_wrap(width="5cm", data=*this*) :results drawer
  digraph{
          a -> b;
          b -> c;
          c -> a;
  }
```

```
#+end_src

#+RESULTS:
:RESULTS:
#+ATTR_LATEX :width 5cm
[[file:/tmp/it.png]]
:END:
```

14.8.2.28 `:prologue`

The value of the **prologue** header argument will be prepended to the code block body before execution. For example, `:prologue "reset"` may be used to reset a gnuplot session before execution of a particular code block, or the following configuration may be used to do this for all gnuplot code blocks. Also see Section 14.8.2.29 [epilogue], page 208.

```
(add-to-list 'org-babel-default-header-args:gnuplot
        '((:prologue . "reset")))
```

14.8.2.29 `:epilogue`

The value of the **epilogue** header argument will be appended to the code block body before execution. Also see Section 14.8.2.28 [prologue], page 208.

14.9 Results of evaluation

The way in which results are handled depends on whether a session is invoked, as well as on whether `:results value` or `:results output` is used. The following table shows the table possibilities. For a full listing of the possible results header arguments see Section 14.8.2.2 [Results], page 197.

	Non-session	**Session**
`:results value`	value of last expression	value of last expression
`:results output`	contents of STDOUT	concatenation of interpreter output

Note: With `:results value`, the result in both `:session` and non-session is returned to Org mode as a table (a one- or two-dimensional vector of strings or numbers) when appropriate.

14.9.1 Non-session

14.9.1.1 `:results value`

This is the default. Internally, the value is obtained by wrapping the code in a function definition in the external language, and evaluating that function. Therefore, code should be written as if it were the body of such a function. In particular, note that Python does not automatically return a value from a function unless a **return** statement is present, and so a 'return' statement will usually be required in Python.

This is the only one of the four evaluation contexts in which the code is automatically wrapped in a function definition.

14.9.1.2 `:results output`

The code is passed to the interpreter as an external process, and the contents of the standard output stream are returned as text. (In certain languages this also contains the error output stream; this is an area for future work.)

14.9.2 Session

14.9.2.1 `:results value`

The code is passed to an interpreter running as an interactive Emacs inferior process. Only languages which provide tools for interactive evaluation of code have session support, so some language (e.g., C and ditaa) do not support the `:session` header argument, and in other languages (e.g., Python and Haskell) which have limitations on the code which may be entered into interactive sessions, those limitations apply to the code in code blocks using the `:session` header argument as well.

Unless the `:results output` option is supplied (see below) the result returned is the result of the last evaluation performed by the interpreter. (This is obtained in a language-specific manner: the value of the variable _ in Python and Ruby, and the value of `.Last.value` in R).

14.9.2.2 `:results output`

The code is passed to the interpreter running as an interactive Emacs inferior process. The result returned is the concatenation of the sequence of (text) output from the interactive interpreter. Notice that this is not necessarily the same as what would be sent to STDOUT if the same code were passed to a non-interactive interpreter running as an external process. For example, compare the following two blocks:

```
#+BEGIN_SRC python :results output
 print "hello"
 2
 print "bye"
#+END_SRC

#+RESULTS:
: hello
: bye
```

In non-session mode, the '2' is not printed and does not appear.

```
#+BEGIN_SRC python :results output :session
 print "hello"
 2
 print "bye"
#+END_SRC

#+RESULTS:
: hello
: 2
: bye
```

But in :session mode, the interactive interpreter receives input '2' and prints out its value, '2'. (Indeed, the other print statements are unnecessary here).

14.10 Noweb reference syntax

The "noweb" (see http://www.cs.tufts.edu/~nr/noweb/) Literate Programming system allows named blocks of code to be referenced by using the familiar Noweb syntax:

        <<code-block-name>>

When a code block is tangled or evaluated, whether or not "noweb" references are expanded depends upon the value of the :noweb header argument. If :noweb yes, then a Noweb reference is expanded before evaluation. If :noweb no, the default, then the reference is not expanded before evaluation. See the Section 14.8.2.16 [noweb-ref], page 202 header argument for a more flexible way to resolve noweb references.

It is possible to include the *results* of a code block rather than the body. This is done by appending parenthesis to the code block name which may optionally contain arguments to the code block as shown below.

        <<code-block-name(optional arguments)>>

Note: the default value, :noweb no, was chosen to ensure that correct code is not broken in a language, such as Ruby, where <<arg>> is a syntactically valid construct. If <<arg>> is not syntactically valid in languages that you use, then please consider setting the default value.

Note: if noweb tangling is slow in large Org mode files consider setting the org-babel-use-quick-and-dirty-noweb-expansion variable to t. This will result in faster noweb reference resolution at the expense of not correctly resolving inherited values of the :noweb-ref header argument.

14.11 Key bindings and useful functions

Many common Org mode key sequences are re-bound depending on the context.

Within a code block, the following key bindings are active:

```
C-c C-c                 org-babel-execute-src-block
C-c C-o                 org-babel-open-src-block-result
M-up                    org-babel-load-in-session
M-down                  org-babel-switch-to-session
```

In an Org mode buffer, the following key bindings are active:

```
C-c C-v p   or   C-c C-v C-p           org-babel-previous-src-block
C-c C-v n   or   C-c C-v C-n           org-babel-next-src-block
C-c C-v e   or   C-c C-v C-e           org-babel-execute-maybe
C-c C-v o   or   C-c C-v C-o           org-babel-open-src-block-result
C-c C-v v   or   C-c C-v C-v           org-babel-expand-src-block
C-c C-v u   or   C-c C-v C-u           org-babel-goto-src-block-head
C-c C-v g   or   C-c C-v C-g           org-babel-goto-named-src-block
C-c C-v r   or   C-c C-v C-r           org-babel-goto-named-result
```

C-c C-v b or *C-c C-v C-b*	org-babel-execute-buffer
C-c C-v s or *C-c C-v C-s*	org-babel-execute-subtree
C-c C-v d or *C-c C-v C-d*	org-babel-demarcate-block
C-c C-v t or *C-c C-v C-t*	org-babel-tangle
C-c C-v f or *C-c C-v C-f*	org-babel-tangle-file
C-c C-v c or *C-c C-v C-c*	org-babel-check-src-block
C-c C-v j or *C-c C-v C-j*	org-babel-insert-header-arg
C-c C-v l or *C-c C-v C-l*	org-babel-load-in-session
C-c C-v i or *C-c C-v C-i*	org-babel-lob-ingest
C-c C-v I or *C-c C-v C-I*	org-babel-view-src-block-info
C-c C-v z or *C-c C-v C-z*	org-babel-switch-to-session-with-code
C-c C-v a or *C-c C-v C-a*	org-babel-sha1-hash
C-c C-v h or *C-c C-v C-h*	org-babel-describe-bindings
C-c C-v x or *C-c C-v C-x*	org-babel-do-key-sequence-in-edit-buffer

14.12 Batch execution

It is possible to call functions from the command line. This shell script calls `org-babel-tangle` on every one of its arguments.

Be sure to adjust the paths to fit your system.

```sh
#!/bin/sh
# -*- mode: shell-script -*-
#
# tangle files with org-mode
#
DIR=`pwd`
FILES=""

# wrap each argument in the code required to call tangle on it
for i in $@; do
    FILES="$FILES \"$i\""
done

emacs -Q --batch \
--eval "(progn
(add-to-list 'load-path (expand-file-name \"~/src/org/lisp/\"))
(add-to-list 'load-path (expand-file-name \"~/src/org/contrib/lisp/\" t))
(require 'org)(require 'org-exp)(require 'ob)(require 'ob-tangle)
(mapc (lambda (file)
        (find-file (expand-file-name file \"$DIR\"))
        (org-babel-tangle)
        (kill-buffer)) '($FILES)))" 2>&1 |grep tangled
```

15 Miscellaneous

15.1 Completion

Emacs would not be Emacs without completion, and Org mode uses it whenever it makes sense. If you prefer an *iswitchb-* or *ido-*like interface for some of the completion prompts, you can specify your preference by setting at most one of the variables `org-completion-use-iswitchb org-completion-use-ido`.

Org supports in-buffer completion. This type of completion does not make use of the minibuffer. You simply type a few letters into the buffer and use the key to complete text right there.

M-TAB   Complete word at point

- At the beginning of a headline, complete TODO keywords.
- After '\', complete TEX symbols supported by the exporter.
- After '*', complete headlines in the current buffer so that they can be used in search links like '[[*find this headline]]'.
- After ':' in a headline, complete tags. The list of tags is taken from the variable `org-tag-alist` (possibly set through the '#+TAGS' in-buffer option, see Section 6.2 [Setting tags], page 58), or it is created dynamically from all tags used in the current buffer.
- After ':' and not in a headline, complete property keys. The list of keys is constructed dynamically from all keys used in the current buffer.
- After '[', complete link abbreviations (see Section 4.6 [Link abbreviations], page 43).
- After '#+', complete the special keywords like 'TYP_TODO' or 'OPTIONS' which set file-specific options for Org mode. When the option keyword is already complete, pressing *M-TAB* again will insert example settings for this keyword.
- In the line after '#+STARTUP: ', complete startup keywords, i.e., valid keys for this line.
- Elsewhere, complete dictionary words using Ispell.

15.2 Easy templates

Org mode supports insertion of empty structural elements (like #+BEGIN_SRC and #+END_SRC pairs) with just a few key strokes. This is achieved through a native template expansion mechanism. Note that Emacs has several other template mechanisms which could be used in a similar way, for example yasnippet.

To insert a structural element, type a '<', followed by a template selector and TAB. Completion takes effect only when the above keystrokes are typed on a line by itself.

The following template selectors are currently supported.

```
s        #+BEGIN_SRC ... #+END_SRC
e        #+BEGIN_EXAMPLE ... #+END_EXAMPLE
```

```
q          #+BEGIN_QUOTE ... #+END_QUOTE
v          #+BEGIN_VERSE ... #+END_VERSE
c          #+BEGIN_CENTER ... #+END_CENTER
l          #+BEGIN_LaTeX ... #+END_LaTeX
L          #+LaTeX:
h          #+BEGIN_HTML ... #+END_HTML
H          #+HTML:
a          #+BEGIN_ASCII ... #+END_ASCII
A          #+ASCII:
i          #+INDEX: line
I          #+INCLUDE: line
```

For example, on an empty line, typing "<e" and then pressing TAB, will expand into a complete EXAMPLE template.

You can install additional templates by customizing the variable `org-structure-template-alist`. See the docstring of the variable for additional details.

15.3 Speed keys

Single keys can be made to execute commands when the cursor is at the beginning of a headline, i.e., before the first star. Configure the variable `org-use-speed-commands` to activate this feature. There is a pre-defined list of commands, and you can add more such commands using the variable `org-speed-commands-user`. Speed keys not only speed up navigation and other commands, but they also provide an alternative way to execute commands bound to keys that are not or not easily available on a TTY, or on a small mobile device with a limited keyboard.

To see which commands are available, activate the feature and press **?** with the cursor at the beginning of a headline.

15.4 Code evaluation and security issues

Org provides tools to work with code snippets, including evaluating them.

Running code on your machine always comes with a security risk. Badly written or malicious code can be executed on purpose or by accident. Org has default settings which will only evaluate such code if you give explicit permission to do so, and as a casual user of these features you should leave these precautions intact.

For people who regularly work with such code, the confirmation prompts can become annoying, and you might want to turn them off. This can be done, but you must be aware of the risks that are involved.

Code evaluation can happen under the following circumstances:

Source code blocks

Source code blocks can be evaluated during export, or when pressing *C-c C-c* in the block. The most important thing to realize here is that Org mode files which contain code snippets are, in a certain sense, like executable files. So you should accept them and load them into Emacs only from trusted sources—just like you would do with a program you install on your computer.

Make sure you know what you are doing before customizing the variables which take off the default security brakes.

org-confirm-babel-evaluate   [User Option]
> When t (the default), the user is asked before every code block evaluation. When `nil`, the user is not asked. When set to a function, it is called with two arguments (language and body of the code block) and should return t to ask and `nil` not to ask.

For example, here is how to execute "ditaa" code (which is considered safe) without asking:

(defun my-org-confirm-babel-evaluate (lang body)
  (not (string= lang "ditaa"))) ; don't ask for ditaa
(setq org-confirm-babel-evaluate 'my-org-confirm-babel-evaluate)

Following `shell` *and* `elisp` *links*
> Org has two link types that can directly evaluate code (see Section 4.3 [External links], page 38). These links can be problematic because the code to be evaluated is not visible.

org-confirm-shell-link-function   [User Option]
> Function to queries user about shell link execution.

org-confirm-elisp-link-function   [User Option]
> Functions to query user for Emacs Lisp link execution.

Formulas in tables
> Formulas in tables (see Section 3.5 [The spreadsheet], page 24) are code that is evaluated either by the *calc* interpreter, or by the *Emacs Lisp* interpreter.

15.5 Customization

There are more than 500 variables that can be used to customize Org. For the sake of compactness of the manual, I am not describing the variables here. A structured overview of customization variables is available with *M-x org-customize RET*. Or select `Browse Org Group` from the `Org->Customization` menu. Many settings can also be activated on a per-file basis, by putting special lines into the buffer (see Section 15.6 [In-buffer settings], page 214).

15.6 Summary of in-buffer settings

Org mode uses special lines in the buffer to define settings on a per-file basis. These lines start with a '#+' followed by a keyword, a colon, and then individual words defining a setting. Several setting words can be in the same line, but you can also have multiple lines for the keyword. While these settings are described throughout the manual, here is a summary. After changing any of these lines in the buffer, press *C-c C-c* with the cursor still in the line to activate the changes immediately. Otherwise they become effective only when the file is visited again in a new Emacs session.

#+ARCHIVE: %s_done::
> This line sets the archive location for the agenda file. It applies for all subsequent lines until the next '#+ARCHIVE' line, or the end of the file. The first such line also applies to any entries before it. The corresponding variable is `org-archive-location`.

#+CATEGORY:
> This line sets the category for the agenda file. The category applies for all subsequent lines until the next '#+CATEGORY' line, or the end of the file. The first such line also applies to any entries before it.

#+COLUMNS: %25ITEM ...
> Set the default format for columns view. This format applies when columns view is invoked in locations where no `COLUMNS` property applies.

#+CONSTANTS: name1=value1 ...
> Set file-local values for constants to be used in table formulas. This line sets the local variable `org-table-formula-constants-local`. The global version of this variable is `org-table-formula-constants`.

#+FILETAGS: :tag1:tag2:tag3:
> Set tags that can be inherited by any entry in the file, including the top-level entries.

#+LINK: linkword replace
> These lines (several are allowed) specify link abbreviations. See Section 4.6 [Link abbreviations], page 43. The corresponding variable is `org-link-abbrev-alist`.

#+PRIORITIES: highest lowest default
> This line sets the limits and the default for the priorities. All three must be either letters A–Z or numbers 0–9. The highest priority must have a lower ASCII number than the lowest priority.

#+PROPERTY: Property_Name Value
> This line sets a default inheritance value for entries in the current buffer, most useful for specifying the allowed values of a property.

#+SETUPFILE: file
> This line defines a file that holds more in-buffer setup. Normally this is entirely ignored. Only when the buffer is parsed for option-setting lines (i.e., when starting Org mode for a file, when pressing C-c C-c in a settings line, or when exporting), then the contents of this file are parsed as if they had been included in the buffer. In particular, the file can be any other Org mode file with internal setup. You can visit the file the cursor is in the line with C-c '.

#+STARTUP:
> This line sets options to be used at startup of Org mode, when an Org file is being visited.

> The first set of options deals with the initial visibility of the outline tree. The corresponding variable for global default settings is `org-startup-folded`, with a default value t, which means overview.

`overview`	top-level headlines only
`content`	all headlines
`showall`	no folding of any entries
`showeverything`	show even drawer contents

Dynamic virtual indentation is controlled by the variable `org-startup-indented`[1]

`indent`	start with `org-indent-mode` turned on
`noindent`	start with `org-indent-mode` turned off

Then there are options for aligning tables upon visiting a file. This is useful in files containing narrowed table columns. The corresponding variable is `org-startup-align-all-tables`, with a default value `nil`.

`align`	align all tables
`noalign`	don't align tables on startup

When visiting a file, inline images can be automatically displayed. The corresponding variable is `org-startup-with-inline-images`, with a default value `nil` to avoid delays when visiting a file.

`inlineimages`	show inline images
`noinlineimages`	don't show inline images on startup

When visiting a file, LaTeX fragments can be converted to images automatically. The variable `org-startup-with-latex-preview` which controls this behavior, is set to `nil` by default to avoid delays on startup.

`latexpreview`	preview LaTeX fragments
`nolatexpreview`	don't preview LaTeX fragments

Logging the closing and reopening of TODO items and clock intervals can be configured using these options (see variables `org-log-done`, `org-log-note-clock-out` and `org-log-repeat`)

`logdone`	record a timestamp when an item is marked DONE
`lognotedone`	record timestamp and a note when DONE
`nologdone`	don't record when items are marked DONE
`logrepeat`	record a time when reinstating a repeating item
`lognoterepeat`	record a note when reinstating a repeating item
`nologrepeat`	do not record when reinstating repeating item
`lognoteclock-out`	record a note when clocking out
`nolognoteclock-out`	don't record a note when clocking out
`logreschedule`	record a timestamp when scheduling time changes
`lognotereschedule`	record a note when scheduling time changes
`nologreschedule`	do not record when a scheduling date changes
`logredeadline`	record a timestamp when deadline changes
`lognoteredeadline`	record a note when deadline changes
`nologredeadline`	do not record when a deadline date changes
`logrefile`	record a timestamp when refiling
`lognoterefile`	record a note when refiling
`nologrefile`	do not record when refiling

---

[1] Emacs 23 and Org mode 6.29 are required

logdrawer	store log into drawer
nologdrawer	store log outside of drawer
logstatesreversed	reverse the order of states notes
nologstatesreversed	do not reverse the order of states notes

Here are the options for hiding leading stars in outline headings, and for indenting outlines. The corresponding variables are `org-hide-leading-stars` and `org-odd-levels-only`, both with a default setting `nil` (meaning `showstars` and `oddeven`).

hidestars	make all but one of the stars starting a headline invisible.
showstars	show all stars starting a headline
indent	virtual indentation according to outline level
noindent	no virtual indentation according to outline level
odd	allow only odd outline levels (1,3,...)
oddeven	allow all outline levels

To turn on custom format overlays over timestamps (variables `org-put-time-stamp-overlays` and `org-time-stamp-overlay-formats`), use

customtime	overlay custom time format

The following options influence the table spreadsheet (variable `constants-unit-system`).

constcgs	`constants.el` should use the c-g-s unit system
constSI	`constants.el` should use the SI unit system

To influence footnote settings, use the following keywords. The corresponding variables are `org-footnote-define-inline`, `org-footnote-auto-label`, and `org-footnote-auto-adjust`.

fninline	define footnotes inline
fnnoinline	define footnotes in separate section
fnlocal	define footnotes near first reference, but not inline
fnprompt	prompt for footnote labels
fnauto	create `[fn:1]`-like labels automatically (default)
fnconfirm	offer automatic label for editing or confirmation
fnplain	create `[1]`-like labels automatically
fnadjust	automatically renumber and sort footnotes
nofnadjust	do not renumber and sort automatically

To hide blocks on startup, use these keywords. The corresponding variable is `org-hide-block-startup`.

hideblocks	Hide all begin/end blocks on startup
nohideblocks	Do not hide blocks on startup

The display of entities as UTF-8 characters is governed by the variable `org-pretty-entities` and the keywords

entitiespretty	Show entities as UTF-8 characters where possible
entitiesplain	Leave entities plain

#+TAGS: TAG1(c1) TAG2(c2)

These lines (several such lines are allowed) specify the valid tags in this file, and (potentially) the corresponding *fast tag selection* keys. The corresponding variable is `org-tag-alist`.

#+TBLFM: This line contains the formulas for the table directly above the line.

Table can have multiple lines containing '#+TBLFM:'. Note that only the first line of '#+TBLFM:' will be applied when you recalculate the table. For more details see [Using multiple #+TBLFM lines], page 32 in Section 3.5.8 [Editing and debugging formulas], page 31.

#+TITLE:, #+AUTHOR:, #+EMAIL:, #+LANGUAGE:, #+DATE:,
#+OPTIONS:, #+BIND:,
#+DESCRIPTION:, #+KEYWORDS:,
#+LaTeX_HEADER:, #+LaTeX_HEADER_EXTRA:,
#+HTML_HEAD:, #+HTML_HEAD_EXTRA:, #+HTML_LINK_UP:, #+HTML_LINK_HOME:,
#+SELECT_TAGS:, #+EXCLUDE_TAGS:

These lines provide settings for exporting files. For more details see Section 12.3 [Export settings], page 138.

#+TODO: #+SEQ_TODO: #+TYP_TODO:

These lines set the TODO keywords and their interpretation in the current file. The corresponding variable is `org-todo-keywords`.

15.7 The very busy C-c C-c key

The key `C-c C-c` has many purposes in Org, which are all mentioned scattered throughout this manual. One specific function of this key is to add *tags* to a headline (see Chapter 6 [Tags], page 58). In many other circumstances it means something like *"Hey Org, look here and update according to what you see here"*. Here is a summary of what this means in different contexts.

— If there are highlights in the buffer from the creation of a sparse tree, or from clock display, remove these highlights.

— If the cursor is in one of the special #+KEYWORD lines, this triggers scanning the buffer for these lines and updating the information.

— If the cursor is inside a table, realign the table. This command works even if the automatic table editor has been turned off.

— If the cursor is on a #+TBLFM line, re-apply the formulas to the entire table.

— If the current buffer is a capture buffer, close the note and file it. With a prefix argument, file it, without further interaction, to the default location.

— If the cursor is on a <<<target>>>, update radio targets and corresponding links in this buffer.

— If the cursor is in a property line or at the start or end of a property drawer, offer property commands.

— If the cursor is at a footnote reference, go to the corresponding definition, and *vice versa*.

— If the cursor is on a statistics cookie, update it.

— If the cursor is in a plain list item with a checkbox, toggle the status of the checkbox.

— If the cursor is on a numbered item in a plain list, renumber the ordered list.

— If the cursor is on the `#+BEGIN` line of a dynamic block, the block is updated.

— If the cursor is at a timestamp, fix the day name in the timestamp.

15.8 A cleaner outline view

Some people find it noisy and distracting that the Org headlines start with a potentially large number of stars, and that text below the headlines is not indented. While this is no problem when writing a *book-like* document where the outline headings are really section headings, in a more *list-oriented* outline, indented structure is a lot cleaner:

```
* Top level headline           |    * Top level headline
** Second level                |      * Second level
*** 3rd level                  |        * 3rd level
some text                      |          some text
*** 3rd level                  |        * 3rd level
more text                      |          more text
* Another top level headline   |    * Another top level headline
```

If you are using at least Emacs 23.2[2] and version 6.29 of Org, this kind of view can be achieved dynamically at display time using **org-indent-mode**. In this minor mode, all lines are prefixed for display with the necessary amount of space[3]. Also headlines are prefixed with additional stars, so that the amount of indentation shifts by two[4] spaces per level. All headline stars but the last one are made invisible using the **org-hide** face[5]; see below under '2.' for more information on how this works. You can turn on **org-indent-mode** for all files by customizing the variable **org-startup-indented**, or you can turn it on for individual files using

> `#+STARTUP: indent`

If you want a similar effect in an earlier version of Emacs and/or Org, or if you want the indentation to be hard space characters so that the plain text file looks as similar as possible to the Emacs display, Org supports you in the following way:

1. *Indentation of text below headlines*
   You may indent text below each headline to make the left boundary line up with the headline, like

   ```
   *** 3rd level
       more text, now indented
   ```

   Org supports this with paragraph filling, line wrapping, and structure editing[6], preserving or adapting the indentation as appropriate.

---

[2] Emacs 23.1 can actually crash with `org-indent-mode`

[3] `org-indent-mode` also sets the `wrap-prefix` property, such that `visual-line-mode` (or purely setting `word-wrap`) wraps long lines (including headlines) correctly indented.

[4] See the variable `org-indent-indentation-per-level`.

[5] Turning on `org-indent-mode` sets `org-hide-leading-stars` to t and `org-adapt-indentation` to nil.

[6] See also the variable `org-adapt-indentation`.

2. *Hiding leading stars*

   You can modify the display in such a way that all leading stars become invisible. To do this in a global way, configure the variable `org-hide-leading-stars` or change this on a per-file basis with

   ```
   #+STARTUP: hidestars
   #+STARTUP: showstars
   ```

   With hidden stars, the tree becomes:

   ```
   * Top level headline
    * Second level
     * 3rd level
       ...
   ```

   The leading stars are not truly replaced by whitespace, they are only fontified with the face `org-hide` that uses the background color as font color. If you are not using either white or black background, you may have to customize this face to get the wanted effect. Another possibility is to set this font such that the extra stars are *almost* invisible, for example using the color `grey90` on a white background.

3. Things become cleaner still if you skip all the even levels and use only odd levels 1, 3, 5..., effectively adding two stars to go from one outline level to the next[7]. In this way we get the outline view shown at the beginning of this section. In order to make the structure editing and export commands handle this convention correctly, configure the variable `org-odd-levels-only`, or set this on a per-file basis with one of the following lines:

   ```
   #+STARTUP: odd
   #+STARTUP: oddeven
   ```

   You can convert an Org file from single-star-per-level to the double-star-per-level convention with *M-x org-convert-to-odd-levels RET* in that file. The reverse operation is *M-x org-convert-to-oddeven-levels*.

15.9 Using Org on a tty

Because Org contains a large number of commands, by default many of Org's core commands are bound to keys that are generally not accessible on a tty, such as the cursor keys (`left`, `right`, `up`, `down`), `TAB` and `RET`, in particular when used together with modifiers like `Meta` and/or `Shift`. To access these commands on a tty when special keys are unavailable, the following alternative bindings can be used. The tty bindings below will likely be more cumbersome; you may find for some of the bindings below that a customized workaround suits you better. For example, changing a timestamp is really only fun with *S-cursor* keys, whereas on a tty you would rather use *C-c .* to re-insert the timestamp.

Default	Alternative 1	Speed key	Alternative 2
S-TAB	*C-u TAB*	C	
M-left	*C-c C-x l*	l	*Esc left*
M-S-left	*C-c C-x L*	L	

---

[7] When you need to specify a level for a property search or refile targets, 'LEVEL=2' will correspond to 3 stars, etc.

M-right	C-c C-x r	r	Esc right
M-S-right	C-c C-x R	R	
M-up	C-c C-x u		Esc up
M-S-up	C-c C-x U	U	
M-down	C-c C-x d		Esc down
M-S-down	C-c C-x D	D	
S-RET	C-c C-x c		
M-RET	C-c C-x m		Esc RET
M-S-RET	C-c C-x M		
S-left	C-c left		
S-right	C-c right		
S-up	C-c up		
S-down	C-c down		
C-S-left	C-c C-x left		
C-S-right	C-c C-x right		

15.10 Interaction with other packages

Org lives in the world of GNU Emacs and interacts in various ways with other code out there.

15.10.1 Packages that Org cooperates with

calc.el by Dave Gillespie

> Org uses the Calc package for implementing spreadsheet functionality in its tables (see Section 3.5 [The spreadsheet], page 24). Org checks for the availability of Calc by looking for the function calc-eval which will have been autoloaded during setup if Calc has been installed properly. As of Emacs 22, Calc is part of the Emacs distribution. Another possibility for interaction between the two packages is using Calc for embedded calculations. See Section "Embedded Mode" in *GNU Emacs Calc Manual*.

constants.el by Carsten Dominik

> In a table formula (see Section 3.5 [The spreadsheet], page 24), it is possible to use names for natural constants or units. Instead of defining your own constants in the variable org-table-formula-constants, install the constants package which defines a large number of constants and units, and lets you use unit prefixes like 'M' for 'Mega', etc. You will need version 2.0 of this package, available at http://www.astro.uva.nl/~dominik/Tools. Org checks for the function constants-get, which has to be autoloaded in your setup. See the installation instructions in the file constants.el.

cdlatex.el by Carsten Dominik

> Org mode can make use of the CDLATEX package to efficiently enter LATEX fragments into Org files. See Section 11.7.5 [CDLaTeX mode], page 135.

imenu.el by Ake Stenhoff and Lars Lindberg

> Imenu allows menu access to an index of items in a file. Org mode supports Imenu—all you need to do to get the index is the following:

```
(add-hook 'org-mode-hook
        (lambda () (imenu-add-to-menubar "Imenu")))
```

By default the index is two levels deep—you can modify the depth using the option `org-imenu-depth`.

`remember.el` by John Wiegley
Org used to use this package for capture, but no longer does.

`speedbar.el` by Eric M. Ludlam
Speedbar is a package that creates a special frame displaying files and index items in files. Org mode supports Speedbar and allows you to drill into Org files directly from the Speedbar. It also allows you to restrict the scope of agenda commands to a file or a subtree by using the command `<` in the Speedbar frame.

`table.el` by Takaaki Ota
Complex ASCII tables with automatic line wrapping, column- and row-spanning, and alignment can be created using the Emacs table package by Takaaki Ota (`http://sourceforge.net/projects/table`, and also part of Emacs 22). Org mode will recognize these tables and export them properly. Because of interference with other Org mode functionality, you unfortunately cannot edit these tables directly in the buffer. Instead, you need to use the command `C-c '` to edit them, similar to source code snippets.

`C-c '`   org-edit-special
Edit a `table.el` table. Works when the cursor is in a table.el table.

`C-c ~`   org-table-create-with-table.el
Insert a `table.el` table. If there is already a table at point, this command converts it between the `table.el` format and the Org mode format. See the documentation string of the command `org-convert-table` for the restrictions under which this is possible.

`table.el` is part of Emacs since Emacs 22.

`footnote.el` by Steven L. Baur
Org mode recognizes numerical footnotes as provided by this package. However, Org mode also has its own footnote support (see Section 2.10 [Footnotes], page 16), which makes using `footnote.el` unnecessary.

15.10.2 Packages that lead to conflicts with Org mode

In Emacs 23, `shift-selection-mode` is on by default, meaning that cursor motions combined with the shift key should start or enlarge regions. This conflicts with the use of *S-cursor* commands in Org to change timestamps, TODO keywords, priorities, and item bullet types if the cursor is at such a location. By default, *S-cursor* commands outside special contexts don't do anything, but you can customize the variable `org-support-shift-select`. Org mode then tries to accommodate shift selection by (i) using it outside of the special contexts where special commands apply, and by (ii) extending an existing active region even if the cursor moves across a special context.

`CUA.el` by Kim. F. Storm

Key bindings in Org conflict with the *S-<cursor>* keys used by CUA mode (as well as `pc-select-mode` and `s-region-mode`) to select and extend the region. In fact, Emacs 23 has this built-in in the form of `shift-selection-mode`, see previous paragraph. If you are using Emacs 23, you probably don't want to use another package for this purpose. However, if you prefer to leave these keys to a different package while working in Org mode, configure the variable `org-replace-disputed-keys`. When set, Org will move the following key bindings in Org files, and in the agenda buffer (but not during date selection).

S-UP	⇒	M-p	S-DOWN	⇒	M-n
S-LEFT	⇒	M--	S-RIGHT	⇒	M-+
C-S-LEFT	⇒	M-S--	C-S-RIGHT	⇒	M-S-+

Yes, these are unfortunately more difficult to remember. If you want to have other replacement keys, look at the variable `org-disputed-keys`.

`ecomplete.el` by Lars Magne Ingebrigtsen `larsi@gnus.org`

Ecomplete provides "electric" address completion in address header lines in message buffers. Sadly Orgtbl mode cuts ecompletes power supply: No completion happens when Orgtbl mode is enabled in message buffers while entering text in address header lines. If one wants to use ecomplete one should *not* follow the advice to automagically turn on Orgtbl mode in message buffers (see Section 3.4 [Orgtbl mode], page 23), but instead—after filling in the message headers—turn on Orgtbl mode manually when needed in the messages body.

`filladapt.el` by Kyle Jones

Org mode tries to do the right thing when filling paragraphs, list items and other elements. Many users reported they had problems using both `filladapt.el` and Org mode, so a safe thing to do is to disable it like this:

(add-hook 'org-mode-hook 'turn-off-filladapt-mode)

`yasnippet.el`

The way Org mode binds the `TAB` key (binding to [tab] instead of "\t") overrules YASnippet's access to this key. The following code fixed this problem:

(add-hook 'org-mode-hook
          (lambda ()
            (org-set-local 'yas/trigger-key [tab])
            (define-key yas/keymap [tab] 'yas/next-field-or-maybe-expand)))

The latest version of yasnippet doesn't play well with Org mode. If the above code does not fix the conflict, start by defining the following function:

(defun yas/org-very-safe-expand ()
  (let ((yas/fallback-behavior 'return-nil)) (yas/expand)))

Then, tell Org mode what to do with the new function:

(add-hook 'org-mode-hook

```
(lambda ()
  (make-variable-buffer-local 'yas/trigger-key)
  (setq yas/trigger-key [tab])
  (add-to-list 'org-tab-first-hook 'yas/org-very-safe-expand)
  (define-key yas/keymap [tab] 'yas/next-field)))
```

`windmove.el` by Hovav Shacham

This package also uses the `S-<cursor>` keys, so everything written in the paragraph above about CUA mode also applies here. If you want make the windmove function active in locations where Org mode does not have special functionality on `S-cursor`, add this to your configuration:

```
;; Make windmove work in org-mode:
(add-hook 'org-shiftup-final-hook 'windmove-up)
(add-hook 'org-shiftleft-final-hook 'windmove-left)
(add-hook 'org-shiftdown-final-hook 'windmove-down)
(add-hook 'org-shiftright-final-hook 'windmove-right)
```

`viper.el` by Michael Kifer

Viper uses `C-c /` and therefore makes this key not access the corresponding Org mode command `org-sparse-tree`. You need to find another key for this command, or override the key in `viper-vi-global-user-map` with

```
(define-key viper-vi-global-user-map "C-c /" 'org-sparse-tree)
```

15.11 org-crypt.el

Org-crypt will encrypt the text of an entry, but not the headline, or properties. Org-crypt uses the Emacs EasyPG library to encrypt and decrypt files.

Any text below a headline that has a ':`crypt`:' tag will be automatically be encrypted when the file is saved. If you want to use a different tag just customize the `org-crypt-tag-matcher` setting.

To use org-crypt it is suggested that you have the following in your `.emacs`:

```
(require 'org-crypt)
(org-crypt-use-before-save-magic)
(setq org-tags-exclude-from-inheritance (quote ("crypt")))

(setq org-crypt-key nil)
  ;; GPG key to use for encryption
  ;; Either the Key ID or set to nil to use symmetric encryption.

(setq auto-save-default nil)
  ;; Auto-saving does not cooperate with org-crypt.el: so you need
  ;; to turn it off if you plan to use org-crypt.el quite often.
  ;; Otherwise, you'll get an (annoying) message each time you
  ;; start Org.

  ;; To turn it off only locally, you can insert this:
  ;;
```

```
;; # -*- buffer-auto-save-file-name: nil; -*-
```

Excluding the crypt tag from inheritance prevents already encrypted text being encrypted again.

Appendix A Hacking

This appendix covers some areas where users can extend the functionality of Org.

A.1 Hooks

Org has a large number of hook variables that can be used to add functionality. This appendix about hacking is going to illustrate the use of some of them. A complete list of all hooks with documentation is maintained by the Worg project and can be found at `http://orgmode.org/worg/org-configs/org-hooks.php`.

A.2 Add-on packages

A large number of add-on packages have been written by various authors.

These packages are not part of Emacs, but they are distributed as contributed packages with the separate release available at `http://orgmode.org`. See the `contrib/README` file in the source code directory for a list of contributed files. You may also find some more information on the Worg page: `http://orgmode.org/worg/org-contrib/`.

A.3 Adding hyperlink types

Org has a large number of hyperlink types built-in (see Chapter 4 [Hyperlinks], page 37). If you would like to add new link types, Org provides an interface for doing so. Let's look at an example file, `org-man.el`, that will add support for creating links like '`[[man:printf][The printf manpage]]`' to show Unix manual pages inside Emacs:

```
;;; org-man.el - Support for links to manpages in Org

(require 'org)

(org-add-link-type "man" 'org-man-open)
(add-hook 'org-store-link-functions 'org-man-store-link)

(defcustom org-man-command 'man
  "The Emacs command to be used to display a man page."
  :group 'org-link
  :type '(choice (const man) (const woman)))

(defun org-man-open (path)
  "Visit the manpage on PATH.
PATH should be a topic that can be thrown at the man command."
  (funcall org-man-command path))

(defun org-man-store-link ()
  "Store a link to a manpage."
  (when (memq major-mode '(Man-mode woman-mode))
    ;; This is a man page, we do make this link
    (let* ((page (org-man-get-page-name))
           (link (concat "man:" page))
```

```
      (description (format "Manpage for %s" page)))
    (org-store-link-props
     :type "man"
     :link link
     :description description)))))

(defun org-man-get-page-name ()
  "Extract the page name from the buffer name."
  ;; This works for both 'Man-mode' and 'woman-mode'.
  (if (string-match " \\(\\S-+\\)\\*" (buffer-name))
      (match-string 1 (buffer-name))
    (error "Cannot create link to this man page")))

(provide 'org-man)

;;; org-man.el ends here
```

You would activate this new link type in `.emacs` with

```
(require 'org-man)
```

Let's go through the file and see what it does.

1. It does (`require 'org`) to make sure that `org.el` has been loaded.

2. The next line calls `org-add-link-type` to define a new link type with prefix 'man'. The call also contains the name of a function that will be called to follow such a link.

3. The next line adds a function to `org-store-link-functions`, in order to allow the command `C-c l` to record a useful link in a buffer displaying a man page.

The rest of the file defines the necessary variables and functions. First there is a customization variable that determines which Emacs command should be used to display man pages. There are two options, `man` and `woman`. Then the function to follow a link is defined. It gets the link path as an argument—in this case the link path is just a topic for the manual command. The function calls the value of `org-man-command` to display the man page.

Finally the function `org-man-store-link` is defined. When you try to store a link with `C-c l`, this function will be called to try to make a link. The function must first decide if it is supposed to create the link for this buffer type; we do this by checking the value of the variable `major-mode`. If not, the function must exit and return the value `nil`. If yes, the link is created by getting the manual topic from the buffer name and prefixing it with the string 'man:'. Then it must call the command `org-store-link-props` and set the `:type` and `:link` properties. Optionally you can also set the `:description` property to provide a default for the link description when the link is later inserted into an Org buffer with `C-c C-l`.

When it makes sense for your new link type, you may also define a function `org-PREFIX-complete-link` that implements special (e.g., completion) support for inserting such a link with `C-c C-l`. Such a function should not accept any arguments, and return the full link with prefix.

A.4 Adding export back-ends

Org 8.0 comes with a completely rewritten export engine which makes it easy to write new export back-ends, either from scratch, or by deriving them from existing ones.

Your two entry points are respectively `org-export-define-backend` and `org-export-define-derived-backend`. To grok these functions, you should first have a look at `ox-latex.el` (for how to define a new back-end from scratch) and `ox-beamer.el` (for how to derive a new back-end from an existing one.

When creating a new back-end from scratch, the basic idea is to set the name of the back-end (as a symbol) and an an alist of elements and export functions. On top of this, you will need to set additional keywords like `:menu-entry` (to display the back-end in the export dispatcher), `:export-block` (to specify what blocks should not be exported by this back-end), and `:options-alist` (to let the user set export options that are specific to this back-end.)

Deriving a new back-end is similar, except that you need to set `:translate-alist` to an alist of export functions that should be used instead of the parent back-end functions.

For a complete reference documentation, see the Org Export Reference on Worg.

A.5 Context-sensitive commands

Org has several commands that act differently depending on context. The most important example is the `C-c C-c` (see Section 15.7 [The very busy C-c C-c key], page 218). Also the `M-cursor` and `M-S-cursor` keys have this property.

Add-ons can tap into this functionality by providing a function that detects special context for that add-on and executes functionality appropriate for the context. Here is an example from Dan Davison's `org-R.el` which allows you to evaluate commands based on the R programming language[1]. For this package, special contexts are lines that start with `#+R:` or `#+RR:`.

```
(defun org-R-apply-maybe ()
  "Detect if this is context for org-R and execute R commands."
  (if (save-excursion
        (beginning-of-line 1)
        (looking-at "#\\+RR?:"))
      (progn (call-interactively 'org-R-apply)
             t) ;; to signal that we took action
    nil)) ;; to signal that we did not


(add-hook 'org-ctrl-c-ctrl-c-hook 'org-R-apply-maybe)
```

The function first checks if the cursor is in such a line. If that is the case, `org-R-apply` is called and the function returns `t` to signal that action was taken, and `C-c C-c` will stop looking for other contexts. If the function finds it should do nothing locally, it returns `nil` so that other, similar functions can have a try.

---

[1] `org-R.el` has been replaced by the Org mode functionality described in Chapter 14 [Working with source code], page 184 and is now obsolete.

A.6 Tables and lists in arbitrary syntax

Since Orgtbl mode can be used as a minor mode in arbitrary buffers, a frequent feature request has been to make it work with native tables in specific languages, for example LaTeX. However, this is extremely hard to do in a general way, would lead to a customization nightmare, and would take away much of the simplicity of the Orgtbl mode table editor.

This appendix describes a different approach. We keep the Orgtbl mode table in its native format (the *source table*), and use a custom function to *translate* the table to the correct syntax, and to *install* it in the right location (the *target table*). This puts the burden of writing conversion functions on the user, but it allows for a very flexible system.

Bastien added the ability to do the same with lists, in Orgstruct mode. You can use Org's facilities to edit and structure lists by turning `orgstruct-mode` on, then locally exporting such lists in another format (HTML, LaTeX or Texinfo.)

A.6.1 Radio tables

To define the location of the target table, you first need to create two lines that are comments in the current mode, but contain magic words `BEGIN/END RECEIVE ORGTBL` for Orgtbl mode to find. Orgtbl mode will insert the translated table between these lines, replacing whatever was there before. For example in C mode where comments are between `/* ... */`:

```
/* BEGIN RECEIVE ORGTBL table_name */
/* END RECEIVE ORGTBL table_name */
```

Just above the source table, we put a special line that tells Orgtbl mode how to translate this table and where to install it. For example:

```
#+ORGTBL: SEND table_name translation_function arguments...
```

`table_name` is the reference name for the table that is also used in the receiver lines. `translation_function` is the Lisp function that does the translation. Furthermore, the line can contain a list of arguments (alternating key and value) at the end. The arguments will be passed as a property list to the translation function for interpretation. A few standard parameters are already recognized and acted upon before the translation function is called:

`:skip N`   Skip the first N lines of the table. Hlines do count as separate lines for this parameter!

`:skipcols (n1 n2 ...)`
             List of columns that should be skipped. If the table has a column with calculation marks, that column is automatically discarded as well. Please note that the translator function sees the table *after* the removal of these columns, the function never knows that there have been additional columns.

`:no-escape t`
             When non-`nil`, do not escape special characters `&%#_^` when exporting the table. The default value is `nil`.

The one problem remaining is how to keep the source table in the buffer without disturbing the normal workings of the file, for example during compilation of a C file or processing of a LaTeX file. There are a number of different solutions:

- The table could be placed in a block comment if that is supported by the language. For example, in C mode you could wrap the table between '/*' and '*/' lines.

- Sometimes it is possible to put the table after some kind of *END* statement, for example '\bye' in TeX and '\end{document}' in LaTeX.

- You can just comment the table line-by-line whenever you want to process the file, and uncomment it whenever you need to edit the table. This only sounds tedious—the command *M-x orgtbl-toggle-comment RET* makes this comment-toggling very easy, in particular if you bind it to a key.

A.6.2 A LaTeX example of radio tables

The best way to wrap the source table in LaTeX is to use the `comment` environment provided by `comment.sty`. It has to be activated by placing \usepackage{comment} into the document header. Orgtbl mode can insert a radio table skeleton[2] with the command *M-x orgtbl-insert-radio-table RET*. You will be prompted for a table name, let's say we use 'salesfigures'. You will then get the following template:

```
% BEGIN RECEIVE ORGTBL salesfigures
% END RECEIVE ORGTBL salesfigures
\begin{comment}
#+ORGTBL: SEND salesfigures orgtbl-to-latex
| | |
\end{comment}
```

The `#+ORGTBL: SEND` line tells Orgtbl mode to use the function `orgtbl-to-latex` to convert the table into LaTeX and to put it into the receiver location with name `salesfigures`. You may now fill in the table—feel free to use the spreadsheet features[3]:

```
% BEGIN RECEIVE ORGTBL salesfigures
% END RECEIVE ORGTBL salesfigures
\begin{comment}
#+ORGTBL: SEND salesfigures orgtbl-to-latex
| Month | Days | Nr sold | per day |
|-------+------+---------+---------|
| Jan   | 23   |    55   |   2.4   |
| Feb   | 21   |    16   |   0.8   |
| March | 22   |   278   |  12.6   |
#+TBLFM: $4=$3/$2;%.1f
% $ (optional extra dollar to keep font-lock happy, see footnote)
\end{comment}
```

When you are done, press *C-c C-c* in the table to get the converted table inserted between the two marker lines.

---

[2] By default this works only for LaTeX, HTML, and Texinfo. Configure the variable `orgtbl-radio-table-templates` to install templates for other modes.

[3] If the '#+TBLFM' line contains an odd number of dollar characters, this may cause problems with font-lock in LaTeX mode. As shown in the example you can fix this by adding an extra line inside the `comment` environment that is used to balance the dollar expressions. If you are using AUCTeX with the font-latex library, a much better solution is to add the `comment` environment to the variable `LaTeX-verbatim-environments`.

Now let's assume you want to make the table header by hand, because you want to control how columns are aligned, etc. In this case we make sure that the table translator skips the first 2 lines of the source table, and tell the command to work as a *splice*, i.e., to not produce header and footer commands of the target table:

```
\begin{tabular}{lrrr}
Month & \multicolumn{1}{c}{Days} & Nr.\ sold & per day\\
% BEGIN RECEIVE ORGTBL salesfigures
% END RECEIVE ORGTBL salesfigures
\end{tabular}
%
\begin{comment}
#+ORGTBL: SEND salesfigures orgtbl-to-latex :splice t :skip 2
| Month | Days | Nr sold | per day |
|-------+------+---------+---------|
| Jan   |   23 |      55 |     2.4 |
| Feb   |   21 |      16 |     0.8 |
| March |   22 |     278 |    12.6 |
#+TBLFM: $4=$3/$2;%.1f
\end{comment}
```

The LATEX translator function `orgtbl-to-latex` is already part of Orgtbl mode. It uses a `tabular` environment to typeset the table and marks horizontal lines with `\hline`. Furthermore, it interprets the following parameters (see also see Section A.6.3 [Translator functions], page 231):

`:splice nil/t`

> When set to t, return only table body lines, don't wrap them into a tabular environment. Default is `nil`.

`:fmt fmt`   A format to be used to wrap each field, it should contain `%s` for the original field value. For example, to wrap each field value in dollars, you could use `:fmt "$%s$"`. This may also be a property list with column numbers and formats, for example `:fmt (2 "$%s$" 4 "%s\\%%")`. A function of one argument can be used in place of the strings; the function must return a formatted string.

`:efmt efmt`

> Use this format to print numbers with exponentials. The format should have `%s` twice for inserting mantissa and exponent, for example `"%s\\times10^{%s}"`. The default is `"%s\\,(%s)"`. This may also be a property list with column numbers and formats, for example `:efmt (2 "$%s\\times10^{%s}$" 4 "$%s\\cdot10^{%s}$")`. After `efmt` has been applied to a value, `fmt` will also be applied. Similar to `fmt`, functions of two arguments can be supplied instead of strings.

A.6.3 Translator functions

Orgtbl mode has several translator functions built-in: `orgtbl-to-csv` (comma-separated values), `orgtbl-to-tsv` (TAB-separated values) `orgtbl-to-latex`, `orgtbl-to-html`, and `orgtbl-to-texinfo`. Except for `orgtbl-to-html`[4], these all use a generic translator,

---

[4] The HTML translator uses the same code that produces tables during HTML export.

`orgtbl-to-generic`. For example, `orgtbl-to-latex` itself is a very short function that computes the column definitions for the `tabular` environment, defines a few field and line separators and then hands processing over to the generic translator. Here is the entire code:

```
(defun orgtbl-to-latex (table params)
  "Convert the Orgtbl mode TABLE to LaTeX."
  (let* ((alignment (mapconcat (lambda (x) (if x "r" "l"))
                               org-table-last-alignment ""))
         (params2
          (list
           :tstart (concat "\\begin{tabular}{" alignment "}")
           :tend "\\end{tabular}"
           :lstart "" :lend " \\\\" :sep " & "
           :efmt "%s\\,(%s)" :hline "\\hline")))
    (orgtbl-to-generic table (org-combine-plists params2 params))))
```

As you can see, the properties passed into the function (variable *PARAMS*) are combined with the ones newly defined in the function (variable *PARAMS2*). The ones passed into the function (i.e., the ones set by the '`ORGTBL SEND`' line) take precedence. So if you would like to use the LaTeX translator, but wanted the line endings to be '`\\[2mm]`' instead of the default '`\\`', you could just overrule the default with

```
#+ORGTBL: SEND test orgtbl-to-latex :lend " \\\\[2mm]"
```

For a new language, you can either write your own converter function in analogy with the LaTeX translator, or you can use the generic function directly. For example, if you have a language where a table is started with '`!BTBL!`', ended with '`!ETBL!`', and where table lines are started with '`!BL!`', ended with '`!EL!`', and where the field separator is a TAB, you could call the generic translator like this (on a single line!):

```
#+ORGTBL: SEND test orgtbl-to-generic :tstart "!BTBL!" :tend "!ETBL!"
                                      :lstart "!BL! " :lend " !EL!" :sep "\t"
```

Please check the documentation string of the function `orgtbl-to-generic` for a full list of parameters understood by that function, and remember that you can pass each of them into `orgtbl-to-latex`, `orgtbl-to-texinfo`, and any other function using the generic function.

Of course you can also write a completely new function doing complicated things the generic translator cannot do. A translator function takes two arguments. The first argument is the table, a list of lines, each line either the symbol `hline` or a list of fields. The second argument is the property list containing all parameters specified in the '`#+ORGTBL: SEND`' line. The function must return a single string containing the formatted table. If you write a generally useful translator, please post it on emacs-orgmode@gnu.org so that others can benefit from your work.

A.6.4 Radio lists

Sending and receiving radio lists works exactly the same way as sending and receiving radio tables (see Section A.6.1 [Radio tables], page 229). As for radio tables, you can insert radio list templates in HTML, LaTeX and Texinfo modes by calling `org-list-insert-radio-list`.

Here are the differences with radio tables:

- Orgstruct mode must be active.

- Use the `ORGLST` keyword instead of `ORGTBL`.
- The available translation functions for radio lists don't take parameters.
- `C-c C-c` will work when pressed on the first item of the list.

Here is a LaTeX example. Let's say that you have this in your LaTeX file:

```
% BEGIN RECEIVE ORGLST to-buy
% END RECEIVE ORGLST to-buy
\begin{comment}
#+ORGLST: SEND to-buy org-list-to-latex
- a new house
- a new computer
  + a new keyboard
  + a new mouse
- a new life
\end{comment}
```

Pressing `C-c C-c` on `a new house` and will insert the converted LaTeX list between the two marker lines.

A.7 Dynamic blocks

Org documents can contain *dynamic blocks*. These are specially marked regions that are updated by some user-written function. A good example for such a block is the clock table inserted by the command `C-c C-x C-r` (see Section 8.4 [Clocking work time], page 78).

Dynamic blocks are enclosed by a BEGIN-END structure that assigns a name to the block and can also specify parameters for the function producing the content of the block.

```
#+BEGIN: myblock :parameter1 value1 :parameter2 value2 ...

#+END:
```

Dynamic blocks are updated with the following commands

`C-c C-x C-u`   org-dblock-update
        Update dynamic block at point.

`C-u C-c C-x C-u`
        Update all dynamic blocks in the current file.

Updating a dynamic block means to remove all the text between BEGIN and END, parse the BEGIN line for parameters and then call the specific writer function for this block to insert the new content. If you want to use the original content in the writer function, you can use the extra parameter `:content`.

For a block with name `myblock`, the writer function is `org-dblock-write:myblock` with as only parameter a property list with the parameters given in the begin line. Here is a trivial example of a block that keeps track of when the block update function was last run:

```
#+BEGIN: block-update-time :format "on %m/%d/%Y at %H:%M"

#+END:
```

The corresponding block writer function could look like this:

```
(defun org-dblock-write:block-update-time (params)
 (let ((fmt (or (plist-get params :format) "%d. %m. %Y")))
   (insert "Last block update at: "
           (format-time-string fmt (current-time)))))
```

If you want to make sure that all dynamic blocks are always up-to-date, you could add the function `org-update-all-dblocks` to a hook, for example `before-save-hook`. `org-update-all-dblocks` is written in a way such that it does nothing in buffers that are not in `org-mode`.

You can narrow the current buffer to the current dynamic block (like any other block) with `org-narrow-to-block`.

A.8 Special agenda views

Org provides a special hook that can be used to narrow down the selection made by these agenda views: `agenda`, `agenda*`[5], `todo`, `alltodo`, `tags`, `tags-todo`, `tags-tree`. You may specify a function that is used at each match to verify if the match should indeed be part of the agenda view, and if not, how much should be skipped. You can specify a global condition that will be applied to all agenda views, this condition would be stored in the variable `org-agenda-skip-function-global`. More commonly, such a definition is applied only to specific custom searches, using `org-agenda-skip-function`.

Let's say you want to produce a list of projects that contain a WAITING tag anywhere in the project tree. Let's further assume that you have marked all tree headings that define a project with the TODO keyword PROJECT. In this case you would run a TODO search for the keyword PROJECT, but skip the match unless there is a WAITING tag anywhere in the subtree belonging to the project line.

To achieve this, you must write a function that searches the subtree for the tag. If the tag is found, the function must return `nil` to indicate that this match should not be skipped. If there is no such tag, return the location of the end of the subtree, to indicate that search should continue from there.

```
(defun my-skip-unless-waiting ()
 "Skip trees that are not waiting"
 (let ((subtree-end (save-excursion (org-end-of-subtree t))))
   (if (re-search-forward ":waiting:" subtree-end t)
       nil         ; tag found, do not skip
     subtree-end))) ; tag not found, continue after end of subtree
```

Now you may use this function in an agenda custom command, for example like this:

```
(org-add-agenda-custom-command
'("b" todo "PROJECT"
  ((org-agenda-skip-function 'my-skip-unless-waiting)
   (org-agenda-overriding-header "Projects waiting for something: "))))
```

Note that this also binds `org-agenda-overriding-header` to get a meaningful header in the agenda view.

---

[5] The `agenda*` view is the same as `agenda` except that it only considers *appointments*, i.e., scheduled and deadline items that have a time specification `[h]h:mm` in their time-stamps.

A general way to create custom searches is to base them on a search for entries with a certain level limit. If you want to study all entries with your custom search function, simply do a search for 'LEVEL>0'[6], and then use `org-agenda-skip-function` to select the entries you really want to have.

You may also put a Lisp form into `org-agenda-skip-function`. In particular, you may use the functions `org-agenda-skip-entry-if` and `org-agenda-skip-subtree-if` in this form, for example:

`(org-agenda-skip-entry-if 'scheduled)`
> Skip current entry if it has been scheduled.

`(org-agenda-skip-entry-if 'notscheduled)`
> Skip current entry if it has not been scheduled.

`(org-agenda-skip-entry-if 'deadline)`
> Skip current entry if it has a deadline.

`(org-agenda-skip-entry-if 'scheduled 'deadline)`
> Skip current entry if it has a deadline, or if it is scheduled.

`(org-agenda-skip-entry-if 'todo '("TODO" "WAITING"))`
> Skip current entry if the TODO keyword is TODO or WAITING.

`(org-agenda-skip-entry-if 'todo 'done)`
> Skip current entry if the TODO keyword marks a DONE state.

`(org-agenda-skip-entry-if 'timestamp)`
> Skip current entry if it has any timestamp, may also be deadline or scheduled.

`(org-agenda-skip-entry-if 'regexp "regular expression")`
> Skip current entry if the regular expression matches in the entry.

`(org-agenda-skip-entry-if 'notregexp "regular expression")`
> Skip current entry unless the regular expression matches.

`(org-agenda-skip-subtree-if 'regexp "regular expression")`
> Same as above, but check and skip the entire subtree.

Therefore we could also have written the search for WAITING projects like this, even without defining a special function:

```
(org-add-agenda-custom-command
 '("b" todo "PROJECT"
   ((org-agenda-skip-function '(org-agenda-skip-subtree-if
                        'regexp ":waiting:"))
   (org-agenda-overriding-header "Projects waiting for something: "))))
```

---

[6] Note that, when using `org-odd-levels-only`, a level number corresponds to order in the hierarchy, not to the number of stars.

A.9 Speeding up your agendas

When your Org files grow in both number and size, agenda commands may start to become slow. Below are some tips on how to speed up the agenda commands.

1. Reduce the number of Org agenda files: this will reduce the slowdown caused by accessing a hard drive.

2. Reduce the number of DONE and archived headlines: this way the agenda does not need to skip them.

3. Inhibit the dimming of blocked tasks:

   (setq org-agenda-dim-blocked-tasks nil)

4. Inhibit agenda files startup options:

   (setq org-agenda-inhibit-startup nil)

5. Disable tag inheritance in agenda:

   (setq org-agenda-use-tag-inheritance nil)

You can set these options for specific agenda views only. See the docstrings of these variables for details on why they affect the agenda generation, and this dedicated Worg page for further explanations.

A.10 Extracting agenda information

Org provides commands to access agenda information for the command line in Emacs batch mode. This extracted information can be sent directly to a printer, or it can be read by a program that does further processing of the data. The first of these commands is the function **org-batch-agenda**, that produces an agenda view and sends it as ASCII text to STDOUT. The command takes a single string as parameter. If the string has length 1, it is used as a key to one of the commands you have configured in **org-agenda-custom-commands**, basically any key you can use after *C-c a*. For example, to directly print the current TODO list, you could use

```
emacs -batch -l ~/.emacs -eval '(org-batch-agenda "t")' | lpr
```

If the parameter is a string with 2 or more characters, it is used as a tags/TODO match string. For example, to print your local shopping list (all items with the tag 'shop', but excluding the tag 'NewYork'), you could use

```
emacs -batch -l ~/.emacs                                          \
      -eval '(org-batch-agenda "+shop-NewYork")' | lpr
```

You may also modify parameters on the fly like this:

```
emacs -batch -l ~/.emacs                                          \
   -eval '(org-batch-agenda "a"                                   \
            org-agenda-span (quote month)                         \
            org-agenda-include-diary nil                          \
            org-agenda-files (quote ("~/org/project.org")))'      \
   | lpr
```

which will produce a 30-day agenda, fully restricted to the Org file ~/org/projects.org, not even including the diary.

If you want to process the agenda data in more sophisticated ways, you can use the command **org-batch-agenda-csv** to get a comma-separated list of values for each agenda item. Each line in the output will contain a number of fields separated by commas. The fields in a line are:

category	The category of the item
head	The headline, without TODO keyword, TAGS and PRIORITY
type	The type of the agenda entry, can be

todo	selected in TODO match
tagsmatch	selected in tags match
diary	imported from diary
deadline	a deadline
scheduled	scheduled
timestamp	appointment, selected by timestamp
closed	entry was closed on date
upcoming-deadline	warning about nearing deadline
past-scheduled	forwarded scheduled item
block	entry has date block including date

todo	The TODO keyword, if any
tags	All tags including inherited ones, separated by colons
date	The relevant date, like 2007-2-14
time	The time, like 15:00-16:50
extra	String with extra planning info
priority-l	The priority letter if any was given
priority-n	The computed numerical priority

Time and date will only be given if a timestamp (or deadline/scheduled) led to the selection of the item.

A CSV list like this is very easy to use in a post-processing script. For example, here is a Perl program that gets the TODO list from Emacs/Org and prints all the items, preceded by a checkbox:

```
#!/usr/bin/perl

# define the Emacs command to run
$cmd = "emacs -batch -l ~/.emacs -eval '(org-batch-agenda-csv \"t\")'";

# run it and capture the output
$agenda = qx{$cmd 2>/dev/null};

# loop over all lines
foreach $line (split(/\n/,$agenda)) {
  # get the individual values
  ($category,$head,$type,$todo,$tags,$date,$time,$extra,
   $priority_l,$priority_n) = split(/,/,$line);
  # process and print
  print "[ ] $head\n";
}
```

A.11 Using the property API

Here is a description of the functions that can be used to work with properties.

org-entry-properties **&optional** *pom which*   [Function]
> Get all properties of the entry at point-or-marker POM.
> This includes the TODO keyword, the tags, time strings for deadline, scheduled, and clocking, and any additional properties defined in the entry. The return value is an alist. Keys may occur multiple times if the property key was used several times. POM may also be `nil`, in which case the current entry is used. If WHICH is `nil` or 'all', get all properties. If WHICH is 'special' or 'standard', only get that subclass.

org-entry-get *pom property* **&optional** *inherit*   [Function]
> Get value of `PROPERTY` for entry at point-or-marker `POM`. By default, this only looks at properties defined locally in the entry. If `INHERIT` is non-`nil` and the entry does not have the property, then also check higher levels of the hierarchy. If `INHERIT` is the symbol `selective`, use inheritance if and only if the setting of `org-use-property-inheritance` selects `PROPERTY` for inheritance.

org-entry-delete *pom property*   [Function]
> Delete the property `PROPERTY` from entry at point-or-marker `POM`.

org-entry-put *pom property value*   [Function]
> Set `PROPERTY` to `VALUE` for entry at point-or-marker POM.

org-buffer-property-keys **&optional** *include-specials*   [Function]
> Get all property keys in the current buffer.

org-insert-property-drawer   [Function]
> Insert a property drawer for the current entry. Also

org-entry-put-multivalued-property *pom property* **&rest** *values*   [Function]
> Set `PROPERTY` at point-or-marker `POM` to `VALUES`. `VALUES` should be a list of strings. They will be concatenated, with spaces as separators.

org-entry-get-multivalued-property *pom property*   [Function]
> Treat the value of the property `PROPERTY` as a whitespace-separated list of values and return the values as a list of strings.

org-entry-add-to-multivalued-property *pom property value*   [Function]
> Treat the value of the property `PROPERTY` as a whitespace-separated list of values and make sure that `VALUE` is in this list.

org-entry-remove-from-multivalued-property *pom property value*   [Function]
> Treat the value of the property `PROPERTY` as a whitespace-separated list of values and make sure that `VALUE` is *not* in this list.

org-entry-member-in-multivalued-property *pom property value*   [Function]
> Treat the value of the property `PROPERTY` as a whitespace-separated list of values and check if `VALUE` is in this list.

`org-property-allowed-value-functions`   [User Option]
>   Hook for functions supplying allowed values for a specific property. The functions
>   must take a single argument, the name of the property, and return a flat list of
>   allowed values. If ':ETC' is one of the values, use the values as completion help, but
>   allow also other values to be entered. The functions must return `nil` if they are not
>   responsible for this property.

A.12 Using the mapping API

Org has sophisticated mapping capabilities to find all entries satisfying certain criteria.
Internally, this functionality is used to produce agenda views, but there is also an API that
can be used to execute arbitrary functions for each or selected entries. The main entry
point for this API is:

`org-map-entries` *func* **&optional** *match scope* **&rest** *skip*   [Function]
>   Call `FUNC` at each headline selected by `MATCH` in `SCOPE`.
>
>   `FUNC` is a function or a Lisp form. The function will be called without arguments,
>   with the cursor positioned at the beginning of the headline. The return values of all
>   calls to the function will be collected and returned as a list.
>
>   The call to `FUNC` will be wrapped into a save-excursion form, so `FUNC` does not need
>   to preserve point. After evaluation, the cursor will be moved to the end of the line
>   (presumably of the headline of the processed entry) and search continues from there.
>   Under some circumstances, this may not produce the wanted results. For example, if
>   you have removed (e.g., archived) the current (sub)tree it could mean that the next
>   entry will be skipped entirely. In such cases, you can specify the position from where
>   search should continue by making `FUNC` set the variable `org-map-continue-from` to
>   the desired buffer position.
>
>   `MATCH` is a tags/property/todo match as it is used in the agenda match view. Only
>   headlines that are matched by this query will be considered during the iteration.
>   When `MATCH` is `nil` or `t`, all headlines will be visited by the iteration.
>
>   `SCOPE` determines the scope of this command. It can be any of:
>
> | | |
> |---|---|
> | `nil` | the current buffer, respecting the restriction if any |
> | `tree` | the subtree started with the entry at point |
> | `region` | The entries within the active region, if any |
> | `file` | the current buffer, without restriction |
> | `file-with-archives` | |
> | | the current buffer, and any archives associated with it |
> | `agenda` | all agenda files |
> | `agenda-with-archives` | |
> | | all agenda files with any archive files associated with them |
> | `(file1 file2 ...)` | |
> | | if this is a list, all files in the list will be scanned |
>
>   The remaining args are treated as settings for the skipping facilities of the scanner.
>   The following items can be given here:
>
> | | |
> |---|---|
> | `archive` | skip trees with the archive tag |
> | `comment` | skip trees with the COMMENT keyword |

```
function or Lisp form
```
> will be used as value for `org-agenda-skip-function`, so whenever the function returns t, FUNC will not be called for that entry and search will continue from the point where the function leaves it

The function given to that mapping routine can really do anything you like. It can use the property API (see Section A.11 [Using the property API], page 238) to gather more information about the entry, or in order to change metadata in the entry. Here are a couple of functions that might be handy:

org-todo **&optional** *arg*   [Function]
> Change the TODO state of the entry. See the docstring of the functions for the many possible values for the argument `ARG`.

org-priority **&optional** *action*   [Function]
> Change the priority of the entry. See the docstring of this function for the possible values for `ACTION`.

org-toggle-tag *tag* **&optional** *onoff*   [Function]
> Toggle the tag `TAG` in the current entry. Setting `ONOFF` to either `on` or `off` will not toggle tag, but ensure that it is either on or off.

org-promote   [Function]
> Promote the current entry.

org-demote   [Function]
> Demote the current entry.

Here is a simple example that will turn all entries in the current file with a tag `TOMORROW` into TODO entries with the keyword `UPCOMING`. Entries in comment trees and in archive trees will be ignored.

```
(org-map-entries
 '(org-todo "UPCOMING")
 "+TOMORROW" 'file 'archive 'comment)
```

The following example counts the number of entries with TODO keyword `WAITING`, in all agenda files.

```
(length (org-map-entries t "/+WAITING" 'agenda))
```

Appendix B MobileOrg

MobileOrg is the name of the mobile companion app for Org mode, currently available for iOS and for Android. *MobileOrg* offers offline viewing and capture support for an Org mode system rooted on a "real" computer. It also allows you to record changes to existing entries. The iOS implementation for the *iPhone/iPod Touch/iPad* series of devices, was started by Richard Moreland and is now in the hands Sean Escriva. Android users should check out MobileOrg Android by Matt Jones. The two implementations are not identical but offer similar features.

This appendix describes the support Org has for creating agenda views in a format that can be displayed by *MobileOrg*, and for integrating notes captured and changes made by *MobileOrg* into the main system.

For changing tags and TODO states in MobileOrg, you should have set up the customization variables `org-todo-keywords` and `org-tag-alist` to cover all important tags and TODO keywords, even if individual files use only part of these. MobileOrg will also offer you states and tags set up with in-buffer settings, but it will understand the logistics of TODO state *sets* (see Section 5.2.5 [Per-file keywords], page 48) and *mutually exclusive* tags (see Section 6.2 [Setting tags], page 58) only for those set in these variables.

B.1 Setting up the staging area

MobileOrg needs to interact with Emacs through a directory on a server. If you are using a public server, you should consider encrypting the files that are uploaded to the server. This can be done with Org mode 7.02 and with *MobileOrg 1.5* (iPhone version), and you need an `openssl` installation on your system. To turn on encryption, set a password in *MobileOrg* and, on the Emacs side, configure the variable `org-mobile-use-encryption`[1].

The easiest way to create that directory is to use a free Dropbox.com account[2]. When MobileOrg first connects to your Dropbox, it will create a directory *MobileOrg* inside the Dropbox. After the directory has been created, tell Emacs about it:

(setq org-mobile-directory "~/Dropbox/MobileOrg")

Org mode has commands to put files for *MobileOrg* into that directory, and to read captured notes from there.

B.2 Pushing to MobileOrg

This operation copies all files currently listed in `org-mobile-files` to the directory `org-mobile-directory`. By default this list contains all agenda files (as listed in `org-agenda-files`), but additional files can be included by customizing `org-mobile-files`. File names will be staged with paths relative to `org-directory`, so all files should be inside this directory[3].

---

[1] If you can safely store the password in your Emacs setup, you might also want to configure `org-mobile-encryption-password`. Please read the docstring of that variable. Note that encryption will apply only to the contents of the `.org` files. The file names themselves will remain visible.

[2] If you cannot use Dropbox, or if your version of MobileOrg does not support it, you can use a webdav server. For more information, check out the documentation of MobileOrg and also this FAQ entry.

[3] Symbolic links in `org-directory` need to have the same name as their targets.

The push operation also creates a special Org file `agendas.org` with all custom agenda view defined by the user[4].

Finally, Org writes the file `index.org`, containing links to all other files. *MobileOrg* first reads this file from the server, and then downloads all agendas and Org files listed in it. To speed up the download, MobileOrg will only read files whose checksums[5] have changed.

B.3 Pulling from MobileOrg

When *MobileOrg* synchronizes with the server, it not only pulls the Org files for viewing. It also appends captured entries and pointers to flagged and changed entries to the file `mobileorg.org` on the server. Org has a *pull* operation that integrates this information into an inbox file and operates on the pointers to flagged entries. Here is how it works:

1. Org moves all entries found in `mobileorg.org`[6] and appends them to the file pointed to by the variable `org-mobile-inbox-for-pull`. Each captured entry and each editing event will be a top-level entry in the inbox file.

2. After moving the entries, Org will attempt to implement the changes made in *MobileOrg*. Some changes are applied directly and without user interaction. Examples are all changes to tags, TODO state, headline and body text that can be cleanly applied. Entries that have been flagged for further action will receive a tag `:FLAGGED:`, so that they can be easily found again. When there is a problem finding an entry or applying the change, the pointer entry will remain in the inbox and will be marked with an error message. You need to later resolve these issues by hand.

3. Org will then generate an agenda view with all flagged entries. The user should then go through these entries and do whatever actions are necessary. If a note has been stored while flagging an entry in *MobileOrg*, that note will be displayed in the echo area when the cursor is on the corresponding agenda line.

   ?   Pressing `?` in that special agenda will display the full flagging note in another window and also push it onto the kill ring. So you could use `?` `z` `C-y` `C-c` `C-c` to store that flagging note as a normal note in the entry. Pressing `?` twice in succession will offer to remove the `:FLAGGED:` tag along with the recorded flagging note (which is stored in a property). In this way you indicate that the intended processing for this flagged entry is finished.

If you are not able to process all flagged entries directly, you can always return to this agenda view[7] using `C-c a ?`.

---

[4] While creating the agendas, Org mode will force ID properties on all referenced entries, so that these entries can be uniquely identified if *MobileOrg* flags them for further action. If you do not want to get these properties in so many entries, you can set the variable `org-mobile-force-id-on-agenda-items` to `nil`. Org mode will then rely on outline paths, in the hope that these will be unique enough.

[5] Checksums are stored automatically in the file `checksums.dat`

[6] `mobileorg.org` will be empty after this operation.

[7] Note, however, that there is a subtle difference. The view created automatically by `M-x org-mobile-pull RET` is guaranteed to search all files that have been addressed by the last pull. This might include a file that is not currently in your list of agenda files. If you later use `C-c a ?` to regenerate the view, only the current agenda files will be searched.

Appendix C History and acknowledgments

C.1 From Carsten

Org was born in 2003, out of frustration over the user interface of the Emacs Outline mode. I was trying to organize my notes and projects, and using Emacs seemed to be the natural way to go. However, having to remember eleven different commands with two or three keys per command, only to hide and show parts of the outline tree, that seemed entirely unacceptable to me. Also, when using outlines to take notes, I constantly wanted to restructure the tree, organizing it parallel to my thoughts and plans. *Visibility cycling* and *structure editing* were originally implemented in the package `outline-magic.el`, but quickly moved to the more general `org.el`. As this environment became comfortable for project planning, the next step was adding *TODO entries*, basic *timestamps*, and *table support*. These areas highlighted the two main goals that Org still has today: to be a new, outline-based, plain text mode with innovative and intuitive editing features, and to incorporate project planning functionality directly into a notes file.

Since the first release, literally thousands of emails to me or to emacs-orgmode@gnu.org have provided a constant stream of bug reports, feedback, new ideas, and sometimes patches and add-on code. Many thanks to everyone who has helped to improve this package. I am trying to keep here a list of the people who had significant influence in shaping one or more aspects of Org. The list may not be complete, if I have forgotten someone, please accept my apologies and let me know.

Before I get to this list, a few special mentions are in order:

Bastien Guerry

> Bastien has written a large number of extensions to Org (most of them integrated into the core by now), including the LaTeX exporter and the plain list parser. His support during the early days was central to the success of this project. Bastien also invented Worg, helped establishing the Web presence of Org, and sponsored hosting costs for the orgmode.org website. Bastien stepped in as maintainer of Org between 2011 and 2013, at a time when I desparately needed a break.

Eric Schulte and Dan Davison

> Eric and Dan are jointly responsible for the Org-babel system, which turns Org into a multi-language environment for evaluating code and doing literate programming and reproducible research. This has become one of Org's killer features that define what Org is today.

John Wiegley

> John has contributed a number of great ideas and patches directly to Org, including the attachment system (`org-attach.el`), integration with Apple Mail (`org-mac-message.el`), hierarchical dependencies of TODO items, habit tracking (`org-habits.el`), and encryption (`org-crypt.el`). Also, the capture system is really an extended copy of his great `remember.el`.

Sebastian Rose

> Without Sebastian, the HTML/XHTML publishing of Org would be the pitiful work of an ignorant amateur. Sebastian has pushed this part of Org onto a

much higher level. He also wrote `org-info.js`, a Java script for displaying web pages derived from Org using an Info-like or a folding interface with single-key navigation.

See below for the full list of contributions! Again, please let me know what I am missing here!

C.2 From Bastien

I (Bastien) have been maintaining Org between 2011 and 2013. This appendix would not be complete without adding a few more acknowledgements and thanks.

I am first grateful to Carsten for his trust while handing me over the maintainership of Org. His unremitting support is what really helped me getting more confident over time, with both the community and the code.

When I took over maintainership, I knew I would have to make Org more collaborative than ever, as I would have to rely on people that are more knowledgeable than I am on many parts of the code. Here is a list of the persons I could rely on, they should really be considered co-maintainers, either of the code or the community:

Eric Schulte

Eric is maintaining the Babel parts of Org. His reactivity here kept me away from worrying about possible bugs here and let me focus on other parts.

Nicolas Goaziou

Nicolas is maintaining the consistency of the deepest parts of Org. His work on `org-element.el` and `ox.el` has been outstanding, and it opened the doors for many new ideas and features. He rewrote many of the old exporters to use the new export engine, and helped with documenting this major change. More importantly (if that's possible), he has been more than reliable during all the work done for Org 8.0, and always very reactive on the mailing list.

Achim Gratz

Achim rewrote the building process of Org, turning some *ad hoc* tools into a flexible and conceptually clean process. He patiently coped with the many hiccups that such a change can create for users.

Nick Dokos

The Org mode mailing list would not be such a nice place without Nick, who patiently helped users so many times. It is impossible to overestimate such a great help, and the list would not be so active without him.

I received support from so many users that it is clearly impossible to be fair when shortlisting a few of them, but Org's history would not be complete if the ones above were not mentioned in this manual.

C.3 List of contributions

- *Russel Adams* came up with the idea for drawers.
- *Suvayu Ali* has steadily helped on the mailing list, providing useful feedback on many features and several patches.

- *Luis Anaya* wrote `ox-man.el`.
- *Thomas Baumann* wrote `org-bbdb.el` and `org-mhe.el`.
- *Michael Brand* helped by reporting many bugs and testing many features. He also implemented the distinction between empty fields and 0-value fields in Org's spreadsheets.
- *Christophe Bataillon* created the great unicorn logo that we use on the Org mode website.
- *Alex Bochannek* provided a patch for rounding timestamps.
- *Jan Böcker* wrote `org-docview.el`.
- *Brad Bozarth* showed how to pull RSS feed data into Org mode files.
- *Tom Breton* wrote `org-choose.el`.
- *Charles Cave*'s suggestion sparked the implementation of templates for Remember, which are now templates for capture.
- *Pavel Chalmoviansky* influenced the agenda treatment of items with specified time.
- *Gregory Chernov* patched support for Lisp forms into table calculations and improved XEmacs compatibility, in particular by porting `nouline.el` to XEmacs.
- *Sacha Chua* suggested copying some linking code from Planner, and helped make Org pupular through her blog.
- *Toby S. Cubitt* contributed to the code for clock formats.
- *Baoqiu Cui* contributed the first DocBook exporter. In Org 8.0, we go a different route: you can now export to Texinfo and export the `.texi` file to DocBook using `makeinfo`.
- *Eddward DeVilla* proposed and tested checkbox statistics. He also came up with the idea of properties, and that there should be an API for them.
- *Nick Dokos* tracked down several nasty bugs.
- *Kees Dullemond* used to edit projects lists directly in HTML and so inspired some of the early development, including HTML export. He also asked for a way to narrow wide table columns.
- *Jason Dunsmore* has been maintaining the Org-Mode server at Rackspace for several years now. He also sponsored the hosting costs until Rackspace started to host us for free.
- *Thomas S. Dye* contributed documentation on Worg and helped integrating the Org-Babel documentation into the manual.
- *Christian Egli* converted the documentation into Texinfo format, inspired the agenda, patched CSS formatting into the HTML exporter, and wrote `org-taskjuggler.el`, which has been rewritten by Nicolas Goaziou as `ox-taskjuggler.el` for Org 8.0.
- *David Emery* provided a patch for custom CSS support in exported HTML agendas.
- *Sean Escriva* took over MobileOrg development on the iPhone platform.
- *Nic Ferrier* contributed mailcap and XOXO support.
- *Miguel A. Figueroa-Villanueva* implemented hierarchical checkboxes.
- *John Foerch* figured out how to make incremental search show context around a match in a hidden outline tree.

- *Raimar Finken* wrote `org-git-line.el`.
- *Mikael Fornius* works as a mailing list moderator.
- *Austin Frank* works as a mailing list moderator.
- *Eric Fraga* drove the development of BEAMER export with ideas and testing.
- *Barry Gidden* did proofreading the manual in preparation for the book publication through Network Theory Ltd.
- *Niels Giesen* had the idea to automatically archive DONE trees.
- *Nicolas Goaziou* rewrote much of the plain list code. He also wrote `org-element.el` and `org-export.el`, which was a huge step forward in implementing a clean framework for Org exporters.
- *Kai Grossjohann* pointed out key-binding conflicts with other packages.
- *Brian Gough* of Network Theory Ltd publishes the Org mode manual as a book.
- *Bernt Hansen* has driven much of the support for auto-repeating tasks, task state change logging, and the clocktable. His clear explanations have been critical when we started to adopt the Git version control system.
- *Manuel Hermenegildo* has contributed various ideas, small fixes and patches.
- *Phil Jackson* wrote `org-irc.el`.
- *Scott Jaderholm* proposed footnotes, control over whitespace between folded entries, and column view for properties.
- *Matt Jones* wrote *MobileOrg Android*.
- *Tokuya Kameshima* wrote `org-wl.el` and `org-mew.el`.
- *Jonathan Leech-Pepin* wrote `ox-texinfo.el`.
- *Shidai Liu* ("Leo") asked for embedded LaTeX and tested it. He also provided frequent feedback and some patches.
- *Matt Lundin* has proposed last-row references for table formulas and named invisible anchors. He has also worked a lot on the FAQ.
- *David Maus* wrote `org-atom.el`, maintains the issues file for Org, and is a prolific contributor on the mailing list with competent replies, small fixes and patches.
- *Jason F. McBrayer* suggested agenda export to CSV format.
- *Max Mikhanosha* came up with the idea of refiling and sticky agendas.
- *Dmitri Minaev* sent a patch to set priority limits on a per-file basis.
- *Stefan Monnier* provided a patch to keep the Emacs-Lisp compiler happy.
- *Richard Moreland* wrote *MobileOrg* for the iPhone.
- *Rick Moynihan* proposed allowing multiple TODO sequences in a file and being able to quickly restrict the agenda to a subtree.
- *Todd Neal* provided patches for links to Info files and Elisp forms.
- *Greg Newman* refreshed the unicorn logo into its current form.
- *Tim O'Callaghan* suggested in-file links, search options for general file links, and TAGS.
- *Osamu Okano* wrote `orgcard2ref.pl`, a Perl program to create a text version of the reference card.
- *Takeshi Okano* translated the manual and David O'Toole's tutorial into Japanese.

- *Oliver Oppitz* suggested multi-state TODO items.

- *Scott Otterson* sparked the introduction of descriptive text for links, among other things.

- *Pete Phillips* helped during the development of the TAGS feature, and provided frequent feedback.

- *Francesco Pizzolante* provided patches that helped speeding up the agenda generation.

- *Martin Pohlack* provided the code snippet to bundle character insertion into bundles of 20 for undo.

- *Rackspace.com* is hosting our website for free. Thank you Rackspace!

- *T.V. Raman* reported bugs and suggested improvements.

- *Matthias Rempe* (Oelde) provided ideas, Windows support, and quality control.

- *Paul Rivier* provided the basic implementation of named footnotes. He also acted as mailing list moderator for some time.

- *Kevin Rogers* contributed code to access VM files on remote hosts.

- *Frank Ruell* solved the mystery of the `keymapp nil` bug, a conflict with `allout.el`.

- *Jason Riedy* generalized the send-receive mechanism for Orgtbl tables with extensive patches.

- *Philip Rooke* created the Org reference card, provided lots of feedback, developed and applied standards to the Org documentation.

- *Christian Schlauer* proposed angular brackets around links, among other things.

- *Christopher Schmidt* reworked `orgstruct-mode` so that users can enjoy folding in non-org buffers by using Org headlines in comments.

- *Paul Sexton* wrote `org-ctags.el`.

- Linking to VM/BBDB/Gnus was first inspired by *Tom Shannon*'s `organizer-mode.el`.

- *Ilya Shlyakhter* proposed the Archive Sibling, line numbering in literal examples, and remote highlighting for referenced code lines.

- *Stathis Sideris* wrote the `ditaa.jar` ASCII to PNG converter that is now packaged into Org's `contrib` directory.

- *Daniel Sinder* came up with the idea of internal archiving by locking subtrees.

- *Dale Smith* proposed link abbreviations.

- *James TD Smith* has contributed a large number of patches for useful tweaks and features.

- *Adam Spiers* asked for global linking commands, inspired the link extension system, added support for mairix, and proposed the mapping API.

- *Ulf Stegemann* created the table to translate special symbols to HTML, LaTeX, UTF-8, Latin-1 and ASCII.

- *Andy Stewart* contributed code to `org-w3m.el`, to copy HTML content with links transformation to Org syntax.

- *David O'Toole* wrote `org-publish.el` and drafted the manual chapter about publishing.

- *Jambunathan K* contributed the ODT exporter and rewrote the HTML exporter.

- *Sebastien Vauban* reported many issues with LaTeX and BEAMER export and enabled source code highlighting in Gnus.
- *Stefan Vollmar* organized a video-recorded talk at the Max-Planck-Institute for Neurology. He also inspired the creation of a concept index for HTML export.
- *Jürgen Vollmer* contributed code generating the table of contents in HTML output.
- *Samuel Wales* has provided important feedback and bug reports.
- *Chris Wallace* provided a patch implementing the 'QUOTE' keyword.
- *David Wainberg* suggested archiving, and improvements to the linking system.
- *Carsten Wimmer* suggested some changes and helped fix a bug in linking to Gnus.
- *Roland Winkler* requested additional key bindings to make Org work on a tty.
- *Piotr Zielinski* wrote `org-mouse.el`, proposed agenda blocks and contributed various ideas and code snippets.
- *Samurai Media Limited* did proofreading and published the manual as a book.

Appendix D GNU Free Documentation License

Version 1.3, 3 November 2008

Copyright © 2000, 2001, 2002, 2007, 2008, 2013, 2014 Free Software Foundation, Inc.
`http://fsf.org/`

Everyone is permitted to copy and distribute verbatim copies
of this license document, but changing it is not allowed.

0. PREAMBLE

The purpose of this License is to make a manual, textbook, or other functional and useful document *free* in the sense of freedom: to assure everyone the effective freedom to copy and redistribute it, with or without modifying it, either commercially or non-commercially. Secondarily, this License preserves for the author and publisher a way to get credit for their work, while not being considered responsible for modifications made by others.

This License is a kind of "copyleft", which means that derivative works of the document must themselves be free in the same sense. It complements the GNU General Public License, which is a copyleft license designed for free software.

We have designed this License in order to use it for manuals for free software, because free software needs free documentation: a free program should come with manuals providing the same freedoms that the software does. But this License is not limited to software manuals; it can be used for any textual work, regardless of subject matter or whether it is published as a printed book. We recommend this License principally for works whose purpose is instruction or reference.

1. APPLICABILITY AND DEFINITIONS

This License applies to any manual or other work, in any medium, that contains a notice placed by the copyright holder saying it can be distributed under the terms of this License. Such a notice grants a world-wide, royalty-free license, unlimited in duration, to use that work under the conditions stated herein. The "Document", below, refers to any such manual or work. Any member of the public is a licensee, and is addressed as "you". You accept the license if you copy, modify or distribute the work in a way requiring permission under copyright law.

A "Modified Version" of the Document means any work containing the Document or a portion of it, either copied verbatim, or with modifications and/or translated into another language.

A "Secondary Section" is a named appendix or a front-matter section of the Document that deals exclusively with the relationship of the publishers or authors of the Document to the Document's overall subject (or to related matters) and contains nothing that could fall directly within that overall subject. (Thus, if the Document is in part a textbook of mathematics, a Secondary Section may not explain any mathematics.) The relationship could be a matter of historical connection with the subject or with related matters, or of legal, commercial, philosophical, ethical or political position regarding them.

The "Invariant Sections" are certain Secondary Sections whose titles are designated, as being those of Invariant Sections, in the notice that says that the Document is released under this License. If a section does not fit the above definition of Secondary then it is not allowed to be designated as Invariant. The Document may contain zero Invariant Sections. If the Document does not identify any Invariant Sections then there are none.

The "Cover Texts" are certain short passages of text that are listed, as Front-Cover Texts or Back-Cover Texts, in the notice that says that the Document is released under this License. A Front-Cover Text may be at most 5 words, and a Back-Cover Text may be at most 25 words.

A "Transparent" copy of the Document means a machine-readable copy, represented in a format whose specification is available to the general public, that is suitable for revising the document straightforwardly with generic text editors or (for images composed of pixels) generic paint programs or (for drawings) some widely available drawing editor, and that is suitable for input to text formatters or for automatic translation to a variety of formats suitable for input to text formatters. A copy made in an otherwise Transparent file format whose markup, or absence of markup, has been arranged to thwart or discourage subsequent modification by readers is not Transparent. An image format is not Transparent if used for any substantial amount of text. A copy that is not "Transparent" is called "Opaque".

Examples of suitable formats for Transparent copies include plain ASCII without markup, Texinfo input format, LaTeX input format, SGML or XML using a publicly available DTD, and standard-conforming simple HTML, PostScript or PDF designed for human modification. Examples of transparent image formats include PNG, XCF and JPG. Opaque formats include proprietary formats that can be read and edited only by proprietary word processors, SGML or XML for which the DTD and/or processing tools are not generally available, and the machine-generated HTML, PostScript or PDF produced by some word processors for output purposes only.

The "Title Page" means, for a printed book, the title page itself, plus such following pages as are needed to hold, legibly, the material this License requires to appear in the title page. For works in formats which do not have any title page as such, "Title Page" means the text near the most prominent appearance of the work's title, preceding the beginning of the body of the text.

The "publisher" means any person or entity that distributes copies of the Document to the public.

A section "Entitled XYZ" means a named subunit of the Document whose title either is precisely XYZ or contains XYZ in parentheses following text that translates XYZ in another language. (Here XYZ stands for a specific section name mentioned below, such as "Acknowledgements", "Dedications", "Endorsements", or "History".) To "Preserve the Title" of such a section when you modify the Document means that it remains a section "Entitled XYZ" according to this definition.

The Document may include Warranty Disclaimers next to the notice which states that this License applies to the Document. These Warranty Disclaimers are considered to be included by reference in this License, but only as regards disclaiming warranties: any other implication that these Warranty Disclaimers may have is void and has no effect on the meaning of this License.

2. VERBATIM COPYING

You may copy and distribute the Document in any medium, either commercially or noncommercially, provided that this License, the copyright notices, and the license notice saying this License applies to the Document are reproduced in all copies, and that you add no other conditions whatsoever to those of this License. You may not use technical measures to obstruct or control the reading or further copying of the copies you make or distribute. However, you may accept compensation in exchange for copies. If you distribute a large enough number of copies you must also follow the conditions in section 3.

You may also lend copies, under the same conditions stated above, and you may publicly display copies.

3. COPYING IN QUANTITY

If you publish printed copies (or copies in media that commonly have printed covers) of the Document, numbering more than 100, and the Document's license notice requires Cover Texts, you must enclose the copies in covers that carry, clearly and legibly, all these Cover Texts: Front-Cover Texts on the front cover, and Back-Cover Texts on the back cover. Both covers must also clearly and legibly identify you as the publisher of these copies. The front cover must present the full title with all words of the title equally prominent and visible. You may add other material on the covers in addition. Copying with changes limited to the covers, as long as they preserve the title of the Document and satisfy these conditions, can be treated as verbatim copying in other respects.

If the required texts for either cover are too voluminous to fit legibly, you should put the first ones listed (as many as fit reasonably) on the actual cover, and continue the rest onto adjacent pages.

If you publish or distribute Opaque copies of the Document numbering more than 100, you must either include a machine-readable Transparent copy along with each Opaque copy, or state in or with each Opaque copy a computer-network location from which the general network-using public has access to download using public-standard network protocols a complete Transparent copy of the Document, free of added material. If you use the latter option, you must take reasonably prudent steps, when you begin distribution of Opaque copies in quantity, to ensure that this Transparent copy will remain thus accessible at the stated location until at least one year after the last time you distribute an Opaque copy (directly or through your agents or retailers) of that edition to the public.

It is requested, but not required, that you contact the authors of the Document well before redistributing any large number of copies, to give them a chance to provide you with an updated version of the Document.

4. MODIFICATIONS

You may copy and distribute a Modified Version of the Document under the conditions of sections 2 and 3 above, provided that you release the Modified Version under precisely this License, with the Modified Version filling the role of the Document, thus licensing distribution and modification of the Modified Version to whoever possesses a copy of it. In addition, you must do these things in the Modified Version:

A. Use in the Title Page (and on the covers, if any) a title distinct from that of the Document, and from those of previous versions (which should, if there were any, be listed in the History section of the Document). You may use the same title as a previous version if the original publisher of that version gives permission.

B. List on the Title Page, as authors, one or more persons or entities responsible for authorship of the modifications in the Modified Version, together with at least five of the principal authors of the Document (all of its principal authors, if it has fewer than five), unless they release you from this requirement.

C. State on the Title page the name of the publisher of the Modified Version, as the publisher.

D. Preserve all the copyright notices of the Document.

E. Add an appropriate copyright notice for your modifications adjacent to the other copyright notices.

F. Include, immediately after the copyright notices, a license notice giving the public permission to use the Modified Version under the terms of this License, in the form shown in the Addendum below.

G. Preserve in that license notice the full lists of Invariant Sections and required Cover Texts given in the Document's license notice.

H. Include an unaltered copy of this License.

I. Preserve the section Entitled "History", Preserve its Title, and add to it an item stating at least the title, year, new authors, and publisher of the Modified Version as given on the Title Page. If there is no section Entitled "History" in the Document, create one stating the title, year, authors, and publisher of the Document as given on its Title Page, then add an item describing the Modified Version as stated in the previous sentence.

J. Preserve the network location, if any, given in the Document for public access to a Transparent copy of the Document, and likewise the network locations given in the Document for previous versions it was based on. These may be placed in the "History" section. You may omit a network location for a work that was published at least four years before the Document itself, or if the original publisher of the version it refers to gives permission.

K. For any section Entitled "Acknowledgements" or "Dedications", Preserve the Title of the section, and preserve in the section all the substance and tone of each of the contributor acknowledgements and/or dedications given therein.

L. Preserve all the Invariant Sections of the Document, unaltered in their text and in their titles. Section numbers or the equivalent are not considered part of the section titles.

M. Delete any section Entitled "Endorsements". Such a section may not be included in the Modified Version.

N. Do not retitle any existing section to be Entitled "Endorsements" or to conflict in title with any Invariant Section.

O. Preserve any Warranty Disclaimers.

If the Modified Version includes new front-matter sections or appendices that qualify as Secondary Sections and contain no material copied from the Document, you may at your option designate some or all of these sections as invariant. To do this, add their titles to the list of Invariant Sections in the Modified Version's license notice. These titles must be distinct from any other section titles.

You may add a section Entitled "Endorsements", provided it contains nothing but endorsements of your Modified Version by various parties—for example, statements of peer review or that the text has been approved by an organization as the authoritative definition of a standard.

You may add a passage of up to five words as a Front-Cover Text, and a passage of up to 25 words as a Back-Cover Text, to the end of the list of Cover Texts in the Modified Version. Only one passage of Front-Cover Text and one of Back-Cover Text may be added by (or through arrangements made by) any one entity. If the Document already includes a cover text for the same cover, previously added by you or by arrangement made by the same entity you are acting on behalf of, you may not add another; but you may replace the old one, on explicit permission from the previous publisher that added the old one.

The author(s) and publisher(s) of the Document do not by this License give permission to use their names for publicity for or to assert or imply endorsement of any Modified Version.

5. COMBINING DOCUMENTS

You may combine the Document with other documents released under this License, under the terms defined in section 4 above for modified versions, provided that you include in the combination all of the Invariant Sections of all of the original documents, unmodified, and list them all as Invariant Sections of your combined work in its license notice, and that you preserve all their Warranty Disclaimers.

The combined work need only contain one copy of this License, and multiple identical Invariant Sections may be replaced with a single copy. If there are multiple Invariant Sections with the same name but different contents, make the title of each such section unique by adding at the end of it, in parentheses, the name of the original author or publisher of that section if known, or else a unique number. Make the same adjustment to the section titles in the list of Invariant Sections in the license notice of the combined work.

In the combination, you must combine any sections Entitled "History" in the various original documents, forming one section Entitled "History"; likewise combine any sections Entitled "Acknowledgements", and any sections Entitled "Dedications". You must delete all sections Entitled "Endorsements."

6. COLLECTIONS OF DOCUMENTS

You may make a collection consisting of the Document and other documents released under this License, and replace the individual copies of this License in the various documents with a single copy that is included in the collection, provided that you follow the rules of this License for verbatim copying of each of the documents in all other respects.

You may extract a single document from such a collection, and distribute it individually under this License, provided you insert a copy of this License into the extracted document, and follow this License in all other respects regarding verbatim copying of that document.

7. AGGREGATION WITH INDEPENDENT WORKS

A compilation of the Document or its derivatives with other separate and independent documents or works, in or on a volume of a storage or distribution medium, is called an "aggregate" if the copyright resulting from the compilation is not used to limit the legal rights of the compilation's users beyond what the individual works permit. When the Document is included in an aggregate, this License does not apply to the other works in the aggregate which are not themselves derivative works of the Document.

If the Cover Text requirement of section 3 is applicable to these copies of the Document, then if the Document is less than one half of the entire aggregate, the Document's Cover Texts may be placed on covers that bracket the Document within the aggregate, or the electronic equivalent of covers if the Document is in electronic form. Otherwise they must appear on printed covers that bracket the whole aggregate.

8. TRANSLATION

Translation is considered a kind of modification, so you may distribute translations of the Document under the terms of section 4. Replacing Invariant Sections with translations requires special permission from their copyright holders, but you may include translations of some or all Invariant Sections in addition to the original versions of these Invariant Sections. You may include a translation of this License, and all the license notices in the Document, and any Warranty Disclaimers, provided that you also include the original English version of this License and the original versions of those notices and disclaimers. In case of a disagreement between the translation and the original version of this License or a notice or disclaimer, the original version will prevail.

If a section in the Document is Entitled "Acknowledgements", "Dedications", or "History", the requirement (section 4) to Preserve its Title (section 1) will typically require changing the actual title.

9. TERMINATION

You may not copy, modify, sublicense, or distribute the Document except as expressly provided under this License. Any attempt otherwise to copy, modify, sublicense, or distribute it is void, and will automatically terminate your rights under this License.

However, if you cease all violation of this License, then your license from a particular copyright holder is reinstated (a) provisionally, unless and until the copyright holder explicitly and finally terminates your license, and (b) permanently, if the copyright holder fails to notify you of the violation by some reasonable means prior to 60 days after the cessation.

Moreover, your license from a particular copyright holder is reinstated permanently if the copyright holder notifies you of the violation by some reasonable means, this is the first time you have received notice of violation of this License (for any work) from that copyright holder, and you cure the violation prior to 30 days after your receipt of the notice.

Termination of your rights under this section does not terminate the licenses of parties who have received copies or rights from you under this License. If your rights have been terminated and not permanently reinstated, receipt of a copy of some or all of the same material does not give you any rights to use it.

10. FUTURE REVISIONS OF THIS LICENSE

The Free Software Foundation may publish new, revised versions of the GNU Free Documentation License from time to time. Such new versions will be similar in spirit to the present version, but may differ in detail to address new problems or concerns. See http://www.gnu.org/copyleft/.

Each version of the License is given a distinguishing version number. If the Document specifies that a particular numbered version of this License "or any later version" applies to it, you have the option of following the terms and conditions either of that specified version or of any later version that has been published (not as a draft) by the Free Software Foundation. If the Document does not specify a version number of this License, you may choose any version ever published (not as a draft) by the Free Software Foundation. If the Document specifies that a proxy can decide which future versions of this License can be used, that proxy's public statement of acceptance of a version permanently authorizes you to choose that version for the Document.

11. RELICENSING

"Massive Multiauthor Collaboration Site" (or "MMC Site") means any World Wide Web server that publishes copyrightable works and also provides prominent facilities for anybody to edit those works. A public wiki that anybody can edit is an example of such a server. A "Massive Multiauthor Collaboration" (or "MMC") contained in the site means any set of copyrightable works thus published on the MMC site.

"CC-BY-SA" means the Creative Commons Attribution-Share Alike 3.0 license published by Creative Commons Corporation, a not-for-profit corporation with a principal place of business in San Francisco, California, as well as future copyleft versions of that license published by that same organization.

"Incorporate" means to publish or republish a Document, in whole or in part, as part of another Document.

An MMC is "eligible for relicensing" if it is licensed under this License, and if all works that were first published under this License somewhere other than this MMC, and subsequently incorporated in whole or in part into the MMC, (1) had no cover texts or invariant sections, and (2) were thus incorporated prior to November 1, 2008.

The operator of an MMC Site may republish an MMC contained in the site under CC-BY-SA on the same site at any time before August 1, 2009, provided the MMC is eligible for relicensing.

ADDENDUM: How to use this License for your documents

To use this License in a document you have written, include a copy of the License in the document and put the following copyright and license notices just after the title page:

```
Copyright (C)  year  your name.
Permission is granted to copy, distribute and/or modify this document
under the terms of the GNU Free Documentation License, Version 1.3
or any later version published by the Free Software Foundation;
with no Invariant Sections, no Front-Cover Texts, and no Back-Cover
Texts.  A copy of the license is included in the section entitled ''GNU
Free Documentation License''.
```

If you have Invariant Sections, Front-Cover Texts and Back-Cover Texts, replace the "with...Texts." line with this:

```
with the Invariant Sections being list their titles, with
the Front-Cover Texts being list, and with the Back-Cover Texts
being list.
```

If you have Invariant Sections without Cover Texts, or some other combination of the three, merge those two alternatives to suit the situation.

If your document contains nontrivial examples of program code, we recommend releasing these examples in parallel under your choice of free software license, such as the GNU General Public License, to permit their use in free software.

Concept index

Key index

C

D

E

F

G

H

I

J

K

L

M

N

O

P

Q

Command and function index

Variable index

This is not a complete index of variables and faces, only the ones that are mentioned in the manual. For a more complete list, use *M-x org-customize RET* and then click yourself through the tree.